WRITING RESEARCH, PEDAGOGY, AND POLICY

Elizabeth Wardle, Series Editor

POLICY REGIMES

College Writing and Public Education Policy in the United States

Tyler S. Branson

Southern Illinois University Press
Carbondale

Southern Illinois University Press
www.siupress.com

Printed in the United States of America

25 24 23 22 4 3 2 1

Publication of books in the Writing Research, Pedagogy, and Policy series is supported by the Roger and Joyce Howe Center for Writing Excellence at Miami University.

Cover illustration: Negroes, school, and classrooms. Courtesy of Bernard Gotfryd photograph collection, Library of Congress Prints and Photographs Division, Library of Congress (cropped).

Library of Congress Cataloging-in-Publication Data
Names: Branson, Tyler S., 1987– author.
Title: Policy regimes: college writing and public education policy in the United States / Tyler S. Branson.
Identifiers: LCCN 2021034261 (print) | LCCN 2021034262 (ebook) | ISBN 9780809338467 (paperback) | ISBN 9780809338474 (ebook)
Subjects: LCSH: English language—Composition and exercises—Study and teaching (Secondary)—United States. | English language—Study and teaching—Standards—United States. | National Council of Teachers of English.
Classification: LCC LB1631.B7635 2022 (print) | LCC LB1631 (ebook) | DDC 808/.0420712—dc23
LC record available at https://lccn.loc.gov/2021034261
LC ebook record available at https://lccn.loc.gov/2021034262

Printed on recycled paper ♻

SIU
Southern Illinois University System

CONTENTS

ACKNOWLEDGMENTS

When I think about the work that went into this book, I think of all the physical places in which the work was completed and the generosity of the folks in those places who supported and mentored my writing along the way. I conducted the archival research in Urbana, Illinois; ethnographic research in northwest Ohio; and I attended professional workshops while researching in Columbus, Ohio. I wrote the first draft of one chapter years ago in Fort Worth, Texas. Another chapter I wrote in my parents living room one summer in a makeshift office in Edmond, Oklahoma. I revised a good chunk of the manuscript with my writing group in Detroit, Michigan. I workshopped chapters at academic conferences in Louisville, Sacramento, Baltimore, and Chicago. Scholars and friends from institutions in California, Vermont, Texas, Oklahoma, Ohio, and Pennsylvania offered their generous feedback and criticism.

I have so much gratitude for the archivists at NCTE's headquarters; the University of Toledo's Office of Research for its generous grant that allowed me to dedicate entire summers to the project; the public school systems in Toledo and beyond; and the individuals Elizabeth Wardle, Carrie Tippen, Joshua Daniel, James Chase Sanchez, Terry Peterman, Tony Edgington, Barbara Schneider, Christine Denecker, Casie Moreland, Ryan Skinnell, and others who read drafts and contributed feedback and advice.

This book is dedicated to my wonderful wife, Jamie, who is my fiercest supporter, and also to our baby, Ramona, who came to us in the middle of writing this book and who motivated me to hurry up and finish so that I could spend time with her. My hope is that Ramona, the most immediate beneficiary of our current educational policies, comes to know the world through a more equitable, empowering, and compassionate public school system that works to prepare everyone, across all grade levels, races, and zip codes, for the messy work of citizenship.

POLICY REGIMES

Introduction: Writing Studies, Policy Regimes, and Public Education Policies

At its heart, this book concerns educational policy for writing instruction as it is promulgated, enforced, engaged, and lived. In the case studies to follow, my goal is to provide frameworks for the field of writing studies to think through how and whether the educational policy work that governs writing and writing instruction is effective (and to consider why it sometimes is not, even when done well by thoughtful and engaged educators).

Throughout the field of writing studies, there is robust work centered around policy. Scholars have taken up specific language policies and their cultural and ideological underpinnings (see Flowers; Gilman; Parks; Wible; Young et al.). Other scholars have approached policy from the broader ideological underpinnings of education reform as they intersect with writing and rhetoric (Webber; Gallagher, *Reclaiming Assessment*; Kynard). Some scholars have researched the institutional policies of academic disciplines (Parks; Scott et al.). Moreover, some of the most important scholarship on policy in the field has to do with the impact of literacy policies on the experience of marginalized communities. For example, Candace Epps-Robertson investigates a county in Virginia that chose to abolish all public schooling in defiance of the 1954 Supreme Court decision that ended school segregation. David Kirkland's *A Search Past Silence: The Literacy of Young Black Men* is an ethnographic account of the literate lives of four Black male students in Michigan and the ways that their social, cultural, and historical contexts for literacy intersect with their educational experiences.

Empirical work on writing policy, however, is less abundant. *Policy Regimes*, then, takes up writing from a *policy studies* approach. My hope is that given the thoughtful work that came before me, this book can extend these discussions and theorize a bit more about what policy actually means to our field and about how we—our discipline, our institutions, and the individuals who compose them—can and should work on policy in the future.

The central questions of this book are, How does education policy shape our experiences with writing and literacy? How do individuals within specific institutional contexts leverage disciplinary knowledge about writing (or what Adler-Kassner and Wardle might call what we *know* about writing) to bridge, partner with, advocate, or resist educational policies? Ultimately, I argue that the slippery and complex topic of policy is a fundamental component of writing studies, and our field would do well to consider both how policies shape the intellectual work of the field and how our own institutions and individual teachers can actively put stress on policies we wish to change. As each case study unfolds, I advocate for doing *kairotic policy work*: a pragmatic, multiscopic rhetorical practice that leverages disciplinary knowledge about writing to put stress on an existing policy regime by taking into account what policy theorists call the *governing arrangements* of education policy and how these arrangements structure—for better or worse—the way writing is taught, researched, and administered in secondary and postsecondary writing classrooms.

I answer these questions through an analysis of case studies of writing and educational policy. First, I analyze the National Council of Teachers of English (NCTE) and its policy work as an organization; next, I explore the role of NCTE in the development of the Common Core State Standards Initiative. I follow these cases with two chapters on dual enrollment: first comes a case study of dual enrollment as an extension of accountability in the state of Ohio; then comes a qualitative case study of a dual enrollment composition course taught in a high school classroom. Together, these chapters provide large-scale views of policy impact combined with a look into a classroom that helps to ground the policy analyses in the lived experiences of students and their teacher.

Through its range of analytic scales and methods, this book will provide readers with a deeper sense of how writing teachers, researchers, and administrators can work together to put stress on accountability-based education policies that do not align with what we know and value about writing across all levels of academic writing instruction.

Above, I described the methodology as *multiscopic*. A multiscopic approach, which I take in part from Bruce McComiskey's work on microhistories, is a strategic process of zooming in and out on the mechanisms through which policies shape the complex interplay between the field's institutional and historical relationship to policy, on the one hand, and the ways that teachers work on a daily basis to carry out those policies on the other. By studying policy from these perspectives, we can see how institutions and individual actors take advantage of *kairotic policy engagement*. As I will show in the following chapters, the ways that institutions and individual actors within those institutions create rhetorical moments for action or take advantage of these opening and closing rhetorical windows can tell us much about how our field can better understand, and ultimately participate in more effectively, the policymaking discussions having to do with writing.

Carolyn Miller once wrote that the revival in rhetoric and composition of the term *kairos*, which is a concept dating back to the Sophistic tradition, is useful for making us "look for the particular opportunity in a given moment, to find—or construct—an opening in the here and now, in order to achieve something there and then" ("Opportunity" 83). According to Miller, kairos can be either *continuous*, which means one can create opportunities for rhetorical intervention at any time, or *discontinuous*, which means the time for one's rhetorical intervention is a rare window in "unprecedented times of radical change" (83). Whether through the institutional efforts of the main professional organization of English Studies, NCTE (which, historically, often took advantage of, yet sometimes fell short of responding to, changes in federal education policy), or through the efforts of individual teachers who create opportunities for rhetorical intervention within prevailing policy regimes—the kairotic element of policy regimes is a persistent theme that emerges from my multiscopic analysis. A *window* is a fitting metaphor for characterizing how policy and writing studies are interconnected. Echoing Lloyd Bitzer, Eric Charles White, in his book about kairos, describes the term as a "right moment" or a "critical time," in which a temporal rhetorical "window" opens up, for one to engage in policy discussions (13).

In writing studies, scholars like Elizabeth Wardle have drawn on this body of work to theorize how policy stakeholders rely on varying levels of kairos to create change in their institutional contexts. For Wardle, theorizing kairos in this way allowed her to consider how the "macro-level disciplinary knowledge" of writing studies can "inform micro-level classroom practices" in the first-year composition curriculum at her university. Thinking kairotically, or rather utilizing both advocates and stakeholders of varying backgrounds and levels of seniority, can help institutions survive precarious changes and "construct, discover, and respond to kairotic openings." Patricia Freitag Ericsson, in her 2003 dissertation, "Beyond the Laments, Beyond the Boundaries: Communicating about Composition," uses the term *polikairos* to describe "an analytical and generative concept, influenced by close attention to problems, policies, and politics, and used for both assessing the opportune time for a political move and guiding the force of that move" (25). A well-developed sense of polikairos, Ericsson writes, can help us "carry on effective policy-oriented learning—to know when to step into 'debate' with other advocacy coalitions, to know what kinds of arguments to make, and to know with what force those arguments must be made to be successful" (111). Throughout the case studies of this book, I explicate how kairotic policy engagement, or polikairos, is a useful temporal-spatial rhetorical practice for writing studies scholars and teachers in a variety of political and material situations to figure out the right responses and the right moments required to put stress on policy regimes of accountability. Polikairotic engagement, in other words, allows us to take stock of the ways that writing policy impacts our institutions as well as our classrooms, and it helps us make critical judgments about the best ways to imagine new policy paradigms, to forge new policymaking arrangements in whatever contexts we inhabit, and to define in kairotic terms what that work can look like.

As Elizabeth Wardle and Linda Adler-Kassner know, writing is an activity *and* a field of study. But writing is also a policy problem. As such, it is important for our field to untangle the ways writing is bound up in what I call the *policy regimes* of education reform. These regimes, which I explain further below, comprise a range of competing interests, ideas, political arrangements, and laws that inform the teaching and research of college composition. If we, as writing teachers, researchers, and administrators, pay close attention to writing policy, we can deepen our understanding of how public education policy helps—and hinders—our commitment to student success at all levels of education.

Whether we like it or not, federal and state education policies are fundamentally entangled with the work of writing studies. In chapters 3 and 4, I focus on the growing number of dual-enrolled students. At my institution, the University of Toledo, the State of Ohio mandates that we partner with local middle and high schools so that they can offer college composition for free to their students. The state pays for dual enrollment by transferring money from the school's budget to ours, and state policy lets students transfer their course credit from our institution to any other public institution in the state. These policies are now components of administering our writing program, for which I serve as the associate director. Moreover, Ohio state law stipulates that all of our dual-enrolled students (those in middle or high school who take our courses) be treated no differently from traditionally enrolled college students. This means that dual enrollment students are to be held to the same standards and assessment criteria as everyone else. At Research 1 land-grant research institutions in the state, this policy probably makes sense because it allows the institutions to maintain their rigorous standards for dual-enrolled students prior to their admission. But for my institution, a regional Research 2 university with an acceptance rate of 93 percent, the mandate has a different impact: essentially *anyone* from seventh to twelfth grade can enroll in our first-year composition course for free. So we enroll both high-achieving and unprepared students in our dual enrollment courses, which creates new, and often straining, pedagogical dynamics for our writing instructors. These dynamics change the way instructors design course content and position themselves to the students in their classes. While all students are welcome in our classes, and our mission as a program is to meet all students where they are regardless of their abilities, the state mandates often leave us perplexed over how to best serve unprepared and at-risk dual enrollment students.

In addition, Ohio's state education policies often differ dramatically from policy platforms and position statements of NCTE. For example, in a 2017 policy analysis from NCTE, Amanda Espinosa-Aguilar writes that the main commonsense argument for dual enrollment—that students can earn credit for college by completing college-level courses in high school—is not entirely accurate: "Many students (and their parents) are actually discovering that these credits/courses are not guaranteed to transfer to a four-year school, and especially not to private institutions." In Ohio, thanks to the passage of House Bill 95, "students can begin higher education at any public institution of higher education and transfer coursework and degrees to any other state institution of higher education without unnecessary duplication or institutional barriers" ("TAG Background"). There can be an issue, however, with transferring credits. If Ohio students with dual enrollment credit transfer out of state, those credits are not guaranteed to transfer with them. Also, there is little evidence to suggest that students who complete a dual enrollment course at the University of Toledo will stay at the university until graduation, which is an alarming fact for an institution like ours where retention is a significant concern (*University Completion Plan*).

Moreover, besides the issue of transferring credits, Espinosa-Aguilar's policy analysis calls into question the rigor of concurrent enrollment courses, a type of dual enrollment where college-level courses are taught *at a high school* by college-approved secondary education instructors. "The evidence seems to suggest that many four-year colleges do not believe that the high school–taught courses are rigorous enough to warrant equivalent transfer credit," she writes. Nevertheless, the Ohio legislature continues to mandate dual enrollment policies to support Attainment Goal 2025, which aims to "increase the number of its [Ohio's] citizens with postsecondary education credentials relevant in the workplace" ("Attainment Goal 2025"). In other words, NCTE's careful policy critiques—which suggest that transferring credits can create barriers for some students or that the rigor of these classes may be suspect—seem to have little to no bearing on Ohio's higher education policy decisions.

Fully understanding that the dual enrollment train was going to move forward despite the reservations of the field, the Conference on College Composition and Communication (CCCC) assembled a task force on dual credit and concurrent enrollment in composition. In 2012 the task force issued a lengthy set of recommendations for curricula, teacher preparation, and assessment for dual enrollment courses, noting the need for "discipline-specific guidelines and high school/college English alliances at the local and state levels . . . to develop and assess the quality of concurrent enrollment/dual-credit composition" ("Statement"). Such discipline-specific recommendations are useful for teachers and administrators when they look for best practices in designing, navigating, and assessing dual enrollment programs, but the State of Ohio's mandated policies do not necessarily align with those recommendations. For example, the task force recommends that

> there should be funds, space, and postsecondary faculty expertise necessary for initial and follow-up discipline-specific training seminars that introduce the selected secondary teachers to the partnering college composition curriculum: course goals, assignments, readings, and assessment, as well as current theory and practices in the field of composition. ("Statement")

The Ohio Department of Education, however, stipulates through its dual enrollment program, called College Credit Plus, that participating secondary instructors are to receive only three hours of "professional development" and that there will be "at least one observation of each" College Credit Plus class (*College Credits Plus: Highlights*). So while there is certainly overlap between the Ohio Department of Education's requirements for dual enrollment and NCTE/CCCC's policy recommendations, this overlap is not always apparent, and it does not seem to be the result of any meaningful dialogue between policymakers at the state level and experts in the field of writing studies. Rather, the requirements seem like an underhanded crafting of policies that merely can be promoted and perceived as "academically rigorous."

The same argument can be made about other policy problems that impact the teaching of composition, such as state education standards, for instance. As I explore in chapter 2, the Common Core State Standards Initiative is an example of how ideological divisions and power imbalances can complicate policymaking strategies despite widespread academic consensus on the inadequacy of a given policy. The Common Core, written in large part by business leaders and policymakers in conjunction with federal grant programs, has come under fire from K–12 teachers and college professors. Detractors from the field of writing studies and elsewhere charge that the English language arts standards do not take into account current research on writing, that the drafting of the standards did not utilize the expertise of teachers, and moreover that the standards benefit the interests of businesses rather than students.

Nevertheless, the website of the Common Core argues that the purpose of the standards is to equip students who graduate from high school with the skills needed to succeed in college and their future career. Developed and maintained by two organizations, the Council of Chief State School Officers and the National Governors Association, the standards were created in response to what they call the stagnation of academic progress in the United States and the "uneven patchwork of academic standards that vary from state to state and do not agree on what students should know and be able to do at each grade level" ("About the Standards"). In 2009 the state school chiefs and state governors from both organizations developed the standards, and in 2010 states began voluntarily adopting them, either by voting through state school boards or by having the standards ratified by state superintendents, legislatures, or governors ("Development Process"). At the time of writing this book, forty-one states have adopted the Common Core, including my state of Ohio.

While the *official* portrayal of the formal processes by which the Common Core was composed, revised, and distributed claims to have had widespread public and academic support, this narrative belies significant critiques of the standards by writing studies scholars. According to the website of the Common Core State Standards Initiative, teachers were involved in developing the standards through the entire process; however, as I show later in the book, there is little evidence that writing teachers played any significant role in the creation, review, and validation of the standards.

Moreover, while the Common Core claims that its English language arts standards are evidence-based, NCTE found that "none of the evidence has been drawn from peer-reviewed research journals or similar sources" (*Report of the NCTE Review Team* 4). Rather, the evidence offered in an early draft of the English language arts standards, NCTE charges, "consists of surveys conducted by the testing companies that stand most immediately to gain from the testing of these standards" (4). In its report, NCTE recommended that "those who are familiar with the relevant research and important practices" be "invited to contribute their insights to the standards," and NCTE even goes so far as to suggest that the authors of the Common Core get rid of *any* "claims that these standards are based in valid evidence, since such claims will only invite skepticism and criticism that cannot be answered" (4). The Common Core's standards for English language arts, according to NCTE, ignored the kinds of writing practices endorsed by academic research and focused instead on the "ease of assessing," which has unfortunately "given rise to distortions in the drafted standards for teaching and learning" (6). Moreover, NCTE concludes that these distortions "misrepresent the nature of composition" and falsely advertise themselves as "standards for learning" instead of what they really are: "standards for assessment," a move that is "extremely costly for the nation" (6). The fact that NCTE's denouncement of the drafted English language arts standards was not heeded by the Common Core's authors exemplifies the efforts of policy elites to rubber-stamp their policies as *rigorous* and *expert-approved* despite the fact that any meaningful dialogue, if it occurred at all, was stymied by a considerable imbalance of power—with government and philanthropic groups, on the one hand, and an organization representing English teachers on the other. These power arrangements, and ideological differences over the role of the federal government in education policy, served to increase, rather than bridge, the gulf between policymakers and composition specialists.

These examples of education policymaking show us how important it is for our field to consider how its professional organizations can contribute meaningfully to policy formation and to consider how policy shapes the teaching of writing. Also, it is important to note that these questions are thorny, and the way forward is not always clear. NCTE's efforts to provide guidance on policy have had their successes and failures over the decades. Similarly, the experiences of teachers, working often in localized, idiosyncratic, and highly political environments, can differ dramatically from the recommendations of NCTE.

One thing I hope readers will glean from the case studies is that we probably cannot craft concrete heuristics for how the field should engage in policy discussions *from now on*. Likewise, the results of my participant observation in a high school dual enrollment classroom should not be interpreted as the definitive answer for how *all* dual enrollment courses in composition should be structured from here on out. Rather, this collection of case studies is meant to point out that meaningful policy work in writing studies should be kairotic or polikairotic in nature. Moreover, the bridges and barriers between institutional engagements with policy on the one hand, and the felt experience of policy by teachers on the other, reveal how policy regimes structure the opportunities, or "windows," we have to put stress on writing policies that do not serve the best interests of teachers or students.

The Accountability Movement and Writing Studies

When talking about policy, we can easily get lost in the capaciousness of the concept. When I speak of *education policy* in this book, I am referring to what Chris Gallagher has described as the "laws (and other judicial decisions), regulations, funding priorities, and other courses of action promulgated by federal, state, and local government bodies and officials" ("At the Precipice" 87). Gallagher's definition of public policy is important because it includes not just the roles as stipulated by government entities but also the "priorities" and "courses of action" of government entities. This inclusion is key when talking about education policy specifically because, as with major education reform issues like *accountability*, their components are not always inscribed in law. They are rather priorities, or what Patrick McGuinn calls *governing arrangements* in which proponents of education reform rhetorically situate their ideas.

The governing arrangements that became known as the accountability movement are a good starting point for a discussion of education policy as it relates to college writing instruction. But many scholars differ on where and when the accountability movement began and what it actually means. Some point to specific pieces of legislation as the beginning of the accountability movement. Diane Ravitch, for example, argues that the accountability movement came to prominence with the passage of the No Child Left Behind Act in 2001 under George W. Bush's administration. From this point forward, she writes, the accountability movement, which she defines as our current culture of "high-stakes testing, data-driven decision making, choice, charter schools, privatization, deregulation, merit pay, and competition among schools," took shape (*Death and Life* 21). In *Reclaiming Assessment: A Better Alternative to the Accountability Movement*, Chris W. Gallagher writes that the accountability movement in public education emerged not necessarily from any one piece of legislation but from several overlapping "literacy crises" in the 1970s where critics bemoaned declining literacy rates and called for more academic rigor in public schools. These crises fed public sentiment and incrementally resulted in public policy aimed at remedying them by strengthening academic expectations.

More recently, Joanne Addison and Sharon James McGee's *Writing and School Reform: Writing Instruction in the Age of Common Core and*

Standardized Testing situates the accountability movement in terms of policy shifts toward standardized testing that began as early as the 1860s, when more diverse Americans were entering college, academic disciplines were becoming defined, and the modern university was taking shape (23). "The mid-1800s and early 1900s," they write, "marked a rapid expansion and development of educational testing and measurement in the United States—much of it through the efforts of our universities to influence curriculum at the secondary level in order to ensure students were prepared for university-level work" (24). Addison and McGee also point to a series of important political and cultural events in America that precipitated the push for more testing and measurement in American schools, such as the launch of the Sputnik satellite by the Soviet Union in 1957. This event became, as literacy scholars later described it, an opportunity for policymakers to "manufacture" a crisis in literacy to justify calls for increasing educational standards to ensure the United States could compete economically with foreign political adversaries (Berliner and Biddle). Shortly after Sputnik's launch, for example, Dwight D. Eisenhower signed the National Defense Education Act in 1958, which set aside funding to strengthen American science curricula (Addison and McGee 28). The cascade of educational reports following the act's passage, they argue, made cases for higher standards and better strategies to measure American students' academic aptitude—reports such as the 1966 Coleman Report and the results of the 1969 National Assessment of Educational Progress test, all the way to modern accountability reform documents such as the 2006 Spellings Report or *A Test of Leadership* of the same year (36–37).

These histories are instructive for tracing the concept of accountability. I tend to fall more in step with Gallagher, though, which is why I do not isolate any policy or piece of legislation as being *the* main driver of accountability, even though I refer to the report *A Nation at Risk* and No Child Left Behind as landmarks in the history of accountability policy regimes. Moreover, in our current accountability moment, driven by efforts to coalesce standards around a "common core" of competencies, it is not policies or laws that color public attitudes toward education as much as the financial influence of private foundations and education philanthropists (Darling-Hammond; McNeil). The current climate is the culmination of a decades-long shift in social, historical, and political understandings of the government's role in education. Framed in terms of "a fear that the United States is falling dangerously behind other countries in global tests of academic achievement" (Addison and McGee 42), our current accountability policies have a stronghold in American public discourse about education. The accountability movement may appeal to democratic platitudes like "leveling the playing field" or "leaving no child behind," yet the movement actually espouses a narrowly defined concern for "getting one's money's worth in a competitive 'free market' of goods and services" (Gallagher, *Reclaiming Assessment* 23).

For Addison and McGee, charting a path forward involves collaboration on all fronts, from high school to college and from teachers to researchers and assessment specialists. For others in the field, charting a way forward in a climate of accountability is about *reframing* public narratives about writing and education policies. In *Activist WPA: Changing Stories about Writing and Writers*, Linda Adler-Kassner reflects on this history of accountability for how it has influenced public discussions of writing and writing instruction. For politicians, pundits, and the media, Adler-Kassner writes, the dominant stories about writing and writing instruction are based in accountability logics, which say that "students can't write" or they "read the wrong things or not at all" or "they aren't prepared or they have to take 'remedial' courses" or, worse yet, that "teachers . . . aren't teaching them 'what they need to know'" (2). Writing studies practitioners should change these narratives because, as Adler-Kassner writes, "these stories have consequences. They encompass every aspect of our work, from placement to curriculum design to classroom instruction to professional development" (18). And in our efforts to intervene and change the prevailing narratives about writing, Adler-Kassner argues that we cannot just "sit and wait to see what happens" (22).

As the scholars quoted above have shown, dominant accountability-based narratives about writing instruction and public education stem from an entrenched *neoliberal* framework that subjects every aspect of education to free-market principles of competition and privatization, a kind of "government through the market, wherein education is viewed as a consumer-driven commodity that ought to be efficient and profitable (e.g., privatized)" (Larson ix). Adler-Kassner and O'Neill argue that writing studies faculty and administrators can combat these neoliberal frameworks by "reframing" public discussions about writing to represent more accurately what we know and value about writing. However, since the current narratives about public education, and about writing in particular, are so entrenched in neoliberal frameworks, what are effective ways for those of us who teach writing to intervene and change these stories? What does it look like to leverage disciplinary knowledge in order to promote education policies that would offer an alternative to accountability?

In his essay "At the Precipice of Speech: English Studies, Science, and Policy (Ir)relevancy," Gallagher tries to answer some of these questions by arguing that, despite our calls to action, "we have a remarkably poor track record of shaping the public policies that shape our work" (74). Gallagher's claim here hits close to home. Writing teachers, researchers, and administrators at all levels are rarely trained in public policy work. And at same time, Gallagher points out, "many policymakers refuse to acknowledge the legitimacy of our knowledge claims" anyway (74). Our professional organizations NCTE and the Modern Language Association—with their many initiatives, campaigns, and advocacy efforts—have had little noticeable impact on public education policies. "While we push for teacher and student empowerment," Gallagher writes,

> educational policy functions by remote control. While we offer complex understandings of reading and writing, educational policy mandates standardized tests that reduce them to discrete, easily measurable skills. While we teach literature as a rich cultural practice, educational policy reduces it to discrete bits of testable knowledge. (75)

These realities can be disheartening to those of us inspired by Adler-Kassner's rallying assertion: "we have the brains, the know-how, and the tools" to change these stories (22). For many of us, the prospects for *actually* changing the stories in our favor seem pretty dim.

So what role does the field of writing studies have to play in shaping education policy, given the scholarship on, interest in, and expertise about writing at our disposal, along with the institutional support of our professional organizations? And, moreover, what does it look like to be engaged in policy work while simultaneously being a teacher, researcher, or administrator? Each institutional alignment, after all, comes with its own thorny bureaucracies and expectations that may run counter to taking an activist stance toward changing policy narratives about writing. What is it really like on the ground for the teachers who are tasked with enacting these policies in their classrooms? What triumphs do they experience? How do they navigate policies they may disagree with? When policy and practice are at odds, what are their workarounds for creating classroom experiences that satisfy districts, states, and assessments while still being true to their own pedagogical philosophies?

Theoretical Lens: A Policy Regime Approach

As a way to answer these questions, the case studies to follow draw on a theoretical concept from political science called policy regimes. A policy regime describes the governing arrangements of a given policy problem. As Peter J. May and Ashley E. Jochim write, traditional approaches to policy studies see policy as a set of specific policymaking strategies and understand politics as an obstacle to the implementation of a given policy. A policy regime approach, on the other hand, analyzes not strategies but *arrangements*, and it sees politics as a fundamental part of the ways that policies achieve legitimacy, coherence, and durability. As an analytical framework, a regime perspective begins with a policy problem and extends outward to the governing arrangements that create the problem. May and Jochim write that policy regimes include the "institutional arrangements, interest alignments, and shared ideas" attached to a policy problem (428).

One of the first scholars to discuss policy regimes was Carter A. Wilson, whose 2000 essay "Policy Regimes and Policy Change" in the *Journal of Public Policy* synthesized the literature on how changes happen in public policy. Wilson begins with a critique of Frank Baumgartner and Bryan Jones's term *punctuated equilibrium*, which characterizes policymaking as having "long periods of stability interrupted by spurts of change" (249). The problem, Wilson writes, is that the literature on policy change focuses on only one dimension at a time. For example, decision theorists highlight only the role of policymakers; state-centered researchers focus endogenously on "the state as the fulcrum of power" (254), while overlooking exogenous factors like inflation or demographic changes; neo-Marxists study "class conflict and economic arrangements" (251) at the expense of "inside institutions which produce policy change" (255); and researchers who link policy and ideology deploy a Gramscian approach that considers policy to be a set of narratives or paradigms but that overlooks other exogenous factors that can initiate policy change.

Instead, Wilson suggests we adopt a regime perspective to explain the relationship between stability and change in public policies. Wilson draws on several scholarly conversations to situate his regime perspective. First, he uses Kratochwil and Ruggi's definition of regimes as "governing arrangements constructed by states to coordinate their expectations and organize aspects of international behavior in various issue-areas" (qtd. in Wilson 256). According to international regime literature, issue areas typically include "trade, monetary policy, food, defense, and others," and they encompass several other dimensions such as the organization of "states, social or political institutions"; "mutually accepted decision-making procedures and agreed upon rules for action"; and "shared principles, norms, and beliefs" (256).

From this scholarship, Wilson proposes four dimensions of a policy regime. The first is what he calls *power arrangements*, or "the presence of one or more powerful interest groups supporting the policy regime" (257). Power arrangements could include any number of both competing or dominant interest groups, coalitions, or professional organizations and may or may not include the state and business sectors. Second, Wilson writes that policy regimes have a *policy paradigm*, a concept that draws heavily from political theorists of ideology and encompasses "the way problems are defined, the types of solutions offered, and the kinds of policies proposed" (257). A policy paradigm encompasses images, assumptions, and narratives about the policy problem, or "ways of seeing, talking and defining problems, which in turn shape policy solutions" (258). Ideological frames are disseminated through the media, in "books, magazines, journals, newspapers, television, and radio—and in every day speech—political campaign speeches, talks and debates on the floor of congress, discussions in the White House, and conservations in the work place, taverns, classrooms, street corners and individual homes" (258). Third, Wilson writes that policy regimes have *policy arrangements*, or mechanisms through which policies are implemented by the government. These arrangements include "leaders of congressional committees, agencies, institutions, professional associations and organized interests involved in developing and maintaining the policy" (258). And fourth and finally, policy regimes cannot survive without the policies themselves, which include the goals, rules, and routines that give the policy legitimacy and durability (258).

According to Wilson, each of these four dimensions—power arrangements, policy paradigms, policy arrangements, and the policies themselves—contributes to the long-term stability of a policy regime. Even in periods of political dispute or instability, Wilson argues, you can still see a relatively stable policy regime. For example, consider the ways that policy arrangements, or the rules and regulations governing policy implementation, ensure a policy regime's stability. Typically, a government agency is established to enforce a policy, which involves hiring officials dedicated to its implementation. These moves strengthen the durability and stability of a policy regime. Wilson writes, "the implementation process operates to sustain the policy and becomes part of the policy regime" (259).

As a specific example, we can look at the career of Diane Ravitch, mentioned above, who championed progressive education policies for much of her early career; yet when she was hired as the assistant secretary of education during the Clinton administration, she became a defender of charter schools, choice, and testing—hallmarks of accountability education reform. Ravitch has since denounced her support of these policies, but she was nevertheless complicit in the policy regime of accountability for her role in implementing these policies when she was in a position of power.

A reason why the accountability-based policy regime has been so durable over several presidential administrations with differing political stances toward public education is that the policy arrangements of the regime steer people with opposing ideologies toward positions of power within the regime and convert them to being protectors and promoters of the policy paradigms that keep the regime strong. Ravitch herself later wrote that it was

> ironic that a conservative Republican president [George W. Bush] was responsible for the largest expansion of federal control in the history of American Education [with the passage of No Child Left Behind]. It was likewise ironic that Democrats embraced market reforms and other initiatives that traditionally had been favored by Republicans. (Death and Life 24)

Another reason that accountability policies have remained durable over time has to do with a policy paradigm that framed accountability in the public imagination as a *commonsense* approach to education reform. Wilson argues that a policy paradigm plays

> a key role in ensuring the stability of a policy regime because it structures perception in ways that obstruct the emergence of alternative policy definitions and policy solutions. It promotes the belief that existing arrangements are rational and natural, and alternatives are irrational or impossible. It legitimizes the regime and contributes to long term stability. (259)

This explains why Ravitch was initially supportive of No Child Left Behind. "Who could object to ensuring that children mastered the basic skills of reading and mathematics?" she asks, invoking the commonsense framing typical of an entrenched policy paradigm. "Who could object to an annual test of those skills? Certainly not I. Didn't all schools test their students at least once annually?" (*Death and Life* 17).

Despite their durability over time, Wilson argues that a policy regime can weaken for several reasons: when external factors stress or enable change (260); when policy paradigms lose their credibility (262–63); when legitimacy crises cause the public to lose confidence in a policy paradigm (264); when power shifts weaken a policy regime, such as changes in presidential administrations or electorates (264); or when the organization of the policy implementation process changes. Over time, Wilson writes, these "stressors" do in fact weaken policy regimes, leaving them vulnerable to change. For example, Wilson describes the governing arrangements of tobacco use in the United States. The initial stressors to the policy regimes that maintained the arrangements governing widespread acceptance and deregulation of tobacco came in the early 1950s, when some of the first studies of the health risks of smoking were published (261). These studies, although shocking indictments of the tobacco industry, did not immediately instigate a regime change. The policy paradigm legitimizing the safety of tobacco remained strong through the 1950s despite these stressors, and it was not until the early 1960s that the paradigm encountered significant opposition, when the surgeon general finally issued a report detailing the health hazards of smoking. According to Wilson, policy regimes of tobacco reform began, first, with a

> significant increase in the number of published studies *operating within alternative paradigms* demonstrating the health hazards

> of smoking. Second, these studies were accepted by reputable opinion leaders. Third, these studies received media coverage and they were publicized by key individuals and organizations. (263; my italics)

In other words, substantial policy change in a policy regime occurs through a matrix of factors that *put stress* on existing regimes, such as the "shifting of power alignments, the discrediting of dominant paradigms, the ascension of alternative paradigms, the formation of new organizational arrangements, and the setting of new policy goals" (270).

Wilson's framework for understanding public policy through the lens of regimes, as well as the confluence of factors necessary for a regime to fall, are helpful when considering the policy regimes governing education in the United States. Political scientist Patrick J. McGuinn takes this approach in analyzing the shift toward accountability as a specific kind of regime change, or what he calls a shift in the federal government's education policy from a largely hands-off approach, the "equity regime" in his terms, to a reform-oriented approach in the late twentieth century. For McGuinn, a policy regime perspective allows us to take a historical view of governing arrangements by seeing education policy changes as kind of regime change. For example, President Lyndon Johnson's signature education bill, the Elementary and Secondary Education Act of 1965, allocated unprecedented amounts of money to improve education. This piece of legislation, McGuinn writes, is emblematic of the old regime, the equity regime. The policy paradigm invoked by the equity regime was that "most public schools were doing fine, that problems were concentrated in schools located in poor areas, and that issues of school governance and improvement were the responsibility of local and state governments" (22). Despite the government making such a huge investment in education, McGuinn notes that the federal government's relationship to education at this time was still relatively hands-off because there were few mandates for what states were to do with the money they received. The bill merely provided resources for promoting equity and access for poor students.

A key point here is that the policy paradigm of the equity regime held steady beyond the Johnson administration thanks to the power arrangements of Democrats in Congress and interest groups such as civil rights activists and teachers' unions. "As a result," McGuinn writes, while the federal role in schools did expand rapidly in the 1960s and '70s, "its scope and nature did not change significantly" (22). As Wilson reminds us, though, policy regimes can begin to crumble owing in part to stressors that put pressure on old policy paradigms. One stressor for the equity regime was a federal education report, *A Nation at Risk*, issued in 1983 by President Ronald Reagan's Commission on Excellence in Education. Composed primarily by CEOs, politicians, and administrators in higher education, *A Nation at Risk* essentially declared a new literacy crisis in which American students were not prepared to compete with other students internationally. The report argued for higher standards, more accountability, and increased choice for parents as to where they could send their children to school. By encouraging the establishment of national education standards, McGuinn writes, this report "undermined the old policy paradigm in education and generated momentum for reform" (22). McGuinn and others link this document to later efforts in the 1990s to tie school performance to federal aid and to actual legislation, namely the No Child Left Behind Act of 2001, which was a reauthorization of Johnson's bill but with new features like increased testing and punitive sanctions for schools with poor test scores. As Gallagher argues, *A Nation at Risk* was important for setting the tone of subsequent education reform efforts, particularly in the way it was "heavily influenced by the nation's business community and its commitment to improving America's competitiveness in the global marketplace" (20–21). Despite the stressors of the early 1980s, though, the equity regime remained the prevailing set of policy arrangements for almost two more decades, thanks in part to members of the Republican Party who insisted on "state and local responsibility and [on being] opposed [to] federal mandates and spending in education" (22). Many Democrats continued to defend the equity regime, too, advocating for the expansion of federal support for education but only in terms of providing equity for underfunded areas (23).

As the equity regime faced continued public pressure, though, Democrats slowly began to support accountability-based reforms despite teachers' unions and civil rights groups having long opposed them. Over time, Republicans also began to support reforms such as increased federal spending, despite their prior views on limited government and states' rights (23). "The old policy regime," McGuinn writes,

> was narrowly focused on helping disadvantaged students by promoting equity and access, and it had been governed by a largely congressional and interest group-dominated policymaking process made possible by the issue's low salience with the public. The new educational policy regime embraces a broad federal commitment to promoting academic achievement for all students and features a very visible and open policymaking process that is responsive to public pressures and directed by presidential leadership. (23)

According to McGuinn, No Child Left Behind was the breaking point of a policy regime that had held strong for nearly five decades. What is particularly noteworthy about McGuinn's methodology is that he did not just analyze the law itself or even the ways in which an already-established policy paradigm inevitably led to the accountability movement. Instead, he traced how the equity regime set up by Johnson's bill was overthrown thanks to an interplay of "ideas, interests, and institutions" in a new policy regime that favored accountability. And in response to political science theories that see policy problems from government activity as more or less stable and durable over time (11), a regime perspective shows us that, actually, "the tendency of the policymaking system is not toward equilibrium but toward disequilibrium" (19).

Moreover, McGuinn's methodology, which I extend in upcoming chapters, presumes that we need to understand policy in terms of a "historical analysis of politics and policymaking over an extended period of time," which includes a "wide variety of actors and factors at work in American politics and the ways in which they interact to produce policy" (19). Similarly, I analyze the role of writing studies in education policy from a regime framework and take into account a wide variety of actors and factors that affect how institutions and individuals interact with and experience writing instruction policy. Thus, this book is not so much interested in outlining policymaking strategies for the field as it is in describing the governing arrangements—the laws, actors, actions, and alignments—that have informed writing studies' role in effecting public education policies so far and in accounting for the ways our institutions intersect with individual teachers' experiences to put stress on an accountability regime that, while "vigorously defended and often quite durable," is not inevitable (19).

Structure of the Book

To apply a policy regime perspective to writing studies' role in federal and state education policies, I use a mixed-method approach that zooms in and out, from the role that the academic discipline of writing studies plays in effecting educational policy, to the individual experiences of teachers in the classrooms where those policies are implemented. In this way, my analysis moves away from critiquing specific strategies of policy implementation or pieces of legislation that impact writing studies and moves toward broader understandings of the policy regimes that give these policies durability and legitimacy. In other words, like McGuinn or Wilson, I analyze authoritative actions like statutes and executive orders, as well as the histories, institutional arrangements, and shared ideas that constitute the paradigm of writing policy.

Drawing on archival research from NCTE's headquarters in Urbana, Illinois, chapter 1 analyzes NCTE's work as an institution to bridge, partner with, advocate, or resist education policy. As Wilson writes, power arrangements encompass "the presence of one or more powerful interest groups supporting the policy regime" (257). Chapter 1 asks, How does NCTE fit into the power arrangements of accountability? How has NCTE historically fit into the governing arrangements of education policy, whether as an agent of opposition, a negotiator that reinforced dominant policy paradigms, or an activist that bridged, dictated, informed, or resisted the implementation of education policy?

To answer this, I present a case study of a small group of NCTE members who worked as literacy lobbyists in the late 1970s and early '80s to gain influence and build relationships with leaders at the Capitol. This Washington Task Force worked diligently over a six-year period to live up to many of NCTE's stated goals in the 1950s and '60s and to maintain sway in the education policy world. However, as McGuinn has pointed out, the policy paradigm dictating the government's role in education reform was shifting during this period from an equity regime to an accountability regime, and NCTE's archives reveal the Washington Task Force bound up in this shift, as stressors aplenty began to change the US government's position on education in favor of testing, choice, and efficiency, all hallmarks of the accountability regime (even though these hallmarks are often couched in terms of equity and social justice). Through an analysis of meeting minutes and personal papers, as well as commission, committee, and Washington Task Force files, this chapter paints a picture of the field's power arrangements in relation to national policymaking in the midst of a regime change. As I show, organizations like NCTE are often critiqued for not being involved enough in policy formation—at least not as much as they were in previous decades. I argue that the reason for this is not ineptitude or a lack of commitment to policymaking. The Washington Task Force's efforts to engage in policy work did not necessarily fail to enact NCTE's vision; rather, the efforts came at a time when the rules of policy work were in flux, and the policy regimes at play had not just political but also ideological consequences. NCTE, too, was bound up in the policy paradigms of the time, which shaped its strategies of policy engagement.

Next, in chapter 2, I focus on a specific case of NCTE's efforts at policy work several decades later, when the accountability regime was in full swing. In 2009 NCTE consulted on an early draft of the English language arts component of the Common Core State Standards, a set of academic standards in math and English designed to equip students who graduate from high school with the skills necessary to succeed in college and their future careers. In one sense, the story of NCTE's feedback on this draft could be described as one of failure, an attempt at dialogue that did not result in a multi-stakeholder policymaking experience, as NCTE hoped, but was instead a frustrating moment of bureaucracy. Doug Hesse notes, in his chapter in the collection *Who Speaks for Writing*, NCTE's work with the authors of the Common Core standards was futile from the very beginning, as "input from experts in writing was missing in the development stages, sought during the end game and pretty much after the fact, then ignored" (11). But this case study also reveals the twenty-first-century power arrangements of writing policy that had been taking shape since the 1980s, highlighting both the current stakes of collaborating with the powerful institutions that now drive writing policy in the United States and the ways that academic disciplines can kairotically put stress on policy regimes in ways other than merely presenting well-researched ideas to the opposition.

The rest of the book focuses on the education policy of dual enrollment. In chapter 3, the case study is Ohio's dual enrollment legislation, College Credit Plus, which is a state-funded program in which students in middle and high school can earn college credit for composition courses for free. They can then transfer their credits to any public institution in the state. This chapter showcases the issues that can emerge within the accountability regime on a local level. The policy paradigm governing accountability characterizes writing as a "set of low-level skills that can and should be fairly and quickly mastered early in college, or even before" and approaches education as a "matter of accumulating credit hours in various categories of instruction" (Hansen, "Composition Marketplace" 2). Through my analysis of state and federal education reports, dual enrollment statistics, and data from the Ohio Board of Regents, this chapter describes a statewide set of policy arrangements that is a direct consequence of the ideas, interests, and arrangements of the accountability regime.

Chapter 4 zooms in even closer by examining teaching and learning in one dual enrollment composition class. I carried out participant observation in a high school class that took part in my university's concurrent enrollment program. My data come from observations of classroom pedagogies and interactions over the course of a semester, along with post-semester interviews I conducted with students. I showcase how policy regimes are *felt, experienced, and enacted* in a classroom context. A policy regime, as McGuinn reminds us, does not just consist of legislation; it consists of the shared ideas that contribute to the regime's ideological justifications. My observations show how individual classroom practices often reinforce but sometimes resist policy regimes of writing. This case study demonstrates how teachers and students are capable of using strategies of kairotic political engagement even as they are tasked with carrying out policies they may or may not support. I argue that, as a field, we need to better understand both how individual classroom pedagogies are bound up in the power arrangements, policy paradigms, and policy arrangements of a given regime and how teachers and students put stress on those regimes in unexpected ways to meet their own needs and interests.

And finally, in a concluding chapter, I discuss, in light of my findings, how writing teachers, researchers, and administrators can complicate calls in our field to "get involved" in policy. In an increasingly precarious time for educators in K–16—whether having to persevere in the face of austerity measures, having to find opportunities for learning amid callous neoliberal agendas, or having to implement a questionable pedagogy or else risk political attacks from ideological critics—what people mean when they admonish us to get involved is vitally important. While we most certainly cannot overstate the importance of writing policy to the field of writing studies, few of us are in a position to actually commit ourselves to full-scale regime change. As the institutional and classroom case studies illustrate, though, policy work in writing studies encompasses a broad range of practices and ideological stances. Putting stress on a regime that appears at first glance to be impenetrable is the first step in this process, but change ultimately takes dedicated collaboration, historical awareness, and an unwavering commitment to students and teachers of writing across all grade levels.

CHAPTER 1

Regime Change: An Overview of NCTE's Policy Advocacy from ESEA to *A Nation at Risk*

Introduction

A policy regime approach to writing studies goes beyond analyzing key pieces of legislation, even though I do discuss several landmark laws that defined the federal government's role in accountability policy. Equally important to a policy regime approach is taking a historical view of how powerful interest groups (power arrangements), ideological paradigms that justify policy approaches (policy paradigms), and bureaucratic mechanisms through which the government enacts its education policies (policy arrangements) maintain the legitimacy of policy regimes over time. Throughout the history of English studies (the disciplinary umbrella for writing studies), several key moments showcase how policy regimes of writing have shaped the way we think about and engage with policy as a field.

This chapter investigates the ways that institutions representing writing studies have engaged in policy work and illustrates how policy regimes of writing have made that engagement effective or ineffective. I analyze the main professional organization representing the interests of literacy instructors and writing researchers: the National Council of Teachers of English, or NCTE. It is the largest professional organization for English teachers in the world, and the Conference on College Composition and Communication (CCCC) is a part of it. I argue that, contrary to the common narrative in our field that says NCTE—and by extension the field itself—is not doing enough to engage in policy, the real story is a lot more complicated. NCTE actually has a long history of working as a bridge, partner, advocate, and responder to federal education policies and has, on many occasions, played a significant role in policy formation. As an institution, though, NCTE is nevertheless bound up in the prevailing policy paradigms of the moment, and throughout its history NCTE has engaged in various political strategies that include aligning itself with the ideological interests of the federal government. In other words, the ways that NCTE has or has not persuaded policy stakeholders have largely depended on the policy regimes governing education policy at the time and the rhetorical choices made by NCTE's leaders about the best ways to cultivate institutional power within those regimes.

As McGuinn has shown, the *equity regime* in the 1950s and '60s saw the federal government's role in education as limited to distributing federal funds for students in poverty to the students' school districts. This regime began to shift in the early 1980s toward an *accountability regime*. Unlike the equity regime, the accountability regime saw the federal government's role in education as ensuring that schooling serves the interests of the economic good instead of the public good. In other words, an accountability regime prioritizes governing arrangements that value workplace readiness, efficiency, or what Piper and Sikes call *managerialism*. The time period analyzed in this chapter captures the transition between these two periods and shows NCTE serving as a sounding board for issues in English studies, sometimes speaking out in resistance to accountability policies but other times working to align its interests with the government's in an appeal for more federal funding for English teaching. This chapter analyzes how NCTE rhetorically positioned itself in the kairos of a *regime change* from equity to accountability, amidst shifting policies, power arrangements, and ideological paradigms.

As the case study of the chapter, I focus on a dedicated group of NCTE members known as the Washington Task Force, who, in the late 1970s and early '80s, struggled to assert NCTE's institutional power during the shift. They worked diligently in Washington, DC to advocate for the interests of English teachers across all grade levels. Basing its engagement strategies on the equity regime logics that had informed federal education policies for the past several decades, NCTE had, up until that point, enjoyed relative success in maintaining its presence among education policy stakeholders. However, a variety of *stressors* began to reframe the equity policy regime around concepts of school choice, standardized testing, and market-based models of efficiency, which ultimately resulted in the construction of new power dynamics and policy arrangements in Washington. NCTE's Washington Task Force therefore encountered more and more obstacles to influencing policymakers on Capitol Hill. By 1984 the new accountability regime had achieved legitimacy in public discourse, and it all but nullified the relationships that NCTE had built in Washington over the previous five years. As such, NCTE's vast disciplinary expertise was no longer persuasive to political insiders, and the Washington Task Force dissolved.

In writing studies scholarship, organizations like NCTE are often critiqued for not being involved enough in policy formation—or at least not as much as they were in earlier decades of their existence. And while there is some truth to those claims, I argue that the reason is not because NCTE as an organization or its leadership has lacked commitment or the political will to engage in policy work, as some have suggested. In fact, when we examine the Washington Task Force's efforts to engage in policy at a time of regime change in education policy, we see that Task Force members were not failing to enact NCTE's vision so much as they were unfortunate spectators in a political climate where the "rules" of policy work were in flux. NCTE, moreover, was just as bound up as any educational organization in the prevailing policy paradigms of the time, and as new power structures and ideological paradigms formed new political arrangements, NCTE was no longer able to wield the political cachet it once had. This unique moment in NCTE's history of political engagement paints a more complicated picture of the role of institutions in shaping and responding to writing policy.

As a prelude to my case study, I provide a brief history of NCTE. Next, I focus on the Washington Task Force. I argue that in this historical case study, we see the triumphs, pitfalls, and ethical limitations of writing studies' institutional engagement in policy. In the equity regime of the 1950s and '60s, NCTE worked successfully alongside powerful policy stakeholders in education reform because the governing arrangements of the equity regime, for the most part, valued the judgment of professional disciplinary organizations in deciding *where* and *how* education funding was spent. NCTE leveraged this arrangement to cultivate institutional power, which made room for a handful of successful policymaking experiences. In the 1970s and '80s, though, those governing arrangements began to shift, and the Washington Task Force found itself no longer able to exert influence like it once had.

As I describe NCTE's institutional efforts to influence education policy, my goal is not necessarily to hold NCTE responsible for poor policy engagement in the accountability era. On the contrary, despite what some in our field have argued, NCTE's efforts over the decades were fruitful. However, as Porter et al. suggest, an institutional critique can be useful, for "institutions, as unchangeable as they may seem (and, indeed, often are), do contain spaces for reflection, resistance, revision, and productive action" (612). There are other benefits to looking at institutions, too. Ryan Skinnell's *Conceding Composition* focuses on what he calls "non-disciplinary institutional exigencies" for reconsidering common assumptions about the history of the field, even though these concerns "often seem distant from the specific demands of composition classrooms" (11). In Skinnell's case, he considered the field's institutional agency over the past one hundred years as a way to disrupt conventional narratives that explain composition's origin story as a kind of cause and effect. (For example, the common story is that an influx of new college students, thanks to the GI Bill, *caused* the field to initiate pedagogical changes). Instead, he asserts that the field was "conceded" in the service of institutional forces. As Skinnell argues, with a desire to receive GI Bill funding, colleges and universities revitalized composition and devoted more resources to the required writing class. Skinnell's aim to understand composition's persistence in the academy by looking at the discipline institutionally—or rather by analyzing "non-disciplinary institutional exigencies and their simultaneously momentous and mundane consequences for composition in American higher education" (27)—resonates with the questions in this chapter. Like Skinnell, I am interested in the non-disciplinary institutional exigencies of education policy, like for example the ways that changing policy regimes created consequences for the teaching, research, and administration of college writing. And moreover, it is important to consider how the institutions of writing studies have historically positioned themselves with regard to policy and how policy regimes have shaped and reshaped those disciplinary commitments.

NCTE and Disciplinary Power

Today, when you visit NCTE's website, its home page explains that the group "amplifies the voice of educators through personal connection, collaboration, and a shared mission to improve the teaching and learning of English and language arts at all levels." Indeed, NCTE's scope and reach extend to most corners of the English teaching profession, from elementary school to college. Another page of the website expands the organization's mission even further, from "amplifying the voice[s]" of educators to "further[ing] the voice and expertise of educators as advocates for their students at the local and federal levels; and to share lesson ideas, research, and teaching strategies through its Annual Convention and other professional learning events" ("About Us"). Of note here is that throughout NCTE's self-description, there is an emphasis on amplifying teachers' voices and extending their influence from local to federal levels. With such a broad vision for access, power, agency, affiliation, and impact, NCTE today is an incredibly far-reaching representative body.

Structurally, NCTE has a Board of Directors, which serves an advisory role in coordination with its Executive Committee. The committee is responsible for approving policies and making decisions regarding NCTE's operations ("Constitution"). Members of the Executive Committee comprise the Presidential Team, which includes a past president, the president-elect, and the current president. The president chairs the Executive Committee, makes at least ten appearances at conferences and conventions throughout the year, and works with the executive director on a host of issues related to NCTE. The executive director is considered the "the face of the organization." A job advertisement in 2015 described the executive director as one who "oversees implementation of the strategic plan and operations across the organization. Identifying short- and long-term opportunities for growth, staff development and management, and financial stewardship will be essential components of the position" ("NCTE Position Profile").

The Executive Committee also includes section directors for elementary, middle, secondary, and college. There are also representatives at large and conference chairs, which include leaders from CCCC, the English Language Arts Teacher Educators conference, the Conference on English Leadership, the conference of the Two-Year College English Association, and the Whole Language Umbrella. Members of

NCTE attend any number of these conferences, depending on their interests, in addition to joining the elementary, middle, secondary, or college sections. There are also geographically based affiliates dedicated to English language arts and literacy; there are caucuses, special-interest groups, and self-organized collaboratives. NCTE also publishes a range of peer-reviewed journals, such as *College Composition and Communication*, *College English*, *Research on the Teaching of English*, *English Education*, and *English Journal*. As an umbrella institution over the last one hundred years, NCTE has been vital for offering "lessons about what it means to establish a discipline and maintain its vitality" (Lindemann 504).

NCTE is also a powerful institution. In the edited collection *Language and Power: An Introduction to Institutional Discourse*, Andrea Mayr argues that institutions are "primary sites for 'reality construction'" (3). Michel Foucault, moreover, in *Discipline and Punish*, describes how the modern prison emerged as an instrument of power through which prisoners began to regulate their own thoughts and behaviors—and hence, their conceptions of truth—through continuous systems of surveillance, or what Foucault called *disciplinary power*. In contrast to brute force, disciplinary power is exercised by the production of knowledge through our institutions. In the edited collection *Foucault and the Critique of Institutions*, editors John Caputo and Mark Yount write that power, as far as Foucault saw it, uses knowledge to normalize behavior, but not in the sense of homogeneity. Normalization, they write, "keeps watch over the excessive and the exceptional"; institutions, in other words, form to "produce legions of adapted, ambient individuals to move easily through the manifold channels of modern social relations" (6). To say that NCTE is a powerful institution is to draw on this intellectual tradition: In a literal sense, particularly through its peer-reviewed journals, annual conferences and conventions, and the bureaucratic mechanisms through which its policy statements and curriculum guidelines are written, approved, and disseminated, NCTE functions as a source of disciplinary power for the field of writing studies. The organization normalizes knowledge production for literacy teachers, it "keeps watch" over the boundaries of truth, and it advocates for those truths in various political and social channels. It is important also to remember that, for Foucault, knowledge and power are two in the same, so to say that NCTE is a source of disciplinary power means that the organization plays a part both in creating social relations and in producing knowledge: "knowledge is what power relations produce in order to spread and disseminate all the more effectively" (Caputo and Yount 7).

Foucault's concepts of disciplinary power and power-knowledge, for Caputo and Yount, also foreground what they call institutional critique, a method designed "to expose the intelligible structure of a local power regime, to show how the differentials in power relations work from their microstructures to their larger effects" (7). In this sense, to say that NCTE *is an institution* is at once to describe the breadth if its influence on writing studies and also to understand it as imbued in a matrix of power relations by which regimes of truth are produced and legitimized. While NCTE is an advocate of teachers' voices—and it certainly is important to acknowledge NCTE's long history of advocacy—analyzing how the organization is bound up in regimes of truth is important as well. For, as Foucault explained in an interview, power does not just "weigh on us as a force that says no"; rather it "traverses and produces things" ("Truth and Power" 61). To quote from Caputo and Yount again, power "does not prevent but invent; does not prohibit but promote; does not negate but affirm; does not annihilate but create" (6). As I briefly trace NCTE's history of policy advocacy below, and as I analyze how the organization effected education policy, these theories can help us situate the history in a context of how policy regimes are produced and legitimized.

Brief History of NCTE

There are several book-length works and articles that discuss NCTE's long history. The most thorough to date is J. N. Hook's 1979 *A Long Way Together*. For Hook, NCTE began as a direct response to education policies. He writes that the very first meeting of NCTE in 1911 was "a meeting of protesters." There, a handful of college professors and secondary educators convened to discuss their disapproval of curricular mandates that were being handed down to them by the nation's colleges and universities.

Colleges and universities, beginning most notably with Harvard in the late nineteenth century, required college entrance examinations in English composition, punctuation, spelling, and literature. Harvard first instituted a "standard authors" list in 1874 to help students prepare for the examination. This list included *Ivanhoe*, *The Lay of the Last Minstrel*, *The Vicar of Wakefield*, and plays by Shakespeare (Hook 8). As other colleges began producing similar lists, the nation's high schools followed suit and began teaching these works of literature as part of their curriculum. As Hook points out, it is important to recognize that the modern high school at this time was a recent phenomenon. The English Classical High School opened in Boston in 1821, and the first court case allowing tax money to be used to support public schools was decided in 1874.

Thus, when Harvard's written entrance exam became the de facto standard for most of the country's colleges and universities, the standard authors list for incoming students frustrated secondary English teachers, who until that time had taught an assortment of subjects in rhetoric, grammar, elocution, and penmanship that they deemed necessary for students (Hook 9). As secondary schools began developing curricula to align with the standard authors lists of the nation's postsecondary institutions, high school teachers became increasingly frustrated by a lack of unity: the standard authors list from Harvard differed from Yale's, which in turn differed from Princeton's and Illinois's. While frustrated calls for uniformity led to the establishment of the College Entrance Examination Board in 1900, which produced a list of literary works for all high school students across the country, secondary school teachers continued to feel constrained by colleges and universities. Moreover, as more and more working-class students began attending high school and as compulsory education laws became the norm (for more on this, see Katz's history of compulsory education laws), teachers were also starting to worry about the relevance of high literary works like those of Shakespeare. As Hook writes,

> Not all high school students, however, could read and understand Shakespeare, Sir Walter Scott, Thackeray, and the rest. A few could not read well at all. Usually discouraged, they dropped out. Else they sat comprehending but a fraction of what was going on. Some could write about baseball or the coal mines but not yet about literature. Some, from foreign families coming in by the tens of thousands, knew so little English that the current prescription was entirely useless. (12)

Thus, in 1892, the National Education Association established a Committee of Ten to make specific recommendations about how secondary schools could better prepare students for college. The committee recommended, among other things, that all work in the secondary schools be identical. In essence, this recommendation effectively inaugurated English as a required course at all high schools in the United States. English, according to the Committee of Ten, involved teaching "the pupil to understand the expressed thoughts of others and to give expression to thoughts of his own" and, also, "to cultivate a taste for reading, to give the pupil some acquaintance with good literature, and to furnish him with the means of extending that acquaintance" (Hook 11). As Carol Aulbach writes, this recommendation from the Committee of Ten was significant because, barely a hundred years before, American university students were not even allowed to *speak* English on campus. However, despite the efforts of the Committee of Ten in the 1890s, the policy nevertheless resulted in understaffed, unprepared teachers who ultimately began relying on "newly developed textbooks," which derived their content from literature "found in college-entrance examinations." Ultimately, says Aulbach, it was still the case that colleges maintained "tight control of [the] high-school English curriculum" (16).

Thus, at the 1911 meeting of the National Education Association, the English Roundtable, a small group of teachers in the association's Secondary Division, appointed a committee to analyze college entrance requirements (Hook 14). The committee decided that it was in their best interest to establish a permanent group for teachers of English and, later that year, created the National Council of Teachers of English, which convened its first meeting in Chicago (16). According to Aulbach, NCTE's founding correlated with increased numbers of immigrants and working-class students attending America's public high schools. NCTE was indeed formed in protest over unfair mandates from colleges, but the organization was also protesting the "high culture as described by Mathew Arnold in 1860 and as represented in the universities' lists," which were, according to Aulbach, "not appropriate for all segments of a democratic society" (17).

A hundred years later, in 2011, *College Composition and Communication* published a special symposium on NCTE's centennial, dedicated to understanding the relationship between NCTE and its offshoot CCCC. In the issue, Erika Lindemann echoes many of Hook's arguments from more than thirty years prior, namely, that the organization was "born out of a protest against college entrance examinations" (506) and that a strained relationship between the nation's high schools and colleges led to the creation, in 1911, of an English Roundtable that gathered in Chicago with the goal of respecting "the authority of teachers to determine standards for graduation" (509). Lindemann extends the story a bit, suggesting that we can better understand NCTE by comparing it to the Modern Language Association (MLA), an organization that was founded just twenty-eight years prior in 1883. That NCTE had a distinct focus on teaching and on secondary-postsecondary collaboration was the main difference between the two organizations. While MLA was also formed in protest by disgruntled college professors who opposed curricula dominated by Latin and Greek, Lindemann writes that "most MLA members' concerns were far removed from the circumstances of most high school English teachers" (512). Lindemann argues that early collaborative efforts between college and high school teachers were instrumental to the founding of NCTE, which sets it apart from other professional organizations' origin stories from this time period.

Lindemann also argues that NCTE made several key moves at *institutionalization* that allowed it to rise in prominence. First, she writes, NCTE cultivated spaces for communicating new scholarship by creating journals, conferences, and newsletters for "demonstrating the scientific nature of the intellectual work" (522). Second, NCTE focused its efforts on "the professionalism of its members," which meant shaping the research agendas of its membership and initiating others into the field.[1] And finally, NCTE became prominent by "attending to larger social responsibilities," which involved dialoguing with high school and college instructors to meet the changing literacy expectations of a growing high school population and an even larger growth of college students who "were entering college to prepare themselves for a broader array of professions other than ministry education, medicine, and the law" (524). These key moves, Lindemann writes, successfully institutionalized NCTE as a group responsible for representing the interests of English teachers at all grade levels as well as creating and maintaining knowledge about English teaching.

For considering the political engagements of NCTE and the role of writing studies in effecting education policy, the story of how NCTE became a professional organization is important. As Hook points out, six years after NCTE formed, it responded to college entrance exam policies forcefully. For example, in 1917, in a joint effort with the National Education Association, James Fleming Hosiac, the first secretary of NCTE, published the *Reorganization Report*, which made recommendations for a complete reorganization of high school English classes whereby high schools should no longer be "subservient" to colleges and, in step with Deweyan educational philosophy of the time, that the subject matter would be *student-focused*. In the following decades, "almost every public high school and many private ones were affected by [the *Reorganization Report*] to some degree in philosophy, in course content and arrangement, and in increased attention to student needs" (Hook 47–48). NCTE, in other words, formed as a group of concerned teachers interested in policy as it pertained both to colleges and universities and to secondary English curricula, and the organization had success early on at effecting national education policy arrangements.

While Hook goes into great detail about the early days of NCTE, most relevant to this chapter is the fact that, as a professional organization, NCTE's early goals and actions involved not just an interest in policy but in working to *create policy knowledge*. From a regime perspective, we can take Lindemann's argument about how NCTE became a successful institution and describe it as NCTE leveraging its institutional power to put *stress* on existing policy regimes—whether by advocating alternative policy paradigms to those policy mandates that unfairly impacted secondary school teachers or by putting stress on existing policy arrangements by collectively establishing and asserting boundaries around English pedagogy. These moves are important for understanding the ways that an institution such as NCTE can work rhetorically within and sometimes against education policy regimes.

NCTE Policy Advocacy

As a group that formed out of a concern for education policy, NCTE has continued its work into the present. NCTE's 2018 legislative agenda prioritized securing full funding for Title I and Title II of the Every Student Succeeds Act, Obama's reauthorization of the 1965 Elementary and Secondary Education Act (ESEA), as well as Title IV funding under the Higher Education Act, which provides access to higher education through federal student grants and loans for at-risk students.

Despite the pages and pages of NCTE's policy recommendations and position statements, some in the field have critiqued NCTE's commitment to policy change. In 2007, for instance, Leslie David Burns argued that "NCTE has not taken decisive action related to current state and federal accountability reforms that govern teacher preparation, curriculum design, and assessment for teaching and learning" (128). Burns notes an abundance of ambiguous calls to action, with titles such as "Take Classroom Stories to Capitol Hill," "Deliver the Message to Legislators and to the Media," and "Speak Up!" She writes that these calls typically lack teeth and fail to provide NCTE's members with "ideas necessary for them to take control of conversations" (128). While Burns does mention that NCTE's leadership over the years has indeed partnered with related organizations, produced position statements on English language arts curriculum and funding, and offered pragmatic tips for teachers on meeting accountability mandates in their states, its efforts still implicitly support accountability frameworks and legislation that run counter to the organization's values. These moves, Burns writes, risk "deferring to conservative framing of the achievement gap as a problem that can only be solved by the imposition of higher standards on teachers and schools regardless of the additional resources that would be necessary in order for them to implement those standards" (129). Moreover, as with NCTE's other political initiatives, such as Support for the Learning and Teaching of English, which formed in 1975 to help create grassroots political movements among NCTE's membership, these too lack follow-through. According to Burns, this 1975 initiative is no longer operational, which represents to her "some of the problems of sustaining coherent political advocacy in a large, ecumenical professional organization" (130).

Burns's argument that NCTE's policy efforts resemble acquiescence to prevailing policy regimes rather than an activist stance striving for regime change has to do with framing. As far as she is concerned, NCTE has not done enough to usurp the conservative framing of education policy in America, or what George Lakoff calls the "strict father" morality that sees education as a moral corrective to disobedience. "Strict father morality applied to the problem of the achievement gap," Burns writes, "leads to the conclusion that black students fail in schools and on standardized tests of literacy because they are undisciplined, suffer from 'bad parenting,' and so forth" (122). Burns does concede that NCTE's position statements and policy guides have raised consciousness and at times "helped educators operate within rigid accountability frameworks." However, despite its resources, NCTE has still generally been "locked out of policy discussions at the national level for over a decade, and its political presence has been largely ineffectual in gaining access to decision-making processes for literacy reform" (132).

It is important to unpack some of Burns's claims because of the assumptions she is making about the role of NCTE and, more broadly, the institutions that represent fields like writing studies. These assumptions have profound implications for what we imagine the roles and responsibilities of institutions to be within policy regimes. First, we need to reconsider one of Burns's main claims, which is that NCTE has been "largely ineffectual in gaining access to decision-making processes" for education reform. Of the research analyzing NCTE's policy engagements, Curtis Mason's 2011 dissertation, *The National Council of Teachers of English and Federal Education Policy, 1959–1966*, might take issue with that reasoning, though Mason may agree about the ethics of such a political orientation.

Mason's study, a treatment of NCTE's policy engagements after World War II, shows that NCTE did indeed find success in influencing policy. Mason shows that in light of a major federal education funding bill, the National Defense Education Act, NCTE worked tirelessly and eventually succeeded in getting English included as a named discipline in the aid package. However, for Mason, this move was not necessarily a good thing. His main critique is that NCTE betrayed its organizational roots in protest. Mason argues that NCTE did an about-face after World War II in working directly with policymakers instead of in opposition to them. When Congress drafted and advanced the 1958 National Defense Education Act, which, as Addison and McGee tell us, was a landmark piece of legislation directing federal funds toward science and technology across all levels of education (30), NCTE spent much of its policy energy lobbying Congress to add English as a qualifying subject in the legislation. In this period, NCTE began advocating "academic rigor and a content-centered curriculum" to better position English instruction to receive federal funding (Mason 2). This, Mason writes, was a distinct shift in curricular priorities aimed at changing Congress's perception of the importance of English. By working to mobilize its membership to frame English as vital to the national interest, NCTE switched its value system from "supporting a broadly defined, student-centered curriculum," as the organization had done in the early twentieth century, toward "a specific, subject-centered academic based curriculum" (85–86). This policy shift, Mason argues, aligns not with changing educational fads but with a strategic "rhetoric designed to appeal to the federal government's perspective" by proving that "there was a compelling national interest in supporting the teaching of English" (20).

As another example of policy work, in 1961, NCTE published *The National Interest and the Teaching of English: A Report of the Profession*, which was published, Mason writes, "in time for every Congressman to receive a copy before NDEA [the National Defense Education Act] reauthorization hearings were held in 1961" (109). The report argued that untrained teachers, overcrowded classrooms, and lack of rigor in content were indicators of a national crisis, which put the United States' position in the world in jeopardy. Only with a "large scale, government-funded effort" similar to that for science and math education reforms in the original National Defense Education Act, could these conditions improve (128). After distributing the report to every congressman, initiating extensive letter-writing campaigns, and having its members speak at congressional hearings, NCTE was eventually able to convince Education Commissioner Sterling McMurrin to allocate funds to English in support of a program named Project English, which funded national conferences, study centers, and summer programs aimed at constructing curricular guides to be used in English classrooms. Members of NCTE, Mason writes, had "armed themselves with new data" and disseminated that information widely (136). In pursuit of these efforts, NCTE members occasionally spoke before Congress to request more funding throughout the early 1960s, noting the success of Project English and also stressing that, without funding, they would not be able to conduct or act on their research (136).

The 1964 reauthorization of the National Defense Education Act finally included English as an official funded subject. This was a huge victory for the organization. In NCTE's 1964 annual report, Executive Secretary James Squire wrote that "the passage of the extended NDEA marks the beginning, not the end, of efforts to strengthen our national and local commitment to the humanities" (*Annual Report 1964*). Squire also noted that, thanks in large part to the last decade of increased policy engagement, "the American people, through their representatives in the Congress, seem to have awakened to the importance of English and the humanities." Contrary to Burns's claim that NCTE's policy engagement strategies have often "lacked teeth," Mason's archival analysis of NCTE's policy work in the 1950s and '60s shows that the organization has a track record of working strategically to prioritize policy engagement as a fundamental part of asserting its institutional power. The 1960s, according to Squire, represented a new era of *federally funded English*, which only made NCTE a "stronger professional association and, above all, a stronger curricular program in English than we have ever imagined" (qtd. in Mason 149).

Burns's other argument, though, is even more complicated, as it pertains to NCTE's policy engagement efforts. The very fact that NCTE worked to align its interests with the government's policy paradigm of the 1960s in order to acquire funding for English instruction is exactly the kind of institutional rhetoric that Burns critiques. Rather than maintaining a firm activist commitment to students and to its political roots of protest, NCTE in this era strategically realigned its policy commitments with markedly different policies to gain resources from the federal government. And, as Mason shows, NCTE made this kind of shift often.

In the mid-1960s, for example, as McGuinn's work shows, government approaches to education reform were beginning to turn toward a policy regime centered on various notions of equity and students in poverty. President Lyndon B. Johnson's 1965 bill earmarked an unprecedented amount federal funding for schools across the country as part of his war on poverty. Mason argues that in this period, NCTE's education policy initiatives shifted again, back toward student-centered theories and philosophies. Mason cites NCTE task forces on disadvantaged students, articles in *English Journal*, and the emerging "elective curriculum" movement as examples of how NCTE changed its political platform to serve students of color and students in poverty more broadly. In other words, as the federal government became more and more invested in public education, and as its priorities shifted over the decades, so too did NCTE's policy priorities. For NCTE, maintaining institutional legitimacy was crucial for maintaining disciplinary power.

These kinds of political moves are precisely what Burns is talking about when she critiques NCTE for "deferring to the conservative framing" of the federal government's accountability-era policies of education reform. And as far as Mason's treatment is concerned, his argument is not based in political regimes. He writes that NCTE "lost part of its historical roots" after World War II but then "regained them" in the mid-1960s by re-adopting earlier positions dedicated to serving "ethnically and economically diverse school populations" and advocating curricula designed for "connecting literature to students through creating relevant learning experiences" (183). Both Burns and Mason shed light on really important questions concerning professional organizations' relationship with policymakers.

But how ideologically *pure* should our professional organizations be? What does it mean for an institution to have *political roots*? How *loyal* to its roots should any organization be? To what extent should disciplinary institutions like NCTE engage in policy work at all? If institutions need to acquire institutional power in order to create disciplinary boundaries around the work that teachers and researchers do, within what ethical boundaries should these institutions operate? In the period that Mason covers, he argues that as federal involvement in education increased dramatically in the 1960s in the name of equity, NCTE's activism displayed "the extent that a professional education organization can alter its longtime message in an attempt to acquire institutional power through research funding and policy influence" (165). For Mason, NCTE became "caught up in post-Sputnik reforms in education," but after briefly losing its way, NCTE found itself again and got back on track in the late 1960s. Burns is less forgiving in her analysis; she takes NCTE to task for engaging at all in conservative accountability regime frameworks and for not sustaining a more "coherent political advocacy" (130).

Both Burns and Mason make compelling arguments. But from a policy regime perspective, it is hard to make the case that NCTE briefly got "caught up" in the post-Sputnik education reform movement, only to recover its "true" mission as the civil rights movement got under way, as Mason asserts. I also question whether professional institutions like NCTE that represent a broad academic discipline could ever "break free" from the policy paradigms that structure education policies—especially when the *regimes of truth* that institutions produce are imbued with the governing arrangements of education policy in the first place. Rather, it seems that instead of *finding its way* in the 1960s, NCTE's student-centered policies and task forces for disadvantaged students merely reflect the prevailing policy regime of the time, one centered on equity, which was epitomized by Johnson's education policy agenda for funneling federal resources to students in poverty. The prior education policy regime of the Eisenhower administration in the 1950s cohered around governing arrangements that understood academic disciplines as serving national defense during the Cold War. Indeed, as the federal government became more and more involved in the creation and implementation of federal education policies that focused on disadvantaged students, NCTE's political commitments aligned with the governing arrangements of the current regime—and NCTE actively worked to cultivate institutional leverage to achieve policy influence within those arrangements. To put it another way, from a policy regime perspective, NCTE's political strategies in the 1960s and '70s do not seem all that different from its efforts in the '50s or even in decades prior.

As an illustration, in the next section I present my case study of the Washington Task Force. Members of the Task Force, literacy teachers and scholars from secondary and postsecondary schools, worked diligently between 1979 and 1984 to cultivate relationships with policymakers on Capitol Hill. By looking closely at the group's efforts, I want to call into question some interpretations of NCTE's policy advocacy. The first one I question is that NCTE has been "largely ineffectual in gaining access to decision-making processes for literacy reform" (Burns 132). The second one is that NCTE's political action strategy of aligning its values with those of the federal government was but a brief hiatus from its traditional disciplinary concerns (Mason 169). In fact, as I will show, NCTE indeed found success participating in policy discussions throughout much of its history by engaging in the kind of rhetorical activity that Mason critiques. Moreover, I will argue that questioning whether NCTE's political engagement meets disciplinary purity tests (consider Burns's argument that NCTE reinforces conservative "strict-father" frameworks of education reform) may not be the best way to move the field forward. A new education policy regime emerged in the 1980s that effectively ended the Washington Task Force's abilities to dialogue successfully with powerful policy stakeholders. Now that accountability logics of education are the dominant policy paradigms through which policy is legitimized and enacted, I pose a question for writing studies to answer: What can NCTE do to put *stress* on policies that negatively impact the work of writing teachers and researchers?

Washington Task Force Archival Methodology

I want to begin with a word on method. Archival research in rhetoric and composition has a long and vibrant history. Scholars have worked in the archives to tell the story of our field (Berlin), to uncover the contributions of women and African Americans to rhetorical education (Bordelon; Enoch; Ritter; Royster), and to emphasize the importance of nontraditional sites of literacy learning, as Shirley Wilson Logan did in her study of nineteenth-century Black Americans' language-learning activities, or *sites of rhetorical education*, which contributed to critical training in rhetoric. Moreover, archival researchers in our field often remind us that sites of literacy and literacy instruction *beyond the university* are fundamental to how we think about "writing" in college contexts. For example, scholars have been uncovering more and more about the historical bridges between secondary and postsecondary education, such as Hansen and Farris's *College Credit for Writing in High School* or Ostergaard and Wood's *In the Archives of Composition*. My archival work in this chapter extends from these discussions in an effort to "expand the institutional contexts where we may construct our disciplinary histories" (Ostergaard and Wood 2).

I am also intrigued by the rich tradition of archival research in rhetoric and composition that frequently emphasizes the chaotic and often accidental nature of the work. Robert Connors's famous article "Dreams and Play" called archival research "a kind of directed ramble" (23); Gesa E. Kirsch describes moments of "serendipity," such as randomly finding connections between things she was reading, or even portraits she noticed in a hotel lobby, and her archive-based research questions (21). In her 2002 article "Claiming the Archive for Rhetoric and Composition," Susan Wells uses the word *gifts* to talk about how archives can complicate our original research questions (58). Peter Mortensen describes one of his archival projects as having a "hunch" about things, "striking gold," and then enjoying the "fruits of accidental discoveries" (47). As these scholars can attest, meaningful findings from archival research almost always include an element of luck. When I came upon a box called "The Washington Task Force," which turned out to be historical documents composed by a group of NCTE members who were corresponding during a time of education policy regime change, I was then reading about McGuinn's concept of education policy regimes, while also having just finished the multivolume biography of Lyndon Johnson by Robert Caro and an account of the passage of Johnson's 1965 education bill (Jeffrey). I could not help but see the box of Task Force files as the kind of gift that Wells described: just as I was studying policy regimes and reading about the shift from the equity regime of the 1950s and '60s to our current regime of accountability, here in this box were documents composed by politically engaged literacy educators who were grappling with that shift as it was happening and who were struggling to assert the kind of institutional power that used to give them leverage at effecting education policy. As a researcher interested in the political engagement strategies of the field's professional institutions, I saw right away that this was the kind of serendipity Kirsch was talking about.

The serendipitous nature of archival work notwithstanding, archival scholars in our field remind us that we need to establish a historical ethos with our readers to gain their trust in our evaluation of archival records (Enos). Hui Wu in "Historical Studies of Rhetorical Women Here and There," for instance, writes that pursuing a historical research method involves "the theorization of the goal of research, the selection of subjects in a particular period (the research topic and focus), and the categories for evaluation of historical evidence" (84). To that end, in "An Argument for Archival Research Methods" Barbara E. L'Eplattenier gives some ground rules for an archival research method, such as noting the goals of the research, the location of the materials, the condition of the materials, and even things like the amount of time spent in the archives and the number of linear feet of materials examined (71–72). This information is important, L'Eplattenier writes, because it gives readers "a sense of the archival provenance of the documents used and gives a clearer sense of the archival materials available to the researcher" (74).

Therefore, my "hunch" when I stumbled on the Washington Task Force files at the NCTE archives at the University of Illinois at Urbana-Champaign was based on a guiding question: What did NCTE's efforts to effect federal education policy look like in the period after the passage of President Johnson's education bill, and what can that tell us about the role of professional institutions in an academic discipline's involvement in education policy issues? After an email discussion with an NCTE archivist, we identified several boxes that might speak to these questions. Over a period of three eight-hour days I worked through these boxes, noting anything that seemed relevant to NCTE's political engagement beyond the typical institutional functions of a professional organization. As I wrote in the first part of this chapter, a historical institutional analysis of NCTE's work at policy advocacy shows us that policy regimes of education have historically impacted how NCTE oriented itself toward policy engagement. The most important piece of scholarship in this area—

Mason's analysis of NCTE's engagement with policy in the 1950s and '60s—ends its treatment in 1966. I therefore searched for material from a period that started when Mason left off, the mid-1960s, and ended in the mid-1980s.[2]

As I analyzed the boxes' contents, mostly folders filled with loose papers, some photocopied, some handwritten, I used a funnel approach in my reading. I started broadly by reading administrative documents like annual reports, and, having started in the early 1960s, I systematically moved down the chain in those years to identify task forces that were involved in policy work. Next I analyzed annual administrative reports of the Executive Committee, 1939–1979 (Record Series 15/70/2), about 0.6 cubic feet of material. From there, I read through 1.3 cubic feet of Executive Committee meeting minutes, 1928–1985 (Record Series 15/70/1). And finally, I looked through the subject files (office files) of the executive directors (Record Series 15/71/9), measuring 1.7 cubic feet, in which the Washington Task Force files were located, in box 7 of the record series. Below, I describe in detail my findings.

Case Study: The Washington Task Force

The Washington Task Force emerged out of NCTE's National Relations Program, which was formed in 1978 to dialogue with the federal and executive arms of the government. The Task Force's emergence was made possible by the prevailing policy regime of the 1960s, which McGuinn calls the "equity regime," a set of policy paradigms, policymaking arrangements, and power arrangements that saw the federal government's role in education as a matter of "target[ing] schools with high concentrations of poor and minority students" where "the primary problem facing these schools was a lack of integration and/or adequate funding" (33). In other words, policies born from ESEA had to do with distributing funds in the form of grants to so-called underserved school districts and with using the courts to ensure equal educational opportunity. Success was "measured by the pace of state integration efforts and the size and distribution of school resources" (33). For an academic organization like NCTE, this was also an opportunity to engage with the federal government to make a case for redistributing some of those resources to support the teaching of English.

The 1970s was a turbulent decade socially, culturally, and politically, and amid the turbulence, special-interest groups, lobbyists, and professional organizations like NCTE found openings for dialogue with the federal government about education policy. According to Maris A. Vinovskis, when we consider education policies of the 1970s, we must heed the social, cultural, and political changes taking place in America at the time. Consider the state of the country leading up to the formation of the Washington Task Force: On the heels of Nixon's overwhelming reelection victory in 1972, and his subsequent resignation amid the Watergate scandal in 1974, the American public's confidence in its leaders was at an all-time low. The Vietnam War finally ended in 1975. After Jimmy Carter was elected in 1976, having defeated Gerald Ford, Nixon's vice president and successor, he quickly went to work in an attempt to repair the damage caused over the past half decade. But, as Vinovskis writes, inflation, income decline, and "continued economic stagnation and the failure of the United States to obtain the release of its hostages in Iran plagued" Carter's presidency (13). In the field of education, high hopes for ESEA's core Title I programs Head Start and Follow Through were showing only modest gains, which, Vinovskis writes, were "not enough to close the large gap with the non–Title I students or to help the most disadvantaged" (13). Moreover, President Johnson's Great Society social reforms of the 1960s were but a fading memory, as many social and economic problems had only intensified in the fifteen years since the Civil Rights Act was passed in 1964 and the public remained deeply divided over the issues of integration and busing.

In fact, many educational scholars argue that two issues, integration and busing, were the most important policymaking arrangements of the *equity regime* post-ESEA. As McGuinn writes, "though it was the 1964 Civil Rights Act that declared that federal funds could not be allocated to support segregated institutions or programs, it was ESEA funding that became a key carrot (and stick) for federal integration efforts" (36). States that failed or refused to integrate would lose Title I funding. McGuinn notes that the debate over racial integrating schools was "the decisive issue in U.S. politics during the second half of the twentieth century and led to the unraveling of the coalition that had supported the Great Society and the war on poverty, and ultimately, a partisan electoral realignment" (36). But court precedent made ESEA difficult to kill, and political opposition took the form of discussions about *how much* to fund its programs and with what strings attached, as opposed to whether the law should exist at all. Remember, McGuinn reminds us, that policy regimes denote not just the laws themselves but the paradigms, political arrangements, and power structures that provide policies legitimacy and durability. In the 1960s and '70s, the equity regime that governed the federal government's role in education remained durable even with widespread Republican discontent with ESEA. Thus, opponents of ESEA turned their attention away from repealing the bill and toward legislating *how* districts spent ESEA Title I money or toward strictly monitoring school districts' compliance with ESEA.

By the time NCTE's National Relations Program was created, the federal government was in the midst of these large-scale bureaucratic realignments in education policy aimed at better enforcing the policies that emerged out of the equity regime. McGuinn writes that the 1970s was a time of "large numbers of bureaucratic regulations . . . without any kind of concomitant focus on student or school results—everything was judged by procedure and process" (36). In an eleven-year period the pages of new federal legislation impacting education more than quadrupled, and the policymaking levers of education switched from the state to the federal level, as federal education spending more than doubled between 1965 and 1975 (McGuinn 37). During that time the equity regime, which held that the federal government was morally obligated to provide assistance for "disadvantaged" students, created unprecedented opportunities for NCTE to make a case for "the number and type of students considered 'disadvantaged' and thus eligible to receive federal Title I aid" (37). Dropout prevention programs, funding for disadvantaged students in rural districts, special education programs—and especially important for this chapter, which I note below, bilingual education programs—were areas that organizations lobbied for inclusion in ESEA funding. Groups active at this time included the National Education Association, the National Advisory Council for the Education of Disadvantaged Children, the National Welfare Rights Organization, the Legal Standards and Education Project of the NAACP (National Association for the Advancement of Colored People), the Lawyers Committee for Civil Rights Under Law, and the National Association of Administrators of State and Federally Assisted Education Programs (37–38). The Carter administration continued this path, successfully reauthorizing ESEA in 1978 and adding even more programs such that, by 1980, there were around five hundred education programs that received federal funding (39).

On the heels of the 1978 reauthorization of ESEA, NCTE's National Relations Program sought to speak up about how ESEA might make the teaching of English a more equitable enterprise. In a 1979 editorial from the NCTE publication *English Journal*, John Maxwell, then director of national relations for NCTE, wrote that the best way to engage with the federal government was to consider how English teachers qualified for Title II grants under ESEA. Whereas Title I distributed funding to schools and school districts with low-income populations, Title II funds came from a much smaller allocation of federal money to support teacher professionalization. In 1978 Congress had amended Title II to form "a new program in Basic Skills" and authorized the secretary of health, education, and welfare to "provide assistance designed to demonstrate improved delivery of instructional services in areas of reading, mathematics, and oral and written communication" ("Conference Report"). Maxwell saw this as an opportunity to lobby Congress on behalf of teacher professionalization programs in these areas. According to Maxwell's editorial, original versions of ESEA legislation, particularly the Reading Improvement Act, included only reading as a basic skill ("Taking Action" 9).

Since the 1978 amendments had redefined "the basics" to include *speaking* and *writing*, Maxwell reasoned that this was an opportunity to develop a new set of standards for basic skills in writing, which NCTE could distribute to the US Office of Education. Beyond that, Maxwell writes, the National Relations Program might also use this as an opportunity to get involved in working to define the basics more broadly for the field of English studies. He named a past NCTE president, Marjorie Farmer, as the architect of "a new and humane and a certainly more satisfying definition of 'the basics' than ones currently in vogue" (10). This began the National Relations Program's involvement in federal education policy, which Maxwell hoped would usher in a new era of collaboration with the federal government: "We look forward to several years of educating Congress, the media, and the profession about 'The Essentials of Education,'" Maxwell wrote, "with the hope that a future version of the Elementary and Secondary Education Act will perceive a broader variety of elements as basic" (10).

By the time NCTE's National Relations Program formed in the late 1970s, the political, cultural, and social changes brought on by the momentous reforms of the 1960s were still reverberating throughout the education policy landscape. The equity regime was being challenged on a variety of fronts, chiefly by conservatives opposed to things like the exclusion of busing for nonintegrated schools. Many of these politicians and interest groups used policymaking arrangements to further bureaucratize ESEA in an attempt to stress and poke holes in the prevailing policy paradigm of the equity regime. Nevertheless, the federal government's role in education expanded exponentially in the 1970s, and NCTE, much like it did in securing funding in the late 1950s from the National Defense Education Act, saw this as yet another exigence to "establish an NCTE 'presence' in the minds of the federal legislators and their staffs, association leaders in and around Washington, and in the national media" (10). In his 1979 editorial, Maxwell tells NCTE members that with an increasing amount of participation in federal education issues of late, a new task force was needed to "make appearances, search out information, knock on doors, and contribute generally to the development of an NCTE presence" (10).

The Washington Task Force box in the NCTE archives contains letters, memos, and meeting minutes from the end of the Carter administration to the end of Reagan's first term. We can see in this case study instances of NCTE functioning as a bridge, partner, advocate, and responder to federal education policies. Contrary to some of the academic scholarship that charges NCTE with being ineffectual at gaining a seat at the policy table, this case study shows that this has not always been the case historically. What it also shows is that NCTE lost its seat at the table for reasons beyond merely having ineffectual strategies of political engagement. NCTE became less influential because of shifting policy regimes, as the governing arrangements that legitimized one ideological perspective about the role of the federal government in education policy transitioned into something new. Under the old regime, NCTE had worked with the US Office of Education to lobby for the profession of teaching English to be a beneficiary of education spending packages. The new regime, though, saw the role of the federal government as enforcing accountability within a neoliberal framework of high-stakes standardized testing, performance-based classification, and school choice (Brathwaite). In the new regime, the input of professional organizations was not spurned, but expertise was considered unnecessary. The policy regime change toward accountability shows itself starkly when viewed through archival documents produced during this transition period.

1979: Washington Task Force Gets Its Start

In the first year of its existence, the Washington Task Force was on a mission to learn about existing policies and policymaking, to engage with policymakers on the Hill, and to begin advocating for literacy policies beneficial to NCTE's membership. One of the first documents in the Washington Task Force files is a memo from Maxwell, director of national relations and author of the editorial cited above. The memo was addressed to Charlotte Brooks, Marjorie Farmer, Betty Renshaw, Nancy Sandberg, Roger Shuy, and Charles Allen. Maxwell's memo initiated the Washington Task Force and so began a unique six-year period of political advocacy for NCTE. In his recruiting memo Maxwell writes,

> After a recent review of our National Relations Program, the Executive Committee of NCTE agreed with me that, at this stage, our effort to establish a "presence" in Washington will be served well by forming a cadre of concerned members in or near Washington who can, from time to time, help cover the Congress and certain bureaus and agencies. (Memo to Washington Task Force, Feb. 26, 1979)

In the memo, Maxwell asked committee members if they would like to take part in the Washington Task Force and if they would be willing to meet once a month "for information sharing, discussion of positions and strategies, and what we know about legislation and legislators." Moreover, "from time to time, we might need you for a day to walk the Hill, see legislators or their aides, and in addition to strengthening our presence, make our views known to these persons." One of the important political issues for the National Relations Program in those early years was securing Title II funding for English teachers. In his recruiting memo, Maxwell mentions that the Task Force's immediate goal should be maintaining current levels of education spending by "preventing erosion of the $37 million during the appropriations process this spring." To do this, Maxwell diligently brought prospective Task Force members up to speed on how the federal government worked and how the Task Force could function as literacy lobbyists in Washington.

That first year, the Washington Task Force met at least five times in Washington, DC, thanks to Maxwell's efforts in reaching out to other professional organizations and in educating Task Force members on important areas of Congress. The Task Force and the National Relations Program also began appointing NCTE leaders to important positions elsewhere in DC, such as seats on the board of the Center for the Book, appointments at the Library of Congress, and memberships on the board of directors of the Council of Communication Societies (Letter from Maxwell to James Slevin, Feb. 1983). Maxwell also spearheaded a collaborative initiative with fifteen other professional organizations on *The Essentials of Education* statement in direct response to the federal government's changes to Title II. This document was eventually circulated to policymakers on the Hill. Some of the groups that signed on were the National Science Teachers Association, the National Council of Teachers of Mathematics, the International Reading Association, and the National Council for Social Studies (*Essentials of Education*). The Task Force also added a new member in September 1979, Geraldine LaRocque, who was at the National Institute of Education studying the impact of legislative policy on school practice (Memo to Washington Task Force, Sept. 1979). Also that first year, thanks to their influence campaign, NCTE members were asked to compose documents for the US House Subcommittee on Elementary, Secondary, and Vocational Education (Memo to the Washington Task Force, June 1979), and some Task Force members were even present in the Rose Garden during the ceremony celebrating the creation of the Department of Education (Memo to Washington Task Force, Oct. 17, 1979).

Maxwell was instrumental in the success of the Washington Task Force. His frequent memos to the group during their first year, which almost always included addenda of relevant readings, consisted of assigning roles to group members, soliciting times for meetings, or updating members on new alliances he had made or potential issues that members could tackle in their work. For example, Maxwell's memo to Task Force members in March 1979 passed along materials from *Education Laws, 1978: A Guide to New Directions in Federal Aid*; he asks members to become familiar with the Basic Skills Act. He then calls for a meeting later that month to "talk for a time, have dinner together and continue talking until 8:30 or so" (Memo to Washington Task Force, Mar. 30, 1979). Maxwell sent another memo a couple of weeks later reminding members about the upcoming meeting, and he attached several more readings: this time a revised version of *The Essentials of Education* and a document called "Possible Task Force Specialties," which included potential topics the Task Force could address, with names of Task Force members next to them. Maxwell asked Roger Shuy to work on the reauthorization of the Higher Education Act, which would require him to "develop familiarity with [the] present Act and try to figure out how, if at all, it affects English teaching," and also to "make acquaintances with staff of Congressman Ford (D-MI) who chairs the higher ed committee." Maxwell put Nancy Sandberg in charge of tackling the budget and appropriations process; Charles Allen, the regulations for ESEA; and Charlotte Brooks, the Department of Education legislation (Memo to Washington Task Force," Apr. 16, 1979). With each political issue, Maxwell expected the members to learn about the procedures of Congress, to become friendly with senators and representatives sitting on pertinent committees, and to back NCTE professionally as they advised policymakers.

These archival materials indicate that Maxwell was well versed in the policy arrangements of the equity regime: since the federal government was mainly involved in public education through the distribution of funds to needy school districts, the main task of NCTE, as Maxwell saw it, was to embed itself in the bureaucratic mechanisms of government and build trust with powerful stakeholders in order to secure opportunities to assert its disciplinary expertise and make a case for directing some federal funding to English language arts education. This work on the Hill involved a significant commitment of time on top of the full-time jobs many Task Force members already had. Maxwell requested that Charles Allen, for instance, become an expert on ESEA regulations overnight. "Sorry, Charlie," Maxwell wrote, "It can be dull work, but important." Maxwell's early memos to the Task Force reveal a passion for political engagement and a commitment to embodying the charge of the National Relations Program outlined in his *English Journal* editorial earlier that year, which was to give NCTE a "'presence' in the minds of the federal legislators and their staffs, association leaders in and around Washington." His charges to the Task Force, he hoped, were "congenial and feasible," although implicit in the memos prior to one of their first meetings was that he took this work very seriously and had high, perhaps too high, expectations for the Task Force's members (Memo to Washington Task Force, Apr. 16, 1979).

After the Task Force's first meeting in 1979, Maxwell went to work that summer consulting with colleagues on the Title II implementation of ESEA. James Gray, director of the Bay Area Writing Project, was set to testify in the coming months before the Congressional Subcommittee on Education, Arts, and the Humanities. Maxwell, in helping Gray prepare for his testimony, wrote to him about how equity regime policies worked and the role of professional institutions within those arrangements. For example, as McGuinn writes, the reason why education policy regimes remain durable despite political opposition is that once certain power arrangements, paradigms, and bureaucratic functions of policies become the norm, opposition to the norm is more or less futile. Instead, just like opponents of President Johnson's ESEA spending package had done, Maxwell recommended refocusing lobbying efforts on controlling *how much* to fund Title II programs and with what strings attached. Maxwell wrote to Gray that literacy educators have the power to influence the way money is distributed and the criteria by which the US Office of Education allotted funds to English language arts projects under ESEA.

Maxwell therefore told Gray that he should emphasize in his testimony the need for the House Appropriations Committee to reconsider cutting funding for Title II, especially since the old definition of "the basics" included just *reading*, which was funded at $25 million, and the new definition included three basic skills (reading, math, and oral/written communication). Using this logic, he argued, each individual skill should receive funding, instead of appropriating a block grant for all of them. The current distribution of the administration's proposed allocations, he said, is "pathetic." Maxwell writes:

> effective basic skills programs require sensible and broad-scale attention within the school and community. While the law suggests this truth, it says little about what *kinds* of school programs should be funded. For example, the NCTE statement of standards for basic skills programs (see enclosed) lays out what an effective writing program should look like. There's a similar statement for oral language programs. A comprehensive faculty involvement in improving of basics (in this case writing) is a necessity; and teacher inservice is a critical aspect of making anything happen. (Memo to the Washington Task Force, June 1979)

Maxwell's advice to Gray about his testimony—to make arguments about funding allocations that stress the importance of teacher professionalization and that draw people toward the consensus knowledge in NCTE's policy statements—reveals how the Washington Task Force navigated equity regime policies: maintain influence in Washington by understanding the policy arrangements of the equity regime and by considering how the federal government views its role in public education. As McGuinn has shown, even while the government's involvement in education was expanding in the late 1970s, its involvement was largely focused on distributing funding to needy schools. So professional organizations like NCTE, according to Maxwell, could cultivate institutional power by leveraging its disciplinary expertise to obtain a larger percentage of federal dollars and by making rhetorical appeals to how federal money should be spent on programs aimed at schools and students in need. Moreover, Maxwell was keen on how to build partnerships through the dissemination of disciplinary literature, which is why the Washington Task Force also worked to create and distribute NCTE position statements and policy critiques to Congress and to those who would be communicating with members of Congress.

The Task Force was also involved in drafting letters of support for various government endeavors, such as Senator George McGovern's proposal for a Commission on Literacy in 1979, which Maxwell passed along to those involved with Support for the Learning and Teaching of English (Memo to Slate Representatives, June 22, 1979). He also wanted the Task Force to lobby Congress about the federal education budget. In one memo leading up to their fall 1979 meeting, Maxwell wrote that

> one of the anxious questions will be whether the struggle between the budget committees and the appropriations committee will be resolved and, therefore, whether the Congress will fund new education programs or content themselves with a continuing resolution on funding. That's for starters. (Memo to the Washington Task Force, Sept. 18, 1979)

The next month, Maxwell passed along a "script" that members should use when they lobbied Congress, which included describing who they were (and leaving a membership form behind when they leave); explaining why they were there, such as "an increasing concern with effects of legislation and regulation on schools and colleges"; and using engagement strategies like asking "warmer-upper" questions: "What are the views of the Congressman . . . on the proposed Department of Education?" One question—"How might NCTE help the Congressman? The Government?"—was followed by stock answers like "100,000 members and subscribers, seven journals, 130 affiliates in all fifty states, etc." Maxwell's proposed legislative agenda had a range of items: ensuring that "subject matter organizations will be consulted when programs affecting their disciplines are involved," "providing increasing support for teacher centers as a prime means for teachers' professional growth," and developing more "sophisticated instruments for assessing aspects of the language arts now neglected in standardized tests" (Memo to the Washington Task Force, Oct. 17, 1979). In other words, Maxwell's work with the Task Force that first year resembled a full-time lobbying position that leveraged the role of an institution in an equity regime context. Thanks to the funding and the support of NCTE in the creation of the National Relations Program, Maxwell was able to harness and benefit from the labor of his colleagues, even though he was also serving as deputy executive director of national relations and other Task Force members were full-time professors and teachers.

Another significant role of the Task Force was communicating with leaders in cabinet-level positions. In December 1979, for example, Maxwell wrote a letter on behalf of the Task Force to Shirley Hufstedler, congratulating her on her recent appointment to secretary of the brand-new Department of Education. In the letter, Maxwell follows his own tips for lobbying Congress from his internal handout to NCTE members: he mentions the organization's "heartland perspective," its broad membership across all fifty states, and its journals that reach "tens of thousands of teachers in elementary, secondary schools and colleges and universities" (Letter from Maxwell to Shirley Hufstedler, Dec. 11, 1979). He then makes several arguments for how Hufstedler, as the new secretary of education, could support English teachers; again his arguments mirror the talking points he had passed along to Gray. First, he maintains that the basic skills clarification in the newly amended ESEA needs more federal support. The current appropriation for education, he argues, "represents a retreat from rather than a commitment to, improving basic skills instruction." Other concerns he mentions include a need for more in-service education grants, more research in written communication, and more instruction in writing across the disciplines:

"The English teaching profession is perennially disturbed about being blamed for our national failures in the teaching of writing. We hold that every teacher shares in that responsibility." Nevertheless, Maxwell calls for improving the conditions in which writing is taught:

> The conditions for teaching writing in secondary schools are abominable and are not much better in elementary schools and colleges. The teaching of writing, some have said, is the great, unfinished work in American education. A Federal inquiry into this issue is, in our opinion, not only needed but long overdue. At the least, we need substantial and sophisticated longitudinal studies of how writing can be improved by altering the unsatisfactory conditions under which writing instruction is now conducted.

Maxwell also expressed concern for the "waste of talent" brought on by declining enrollments "in the face of what the press and Senator McGovern refer to as a 'literacy crisis.'" He writes, "From our perspective, 'the world is out of joint.' We would like to confer with appropriate members of your staff, when the dust settles, about appropriate Federal legislation to deal with these two problems in search of a solution." Here, we see Maxwell appealing to equity regime frameworks in which federal interventions can ameliorate a world *out of joint* and allow NCTE to assert its disciplinary expertise more effectively in English classrooms across the country.

Maxwell's efforts were successful. Later in the new year, 1980, NCTE representatives finally were able to meet with Secretary Hufstedler to discuss the Washington Task Force's letter; and two days after the meeting, Alan Purves, president of NCTE at the time, sent along another document to Secretary Hufstedler, this time the revised *Essentials of Education* born from a desire to "revitalize the way curriculum is viewed by education policy makers." This revised statement, Purves wrote to her, offers a solution to the problem; however, "there needs to be a channel for this continuing concern within the structure of the Education Department." Purves then recommended that the Department of Education include English specialists on staff, positions in which NCTE members would happily serve if asked (Letter from Alan Purves to Sec. Shirley Hufstedler, Jan. 18, 1980).

The Task Force's efforts to reach out to, work with, and lobby members of Congress and cabinet officials were not new for NCTE, as

Mason's study documents. However, NCTE members' arguments in the late 1950s for inclusion in funding for the National Defense Education Act had relied on claims that English education was in the interest of national defense. This argument aligned with policy paradigms of the time that saw the federal government's role in education in nationalistic terms. Maxwell's efforts with the Washington Task Force and the National Relations Program in the 1970s were different in that he requested funding in the service of promoting equity for poor students, fixing the conditions in which writing was taught, and preparing literacy instructors to adequately reach those students. Task Force members were rewarded for their efforts by becoming an *official* NCTE committee in October 1979.

The work was intense, though, and by the second year of the Washington Task Force's existence, participation had proved too much for some members who also had work obligations at their home institutions. Roger Shuy, head of sociolinguistics at Georgetown University, wrote to Maxwell in 1980: "I think it's time that I level with you and admit that I don't think it wise for me to continue to be on the Washington Task Force. I just don't have the time these days and I really don't have the commitment either" (Letter from Roger Shuy to Maxwell, Jan. 23, 1980). Four days later, Betty Renshaw, an instructor at Prince George's Community College in Maryland, also wrote to Maxwell: "It is becoming clearer and clearer that I simply cannot make the Task Force one of my real priorities. . . . I simply cannot stay up with everything I see that needs doing" (Letter from Betty Renshaw to Maxwell, Jan. 27, 1980). About a week later, Maxwell backchanneled about the resignations with Charlotte Brooks, a former president of NCTE who taught at Washington, DC, public schools, noting that they needed to discuss hiring a Washington representative full-time at some point in the future. As was customary for any letter from Maxwell, he enclosed a xeroxed copy of an article from *Education Week* that he hoped she would find interesting (Letter from Maxwell to Charlotte Brooks, Feb. 5, 1980).

Despite the attrition, Maxwell pressed forward. In a memo the following spring, he admitted that "we've lost two members, and my instinct is that . . . we need one more and possibly two new members." He nevertheless called for a meeting to strategize about the upcoming event in Washington, which would be a "good time for 'presence' and politicking." He also wanted to hear back from the group on their respective beats, like Charles Allen's work as a reader for ESEA Title II grants and Marjorie Farmer's experience at the Blacks in Education Gala. He also enclosed a reading on impacting policy in Washington. He wrote to members again before the meeting, enclosing a few more readings and agenda items to discuss. One new item was "general discussion of our effectiveness in 'putting across our point' in Washington—an 18-month, no-holds-barred review." This was fairly typical of Maxwell. He was committed and diligent but still aware of the precarity of the work as he tried also to showcase his flexibility (Memo to the Washington Task Force, Apr. 16, 1980).

In an August 1980 letter to Bob Hogan, executive director of NCTE at the time, Maxwell spoke of the Task Force's May meeting positively. Most notably, Marjorie Farmer proposed to seek legislation for funding to train English teachers to work with linguistically diverse populations. The Task Force also welcomed a new member, Ronnie Lowenstein, a public school teacher in Falls Church, Virginia. In addition to meeting with the Washington Task Force in Washington, Maxwell described the rest of his harrowing schedule in Washington: he had met with the Essentials in Education Task Force, union leaders from the American Federation of Teachers, and a host of heads from other professional organizations; he had attended the Music Educators Conference and had breakfasted with leaders of the National Institute of Education and the National Endowment for the Humanities, among other networking events (Letter from Maxwell to Bob Hogan and Charles Suhor, Aug. 3, 1980).

Maxwell's work in Washington that weekend was purposeful, as the presidential election of 1980 was only three months away. Ronald Reagan, former governor of California, was running against incumbent Jimmy Carter, a Democrat who was having a hard time winning over voters. In an early memo to the Task Force back in October 1979, Maxwell had updated the Task Force on the goings-on at headquarters. He noted that the Executive Committee recently discussed the 1982 convention in Washington, DC, which was still three years away, and had tossed around the idea of doing something "internationally significant," like inviting President Carter to attend. "But," he wrote, "with Carter's problems we thought to wait" before sending out the invitation (Memo to the Washington Task Force, Oct. 11, 1979). In Maxwell's August 1980 letter to Hogan, he announced that "politics is much in the air" and that from his discussions in Washington, "I got the sense that everything is hanging on the election. Most insiders don't feel Reagan would eliminate the Department of Education, only eviscerate it. Given the possibility of a Reagan election, most senior-staffers are looking around for something else, just in case" (Letter from Maxwell to Bob Hogan and Charles Suhor, Aug. 3, 1980). Maxwell's observation here is important because this is the first mention in the archival materials of an unease on Capitol Hill, a sign that the tide was turning away from an equity regime toward something new.

By the end of summer in 1980, according to Maxwell's report to the NCTE Executive Committee, the National Relations Program and the Washington Task Force had accomplished much. They had made efforts to extend the Essentials of Education movement by building coalitions with other professional groups and by contributing to the formation of the Council on Basic Education. Members of the Task Force were also prominent members on boards and committees across the country. Members participated in reading ESEA Title II proposals, or what Maxwell described as a "grueling session to review over 700 proposals for funding" (Report on National Relations, May 1980). Though they lost Geraldine LaRocque, a member for only a short time, her replacement, Ronnie B. Lowenstein, helped them set their sights for the 1980s on developing legislation for the professional development of teachers working with "linguistically and culturally different youth," which was an initiative originally developed by Task Force member Marjorie Farmer (Memo from Maxwell to Bob Hogan and Charles Suhor, Aug. 3, 1980). By August 1980 Task Force members had a working draft of the legislation, which they passed along to the executive director of NCTE, Charles Suhor. In the next few months, members of the Task Force met with various professional organizations in the DC area, such as an October 1980 meeting with the International Reading Association to provide guidance on proposing and finding co-sponsors for legislation (Letter from Maxwell to Ralph Staiger, Oct. 17, 1980).

Maxwell reached out to others for guidance and co-sponsorship. For instance, in a December 18, 1980, letter to James Alatis, the director of Teachers of English to Speakers of Other Languages at Georgetown University, Maxwell enclosed the proposed legislation for funding for bilingual education as well as resolutions recently passed by NCTE, noting that this was "the first time that NCTE has clearly stated the obligation of its members to work toward the success of students who are speakers of other languages." NCTE's efforts, Maxwell hoped, were "setting the stage for a conversation sometime this year on the work and stances of our two organizations." While the legislation was "a long way" from being complete, Maxwell wanted to "share drafts with" Alatis to get his advice (Letter from Maxwell to James Alatis, Dec. 18, 1980). In a December 15 memo to the Task Force, Maxwell expressed optimism about the bilingual education bill. However, he noted, considering Reagan's recent defeat of Jimmy Carter and the "slow transition time between administrations," there may be some delay in getting things going. "Right now," he wrote, "the whole topic of bilingual education is under a cloud, and anything referring to it might meet with less than [an] enthusiastic response." Maxwell was nevertheless hopeful that the bilingual education bill would not run into "heavy resistance," and he vowed to "forge ahead" in the new year (Memo to the Washington Task Force, Dec. 15, 1980).

The Task Force Witnesses the Transition to the Accountability Regime

Notwithstanding Maxwell's vow to forge ahead in the new year, there was an abrupt shift in the early 1980s in the tone and optimism of the Washington Task Force correspondence. Throughout 1981, for example, while the Task Force still focused on Marjorie Farmer's draft legislation for allocating funds for in-service education for English teachers working with "linguistically and culturally different youth," the members involved expressed increasing uncertainty about the new presidential administration. According to the minutes from one of the year's first meetings, Charlotte Brooks, who had served as NCTE's Washington representative for a time prior to the Washington Task Force, reported that since the election, "most of our friends have either gone, are planning to go, or are poised in expectations that they will be replaced." Moreover, Task Force members were also concerned that a federal government "freeze in hiring has further confused the situation as have proposed budget cuts and the possible shift to 'block grant' funding to the state in fiscal year 1982." These minutes also note that due to the policy paradigm shift occurring on Capitol Hill—with legislators becoming more concerned with austerity measures in education to improve the economy than with appropriations to combat poverty—the Task Force now needed to "work from 'ground zero' in establishing relationships." Some strategies included strengthening efforts at building coalitions with even more diverse professional organizations or "finding 'hand-hold' persons in the new administration with inclinations consistent with ours" (Brief Minutes of the Washington Task Force Meeting, Feb. 1981).

Nevertheless, the Task Force set an ambitious timeline for getting a bilingual education bill passed in 1982, which included convening meetings in the spring to get the support of other professional organizations, revising draft legislation, and then in the summer months, seeking the support of legislators "depending on the climate for support at that time" (Brief Minutes of the Washington Task Force Meeting, Feb. 1, 1981). From the archival record, though, it appears this vision was never realized. Early in the year, NCTE did manage to send out letters welcoming Terrel H. Bell to his new role as secretary of education (Bell replaced Hufstedler), but the archives are dark for much of the summer (Letter from Robert Squires to Sec. Terrel H. Bell, Feb. 2, 1981). Part of the reason is that Maxwell, who had been appointed the associate executive director of NCTE and director of the National Relations Program in 1978, was newly appointed the executive director in 1981, so he now had obligations beyond the Washington Task Force (Suhor and Allen). As such, his normally loquacious memos and supplemental reading waned in these critical years of the 1980s.

In his 1981 annual report to NCTE members, his first as executive director, Maxwell described the changing political tide away from the equity regime and toward something that members perceived as more ominous. He wrote that 1981 has been "a confusing and often perplexing year for representatives of professional associations in Washington." The Reagan administration, he wrote, worked assiduously to cut funding for education programs, which "has led to extreme uncertainty about changes in the federal educational establishment and, therefore, the appropriate activities of the Washington Task Force." Nevertheless, he noted, the Task Force had continued to attend hearings, serve on boards and as members of other organizations, and maintain a presence in Washington. However, "the future of the educational establishment in Washington is uncertain," he wrote, "and the future of the Washington Task Force is, consequently, uncertain" (*Annual Report 1981*).

One interesting letter from the Washington Task Force archives is from early in 1981, when Marjorie Farmer, a drafter of the proposed bilingual education legislation, received a letter from a professor from Florida Atlantic University named Zola Sullivan. Professor Sullivan, who had taken an interest in Farmer's work and believed in the proposed bill, issued a warning to the Task Force: the Reagan administration's new education agenda, while clearly not a continuation of Carter's vision, was actually an even more radical agenda anchored in a bizarre evangelical Christian interpretation of education reform that prioritized market-based solutions to issues in education. Signaling what Sullivan saw as the early erosion of the equity regime and the emergence of new governing arrangements was an article in the May 1980 issue of *Phi Delta Kappan* by Charles Park, in which he discussed the New Right, an evangelical Christian movement that opposed "abortion, women's rights, gay rights, unionism, big government, and social legislation" (Park 608).

Park essentially argues that in the new political paradigm advocated by the New Right and its offshoots, think tanks like the Heritage Foundation, there is no need for federal funding for education when "private schools funded via a voucher plan" could just as easily provide the so-called equity of failed democratic policies (610). Park goes on to say that

> the chances of a campaign against public school funding, curricula, and philosophy to develop and consolidate right-wing political power cannot be easily dismissed. The evidence reflects with startling clarity that right-wing interests have found the public schools a convenient target for unifying ultra-conservative ideology and traditional morality for political gain. . . . [W]e appear to be inexorably locked into a values conflict centered on the rights of open inquiry in a pluralistic democracy and the imposition of certainty from those who claim to possess absolute truth. (611)

In her letter, Sullivan impresses on Farmer that this new set of governing arrangements in the federal government's relationship with education policy was no longer compatible with the equity regime, and these ominous changes should be a central concern for the Task Force moving forward. Without concerted lobbying for the interests of teachers and students, groups allied with the New Right "will greatly influence the Reagan Administration's position in funding, developing and eliminating various educational programs. Only time will tell" (Letter from Zola Sullivan to Marjorie Farmer, Feb. 17, 1981). Sullivan saw the writing on the wall with the election of Reagan and his radical positions on the utility of the Department of Education. And while Sullivan was not the only one at this time who forecast the changing political, ideological, and bureaucratic governing arrangements of education policy, it was the first time such a statement was made in writing to Washington Task Force members, and the statement was surely a herald of the new policy arrangements and power structures that would impact members' work in the coming months and years.

In a response to Sullivan, Maxwell, who was writing on behalf of the Task Force, was somber in his reflection. He wrote that the current political climate

> is less than sanguine for new education legislation in Washington. Under the circumstances, progress on this topic is less than slow since I, at least, perceive almost no possibility for new legislation until sometime in 1982. We will continue to move along and watch for opportunities. Meanwhile, people like you in the trenches are not going to get very much help from the Federal government and probably less from the state. I wish I had better and happier words. But I don't. (Letter from Maxwell to Sullivan, Mar. 16, 1981)

This exchange could be seen as a premonition of what was to come.

The rest of 1981 saw the Task Force struggling for opportunities to meet. The group welcomed a new member, Joan Gibbons from the Armed Forces Dependent Schools Headquarters in Alexandria, Virginia, and met with coalition members in and near Washington (Letter from Maxwell to Joan Gibbons, Dec. 10, 1981). But the archival material is still scant; chronologically, the next document that describes the activities for the year is the 1982 NCTE annual report, in which Maxwell writes that

> the Reagan administration's attempts to cut educational spending, though by and large successful, were in part resisted by activities of several consortia of which NCTE is a member. Similarly, Administration attempts to abolish the cabinet-level Department of Education were defeated. Washington Task Force members, particularly Charlotte K. Brooks, the Council's Washington Representative, took part in various activities of these coalitions. (*Annual Report 1982*)

Overall, 1981 and 1982 were the beginning of a substantial shift in the government's perspective on, and its role in, education, despite valiant efforts at resistance by members of the Task Force. The Task Force's efforts to participate in education policy had been relatively successful in the not-so-distant past, but now the group was struggling to stay relevant.

Markedly different from earlier correspondence is the tone of archival materials after 1981: somber, resigned, and uneasy about NCTE's role in politics at all, cognizant of a shift in governing arrangements toward accountability-based policies. Late in the year, for example, Maxwell informed the group that a NCTE-wide survey "revealed some distaste among the sample of members for their 'political' concerns and activities" (Memo to Washington Task Force, Nov. 5, 1981). A month later, Maxwell recapped a meeting of the Executive Committee where members outlined a major goal of the Task Force as combating "activities of the radical Right, along with a continuing concern about class-size issues and the ironic fact that English teachers are being riffed when all and sundry are complaining about how poorly youngsters write" (Memo to the Washington Task Force, Dec. 10, 1981). Much in the archives from 1982 onward consists only of correspondence between Task Force members trying to get meetings scheduled. In fall 1982, Maxwell mentions some good news, that the Task Force had been renewed another three years, but he then asks if they even wanted to remain a group at all (Memo to Washington Task Force, Oct. 21, 1982). And early in 1983, Maxwell writes that "the onslaught of Reaganomics . . . has pretty well decimated the points of contact we had with the federal establishment in education." Thus, he asks, for the third time in as many months, "Do we need to continue to have a Task Force? And if so, what shall we perceive as our major functions in the near future?" (Memo to the Washington Task Force, Feb. 14, 1983). Despite adding two new members, James Slevin of Georgetown University and Nancy Sandberg, who recommitted after being largely unavailable for the first three years, the question persisted of whether to remain active as a group amid the Reagan administration's unprecedented political attack on public education (Clabaugh). Maxwell's existential inquiries came up again in a meeting agenda the following month: "Do we even need a Washington Task Force?" (Preliminary Agenda, Washington Task Force, Mar. 24, 1983).

This looming question pervaded the Washington Task Force's meeting minutes throughout the early 1980s. As Task Force members grappled with Reagan's education policy regime, *A Nation at Risk*, which many scholars of accountability point to as a pivotal document in education reform, began breaking the equity regime's hold on public opinion about education. Chris Gallagher asserts that *A Nation at Risk* casts "a long shadow over educational reform" (*Reclaiming Assessment* 20). Other education scholars, David Tyack and Larry Cuban, and scholars in writing studies, Linda Adler-Kassner and also Joanne Addison and Sharon James McGee, similarly note the importance of *A Nation at Risk* as a fundamental stressor on the equity policy regime. Considering Maxwell's frequent complaints about Reaganomics and his lamenting the education policy landscape of the 1980s, one might assume that, by the time April 1983 rolled around and *A Nation at Risk* was released the public, the Task Force would have much to say about it. Yet, that summer, Maxwell wrote only a short memo to the Task Force that simply said, "I imagine you may have already purchased or stolen your own copy of the Commission on Excellence report" (Memo to the Washington Task Force, June 6, 1983). All he said about *A Nation at Risk* was that soon they should meet to discuss it. Three months later, Maxwell wrote again only to say that NCTE was working on ways to respond to it, which included adopting a brand-new slogan, "Toward Excellence in English Teaching," which would be printed on all NCTE "documents, forms, and wherever" else from then on (Memo to Washington Task Force, Sept. 8, 1983).

Why would an organization so disillusioned by Reaganomics and accountability-based education reform embark on rebranding NCTE to be more in line with the new accountability policies, given its previous efforts at resistance or the warning of a comrade like Sullivan? Why capitulate to accountability catchphrases like the *excellence movement* when the organization had fought so long against that kind of policy? To some, this turn of events might indicate ineptitude, a lack of will, or some other failing attributed to academia for not being more politically engaged. However, when you consider NCTE to be an institution enmeshed in prevailing policy regimes, you see that institutions work to influence policy while also being structured by it. NCTE has a history of aligning its position with the political arrangement of the federal government as a way to secure resources. Its efforts to build relationships with lawmakers and policymakers on Capitol Hill helped it leverage disciplinary power to make rhetorical appeals for the relevance of English studies (Mason). Therefore, NCTE's move after *A Nation at*

Risk to rebrand itself as an organization concerned with "excellence" is actually not that surprising. In fact, even though most of NCTE's members, individually, probably abhorred not only Reagan's education agenda but also the various groups and think tanks of the New Right that justified and legitimized Reagan's political agenda, many of the Washington Task Force's efforts on behalf of NCTE at this time demonstrate that the organization decided that the best path forward was to leverage the new excellence movement in its favor. This is yet another example of how policy regimes remain durable over time despite widespread opposition. As the accountability regime supplanted the equity regime, new ideological paradigms that cast American schools as "failing" put stress on the equity regime's focus on allocating government funds to "save" the failing schools. A new reformist presidential administration placed bureaucrats and politicians in power who could influence policy debate and push new agendas that obstructed existing regime policies. And finally, new policies based in these social and cultural attitudes began to expand the federal government's role in education—with the assumption that government was now required to hold schools, teachers, and so-called experts in education accountable for the nation's schools.

When Charlotte K. Brooks, Maxwell's most dedicated Task Force member, resigned in the fall of 1983, the work of the Washington Task Force was effectively over (Letter from Maxwell to Charlotte Brooks, Sept. 27, 1983). Task Force members still went to conferences and had their congressional beats and reading lists, and Maxwell continued to send clippings and relevant stories well into 1984; but, as Maxwell wrote early that year, he now spent only around 5 percent of his time working on issues related to the National Relations Program and the Washington Task Force, for without Brooks, prospects for a healthy Task Force were slim (Letter from Maxwell to Richard Lloyd-Jones, Jan. 3, 1984). And perhaps as a most fitting symbol of NCTE's embrace of accountability logics, the last of the Washington Task Force box includes a memo from Maxwell to fellow NCTE member Charles Allen, asking him to share with the Task Force the new initiative of NCTE, "Excellence in Education," and the creation of a new "Excellence Task Force." As with NCTE's lobbying efforts in the 1950s, '60s, and '70s, the Excellence Task Force of the '80s resembled the way the institution had always been politically active: by aligning its interests with prevailing policy paradigms as a way of leveraging institutional and disciplinary power to compete for resources. The new Excellence Task Force, among other things, sought "funds to support 250 teachers of English language arts to return to summer study in the summer of 1985." Members had created tee shirts and other apparel with the slogan "Toward Excellence in English." In this new era, even some of the awards and other recognitions that NCTE bestowed on its members were stamped with the word "Excellence" (Letter from Maxwell to Charles Allen, May 2, 1984).

Conclusion

This case study from the NCTE archives shows that, despite some writing studies scholars lamenting that NCTE does not do enough to get a seat at the table in policy discussions, there is ample evidence from its history to substantiate that the organization worked to bridge, partner, advocate, and respond to federal education policy in very real ways. On the flip side, documenting the Washington Task Force's capitulation to the accountability regime through its excellence movement of 1984 is somewhat disconcerting, especially considering the organization's sacrifice of what some would call its *core beliefs* in student-centered teaching—beliefs that do not generally align with accountability regime policies. In fact, ascribing "core beliefs" to NCTE affirms the narrative of an organization "born in protest," as historians of NCTE have described it. This idea, however, is a romanticized vision of what a professional organization does and produces. As Mason has shown, NCTE historically worked to align its interests with the federal government's in order to compete for resources. But unlike Mason, who argues that NCTE's interest alignment in the 1950s was merely a momentary departure from its *true* values, my case study of the Washington Task Force reveals NCTE working hard throughout the 1970s and early '80s to do the same kind of thing, only this time NCTE sought resources to fund policies aligned with the equity regime such as bilingual education and Title II funding for professionalizing teachers. As the accountability regime replaced the governing arrangements of the equity regime, NCTE's later moves to form an Excellence in English Task Force and similar programs indicate that NCTE as an institution has always ordered its policy alignments toward prevailing policy paradigms.

As Foucault maintains, this is how institutions are supposed to work. When writing studies scholars call for NCTE to be more politically involved and to work harder to get a seat at the table, or when they critique the organization for being "largely ineffectual" in combating conservative education policies (Burns), they are not altogether wrong. But the reason that NCTE is sometimes locked out of policy discussions, especially since the advent of the accountability regime, is not because NCTE has *lost its way* or because its political engagement strategies are all of a sudden ineffectual. It is because, in an accountability policy regime, the policy paradigms, power arrangements, and policymaking arrangements understand education to be an economic good. As Ross and Gibson write, education reform under an accountability regime seeks to "commodify public education by reducing learning to bits of information and skill to be taught and tested and marketize education through programs that promote privatization and user fees in place of free, public education" (4). In this policy regime, the federal government no longer needs input from education experts on how to invest federal dollars to work toward equity. Experts are not necessary at all to preserving the governing arrangements in an accountability regime. What complicates this picture even further is that accountability regime policies are still promoted rhetorically as a way to advance equity. The best way to serve equity, the logic goes, is through market-based reforms and the commodification of public education.

The issue at hand is not so much whether NCTE can ever gain a seat at the table, because we know for a fact that it has done so before. The frequent calls in writing studies for scholars to "reframe" the debate on school reform away from accountability may also be misguided (Webber). Instead, we need to consider how NCTE is bound up in the policy paradigms, policymaking arrangements, and power arrangements of a given policy regime, and the various ways that an institution aligns its interests with regime logics or, alternatively, works to put "stress" on existing regimes.

NCTE's efforts to embrace the excellence movement were pretty squarely in line with the organization's interest-alignment style of policy engagement strategies since at least the 1950s. In an accountability regime, though, NCTE's engagement strategies were not as persuasive to powerful policy stakeholders. One reason for this has to do with the ways that policy regimes value expert knowledge. In the equity regime, the expert knowledge of NCTE leaders often influenced politicians in deciding how to spend federal money on education initiatives. In an accountability regime, though, the disciplinary knowledge of experts is inconsequential to policy decisions because the regimes of truth that produce policymaking arrangements hold that efficiency, choice, and marketplace logics are better methods of achieving equity in education.

From this exploration of the Washington Task Force, we can see that NCTE has been able in its history to participate in policy discussions in meaningful ways. However, NCTE's institutional influence began to diminish in the early 1980s as a new policy regime emerged nationally, and the Task Force's policy engagement strategies became no longer persuasive. But the takeaway from the Washington Task Force's dissolution should not be that NCTE failed to enact its *core values* or that NCTE simply cannot influence education policy anymore. NCTE, like any institution that cultivates disciplinary power, is always going to be bound up in the prevailing policy regimes, and its strategies of policy engagement in the era of the Washington Task Force reflected the precarity of engagement in a time of policy regime change.

In the next chapter, I fast-forward a few decades to look at another example of NCTE's policy engagement strategies: NCTE's effort in 2009 to provide feedback on a draft of the English language arts standards of the Common Core State Standards. This case study shows again that, in the accountability regime, the expertise of professional disciplinary organizations is no longer influential in policy formation. Part of the problem was NCTE's misguided adherence to the governing arrangements of the old regime—arrangements that granted the importance of professional organizations and the value of their disciplinary expertise—which in the new regime are no longer persuasive for stakeholders. Where, then, do we find inroads of participation in policy debates from an institutional perspective? If expert knowledge about writing is not valued, what kinds of rhetorical strategies can our institutions use to deliberate about policy successfully in the accountability era?

CHAPTER 2

NCTE's Critique of the Draft of the Common Core English Language Arts Standards

Introduction

As the national discourse around education reform shifted to an accountability regime in the late 1970s and early '80s, English studies' main professional organization, NCTE, found itself struggling to maintain the same level of policy influence as it had in the previous two decades. As we saw in the last chapter, in the aftermath of the Reagan-era *A Nation at Risk* report, NCTE continued to align its interests with the so-called "excellence movement" in education as a way to appeal for federal resources. In an accountability regime, where the governing arrangements view the federal government's role in education as ensuring that schools and teachers are held accountable for the efficient completion and economic success of graduates, disciplinary experts and their professional organizations became unpersuasive at best and, in many cases, unimportant.

In this chapter I fast-forward to another important moment in NCTE's education policy history, when, in 2009, a group of business leaders and politicians responsible for the Common Core State Standards (CCSS) asked for NCTE's feedback on a draft of its English language arts (ELA) standards. As in the last chapter, I highlight the important work of a dedicated group of NCTE members who worked diligently on behalf of the organization to craft education policy. At this moment in

2009, the political context briefly resembled the days of the 1960s and '70s when the organization's input in policy decisions was seemingly valued by powerful stakeholders. But, without the clout to build and maintain relationships with the organizations representing the Common Core, NCTE's efforts at policy deliberation in these talks stalled, leaving the organization, and English studies yet again, on the outside looking in.

On the heels of the standards-based reform initiatives of the 1990s, which culminated in one of the most important pieces of education legislation in fifty years—the No Child Left Behind Act (NCLB) of 2001—the Common Core is an integral set of ideas and arrangements in the accountability regime's quest for power. Unlike prior education policies, the Common Core is not actually legislation but rather a set of standards that states *voluntarily adopt*. But, as Diane Kelly-Riley writes, the Common Core nevertheless represents a "pivotal event in the history of US public education" in that it was the first time a majority of states adopted common standards for English and math (193). Another significant difference with the Common Core is that the standards were developed not by educators but by private philanthropists, executives from the standardized testing industry, and politicians with no teaching experience, who also were in charge of designing the assessments of students' attempts to meet those standards. If the National Defense Education Act of 1958 or the Elementary and Secondary Education Act of 1965 epitomize McGuinn's definition of the equity regime, then NCLB and the Common Core epitomize accountability—particularly in the reliance on leaders in *industry* to advance the Common Core as opposed to educators. The CCSS do not only affect K–12 education, of course. As Joanne Addison writes, the Common Core is "the most well-funded and pervasive effort to date at ensuring accountability through standardization not just in our K–12 classrooms but increasingly in our college classrooms as well." Kelly-Riley calls this phenomenon "spill-over effects," that is, the inevitability that Common Core curricula and testing at the elementary and secondary levels will impact teaching in college-level writing classrooms.

The story of NCTE's role in developing the Common Core is important for understanding the role of writing studies' institutions in effecting education policy today. As the archives of the Washington Task Force showed us in the last chapter, the emergence of new political arrangements subverted NCTE's hallmarks of institutionalization—the persuasiveness of disciplinary evidence and expertise—as a new policy regime took shape. In this chapter, at the height of the accountability regime in the early 2000s, we see NCTE experiencing the consequences of this shift in even starker terms. What does a professional organization do when disciplinary knowledge no longer matters to policymakers? How do experts in writing studies respond when having a veneer of expertise—the appearance of a dialogue—is the only precondition to making policy?

Specifically, this chapter analyzes a moment in 2009 when members of NCTE were asked to comment on a draft of the Common Core ELA standards, and leaders from both groups dialogued and even met face to face to exchange ideas. At a moment when the accountability regime was in full swing, NCTE's good-faith efforts at policy deliberation failed because the evidence-based case it made about the standards was unconvincing for the Common Core's representatives; the ideological paradigm of the old regime, holding that disciplinary expertise mattered when deciding how federal education dollars should be spent, was no longer a narrative framework with which stakeholders evaluated and shaped policy solutions. This is not to say that in accountability regimes *evidence itself* is unpersuasive. Rather, accountability regime logics value other kinds of evidence than what NCTE presented. As Jim Webber writes, contemporary education reform values a "globally competitive present," which necessitates the need for "common standards and assessments [to] improve *all* students' access to opportunity" (11). Therefore, when groups like NCTE oppose initiatives like the Common Core, they are unpersuasive because the governing arrangements that privilege industry, competition, and efficiency see NCTE's critiques as a "failure to recognize the way the world is" (11).

This chapter offers an analysis of policy and rhetoric, specifically of two main texts: NCTE's critique of an early draft of the ELA standards (which I call the "July Draft") and the revised draft of those standards published by the Common Core authors several months later. In addition, I analyze nonofficial discourse surrounding this attempted dialogue, including academic scholarship, newspaper articles, essays, and blogs. From this analysis there are two key takeaways. The first is that NCTE's thorough response to the July Draft did not have any noticeable impact, either on the collaborative process or on the final version of the standards. And second, if professional organizations like NCTE want to effect education policy, then sustained dialogue is needed between disciplinary researchers and policymakers so that the research of a professional organization is valued, although the ethics of collaborating with the accountability regime is a matter that English studies will have to consider. What the institutions of English studies need are more kairotic strategies of political engagement for deciding whether and when to participate in policymaking discussions: for example, whether to help create new policy arrangements, to gain the credibility to challenge prevailing policy in public debates about policy problems, or to effect policy change through more overt political strategies in opposition to the power structures through which policy is enacted. But first, it is important to situate these concerns in the history of the Common Core to see how its ELA standards manifest the accountability-based policy regime logics that champion the standards as a good, equitable, and commonsense solution to the problems facing American public schools.

Brief History and Power Arrangements of the Common Core State Standards

There are several detailed histories of the development of the CCSS, both from the developers themselves and from scholars in writing studies, such as Diane Kelly-Riley's essay "Common Core State Standards: A Policy Review for WPAs," Doug Hesse (who attended the meetings between NCTE and Common Core representatives) in his essay "Who Speaks for Writing?," and Joanne Addison's essay "Shifting the Locus of Control." These essays detail the processes, networks, and individual actors involved in drafting and implementing the standards and the matrix of organizations that thrust the standards into the public discourse about education. My overview draws from these scholars and from the Common Core's official discourse. Readers interested in a more thorough history of these events should consult the works referenced above, as well as critical interpretations of the standards from Kristine Hansen or Judith Summerfield and Philip M. Anderson.

The Common Core is emblematic of the concept of policy regimes because of its widespread adoption throughout the nation's schools as a policy itself—even though it is not an actual piece of legislation—and because of its broader power arrangements: the vast network of businesses, government, and educational entrepreneurs who jockey for influence in the Common Core universe. The Common Core remains durable (despite its many critics) because of the policy paradigm it invokes, which legitimizes through public discourse the idea of having national standards. In fact, the Common Core is so embedded in the social and political culture of public education that, even as more and more states opt out of the standards or develop their own standards with a different name, there seems to be no turning back. A vast network of private philanthropists and Common Core–affiliated testing consortia ensure the perpetuation of the Common Core in American education. "Whether or not states adopt or subsequently drop the CCSS is really now a moot point," writes Kelly-Riley. "Textbooks, professional development materials, tests, and other educationally supportive materials have been revised to align with the standards since they have been so widely adopted" (207).

The Common Core casts its official history as a broad collaboration that began in 2009 among politicians, industry leaders, and teachers, with the goal of revamping education standards in the United States so as to better prepare students for college and the workforce and thereby make the country more competitive globally. As I mentioned above, even though the Common Core is emblematic of the accountability policy paradigm, it still invokes the values of access and equity. The evidence that it supports these values, though, comes in the form of words like *choice* or phrases like *college and career readiness* or statements like this: "The standards were created to ensure that all students graduate from high school with the skills and knowledge necessary to succeed in college, career, and life, regardless of where they live" ("About the Standards"). Success is also framed in terms of students' future ability to contribute to the economy: the standards ensure that "students are prepared for today's entry-level careers, freshman-level college courses, and workforce training programs" ("What Parents Should Know").

Developed primarily by two organizations, the Council of Chief State School Officers and the National Governors Association, the Common Core was a response to what they considered to be a crisis in American public education: the "uneven patchwork of academic standards that vary from state to state and do not agree on what students should know and be able to do at each grade level" ("About the Standards").[1] At the time of writing of this book, forty-one states have adopted the Common

Core, and nine states—Alaska, Florida, Indiana, Minnesota, Nebraska, Oklahoma, South Carolina, Texas, and Virginia—are not adopters because they formally withdrew from participation or voted to repeal the standards after having adopted them.[2]

The governing arrangements of the accountability regime prioritize a policy paradigm of advancing equity through interventions of business and industry that value speed, scale, and efficiency and that *devalue* the disciplinary knowledge of experts. A key concept of accountability regime logics is competition. By framing the goals of equity and access in a context of competition, writes Webber, a *successful* policy becomes one that "requires a policy marketplace that invites public *choice* among competing providers of expertise" (12). This means, according to Webber, that the disciplinary knowledge of experts is now in *competition* with the business acumen of philanthropists and executives, who argue that their innovative solutions are better poised to "define the goals and measures of public education in literacy" than any alternative from experts in writing studies (11). Also, despite declarations from the Common Core's discourse that tout the input of teachers, there is little evidence of teachers having played any significant role in how the ELA standards took shape. (This is perhaps one reason why the standards were developed and scaled up so quickly. The CCSS became the nation's de facto national education standards between 2008, when the Council of Chief State School Officers, the National Governors Association, and an accountability-oriented think tank called Achieve Inc. began lobbying powerful policy stakeholders about the need for national standards, and 2011, when states began formally adopting them).[3]

Although the Common Core's discourse claims that teachers were consulted through their national organizations, which included work groups and feedback groups or state-convened teams appointed to provide feedback in local contexts (*Summary of Public Feedback*), in reality, the drafting and adoption of the CCSS happened with barely any input from writing teachers or organizations. Linda Adler-Kassner writes that the CCSS "went from draft to final version in about 14 months"; the standards were "drafted by a relatively small group of educators (largely administrators) and professionals, [and] vetted with minimal input from professional organizations like NCTE or even MLA" ("Companies We Keep" 124). Doug Hesse asserts that "no experts in writing at the college level were involved in any significant way in any phase of the development process" (11). In her 2014 speech to the Modern Language Association, Diane Ravitch, an outspoken critic of Common Core, claimed that the standards were written "behind closed doors" by a small writing group that included "a significant number of representatives of the testing industry," in a process that was "marked by the absence of public participation, transparency, or educator participation" (qtd. in Strauss). And, in 2010, the Common Core Validation Committee (VC), which was convened to review the final draft of the ELA standards and issue an official stamp of approval, also had little representation of ELA experts. Sandra Stotsky, a retired education professor from the University of Arkansas, detailed her experiences on the committee in a paper given at the Consequences of the Common Core conference at Notre Dame in 2013. She claimed that "the VC contained almost no experts on ELA standards. . . . I was the only nationally recognized expert on English language arts standards" (2). Stotsky continued, "It quickly became clear that the VC existed as window-dressing—to rubber-stamp, not improve, whatever standards were declared as college- and career-readiness and grade-level standards" (3).

Consistent with Stotsky's claim, evidence shows that Common Core representatives sought out the advice of content experts to provide the *appearance* of dialogue, while the most significant contributors to the standards were business leaders and philanthropists. When the names of the initial team that developed the college- and career-readiness standards were released in July 2009, the membership was mostly employees from Achieve Inc., ACT, and the College Board ("CCSSI Development Teams"). Education journalist Anthony Cody at *Education Week* notes that, of the feedback groups announced,

> six are associated with the test-makers . . . and four are with Achieve. Zero teachers are on either Work Group. The Feedback Groups have 35 participants, almost all of whom are university professors. There appears to be only one classroom teacher involved in the entire process. ("Secret Sixty")

The lack of teachers runs counter to any responsible process of composing standards: "Would standards for the practice of medicine be written without the participation of doctors?" he asks. "Standards for the practice of law without lawyers? It is not only insulting, it is undemocratic and counterproductive in the extreme."

Doug Hesse informs us that the main author of the Common Core's ELA standards was not a language arts expert but was instead David Coleman, then head of a company called Student Achievement Partners. His company worked in consultation with the governors and chief school officers starting in spring 2009, and by late summer they had achieved three ambitious goals: drafting the standards, convincing (at one time) forty-eight states to adopt them, and, finally, persuading President Barack Obama's administration to tie federal education grants to the adoption of the standards.

These federal grants were part of the Obama-era initiative called Race to the Top, a $4.3 billion competitive grant program funded as part of the American Recovery and Reinvestment Act of 2009; the grant program doled out federal funds to states that promised to meet performance-based standards (*Race to the Top*). Attaching the Common Core to Race to the Top grant applications led to quick, widespread adoption of the standards without any significant input from teachers. All states had to do was commit in their applications to implementing the Common Core, which made them much more likely to secure Race to the Top grants. All of the states that received the grants, in fact, had aligned their state curricula with the Common Core ("Awards"). States that aligned their curricula thus also qualified for waivers "from adequate yearly progress quotas set under the new NCLB law, [which saves] many schools from being categorized as 'failing'" (Perez-Pena). Political scientist Nicholas Tampio writes that the Common Core's loose affiliation with federal law paved the way for some curricula, like New York's for instance, to script word for word what teachers should say all throughout the semester. "The Common Core Curriculum," he writes, "imposes a rigid plan and schedule on teachers and students. In theory, the Common Core standards are not a curriculum; in reality, for millions of children the Common Core Curriculum gives lockstep instructions for the entire school year" (47). The connection between federal funding and the Common Core has signaled to many critics from both sides of the political aisle that the Common Core constitutes de facto national standards. This connection had further embedded accountability-regime logics in the bureaucracy and ideology of American public education by the end of the first decade of the 2000s.

The Common Core emerged from a policy regime of accountability that redefined the federal government's relationship with public education from an older, more hands-off model to a more intrusive, punitive one. As Arthur Applebee asserts, this kind of relationship between the federal government and public education—in which the government imposes punitive sanctions on school systems that do not perform well enough in high-stakes testing and distributes federal funds to districts that prioritize workplace-readiness standards—are hallmarks of accountability-based education reform. Applebee's analysis reveals how the CCSS clearly articulate the goal of accountability regime logics: students should develop the "knowledge and skills needed by a college- and career-ready high school graduate." Applebee also asks us to see the Common Core not as new or revolutionary but rather as embedded with "the vestiges" of older discourses about standards (25); for example, No Child Left Behind, which made standards a state responsibility, set up a framework in which the Common Core could take shape.

One reason why the Common Core was seen as a commonsense solution to education policy was that, since the passage of No Child Left Behind, there had become "50 different visions of what students should know and be able to do" (Applebee 26). Thus, a set of *common* standards was seen as a welcome remedy. As Webber writes, the ideological framework of accountability implies that states, schools, and teachers should be *accountable* through strategic measuring of student success, and therefore "the goals and measures of literacy education must be common."; this reasoning implies a "market model of public policy: since teachers and scholars refuse to standardize, policy development itself must become competitive" (24). These ideological paradigms made accountability policies like the Common Core seem like a natural and inevitable solution, which thus required new power arrangements to legitimize and bureaucratize the policies even further, and the landscape of public education changed dramatically. Now, stakeholders in education policy included fewer and fewer teachers, content experts, and scholars, and more and more of the stakeholders were leaders in industry and educational philanthropy. Jory Brass, in his article "English, Literacy and Neoliberal Policies," argues that the main difference between the CCSS and the standards-based reform of No Child Left Behind is that the Common Core power arrangements had no interest in seeking evidence provided by teachers. The sought-after input came instead from

> overlapping networks of policy entrepreneurs (e.g., Student Achievement Partners), venture philanthropy (e.g., Gates Foundation, Pearson Foundation, GE Foundation), neoconservative think tanks (Fordham Foundation), corporate executives (e.g., Business Roundtable), and non-governmental trade organizations (Achieve, Inc., National Governors Association) in "partnership" or "consortia" with education publishers (e.g., Pearson Corporation, McGraw-Hill) and standardized testing companies (Education Testing Service, ACT, College Board). (126)

It was in this way, explains Hesse, that David Coleman and the Council of Chief State School Officers and the National Governors Association quickly succeeded in their efforts and had already "hitched to the Department of Education train and schedule" by the time they reached out to NCTE (11). By July 2009, when Common Core officials reached out to NCTE for feedback on the ELA standards, architects of the Common Core had already been heavily involved in conversations with governors and the Department of Education about the widespread adoption of standards that had not yet even been vetted.

Case Study: NCTE's Feedback on the CCSS

Throughout the summer of 2009, as the nation's governors and chief state school officers conferred with so-called *work groups* in developing "College and Career Readiness Standards," feedback groups created more specific grade-by-grade standards based on early drafts ("Development Process"). All of this happened *before* NCTE received embargoed copies of the ELA standards. And, despite NCTE's *major* concerns with the standards, which I unpack below, the standards still proceeded relatively unchanged to the twenty-nine-person VC in October 2009. And, to reiterate Adler-Kassner's point, not one person on the VC was a professor of English or an ELA teacher. Cody writes that of the twenty-seven people in the initial work groups, only three were from outside the ACT, College Board, Achieve Inc., Student Achievement Partners, or America's Choice, and only one was a classroom teacher (in the mathematics work group). Moreover, despite the *appearance* of feedback from professional organizations, the drafting, vetting, and implementation of the Common

Core was highly secretive and devoid of scrutiny from content experts (Cody, "Common Core Standards").

NCTE's involvement in the Common Core is embedded within a policy regime that devalues the knowledge of writing experts and questions whether educators with classroom experience in writing, literacy, and language should even contribute to policymaking discussions. And while the National Governors Association and the Council of Chief State School Officers consistently touted the collaborative and inclusive nature of making the standards, the fact that practitioners of English studies felt lost in the shuffle of consultants, business leaders, and philanthropic organizations like the Bill and Melinda Gates Foundation is important. It helps explain why NCTE ultimately accepted an invitation (on short notice) to work with the Common Core authors and provide feedback. Moreover, it is also important to consider the distinct ideological and power differentials between the policymakers and businesspeople crafting the documents, whose interests aligned with the accountability regime's policy paradigm, and the teachers and writing experts, whose approach to education reform was mostly opposed to accountability policies (NCTE as an institution has historically positioned itself in accordance with the government's interests as a way of leveraging institutional power). The daylight visible between these two alignments foreshadows their different approaches to policy and their failed collaborative experience.

NCTE's short relationship with the Common Core authors is not a model of meaningful and transformative collaboration. Rather, their partnership highlights a moment when efforts at collaboration failed, ostensibly because one side valued disciplinary expertise and the other saw improving student success and achieving equity only in terms of creating economic efficiency. On August 17, 2009, Kylene Beers, then president of NCTE, released a memo to members in which she confirmed that an NCTE committee had met with the National Governors Association and the Council of Chief State School Officers earlier that month to review a draft of the Common Core ELA standards. The committee, she writes, judged the July Draft to be "against existing NCTE policies and practices." The review panel crafted a response and met with Common Core representatives on August 10; the panelists "brought to the table many years of classroom experience both in secondary education and higher education." After a "frank" conversation, Beers notes that the "90-minute meeting was, at times, blunt and by the end of the meeting, it was obvious that all were very impressed by the thoroughness of the NCTE review." Moreover, Beers writes,

> Though I do not know how influential the NCTE review of the document will prove to be, I do know that of the 300 or so groups or individuals who have offered response to the [Council of Chief State School Officers], only six groups were invited to a face-to-face meeting regarding the draft document. NCTE was one of those six. The Executive Committee is appreciative of the meeting.

Finally, Beers notes that the committee now waits with "cautious optimism" for the release of the final documents. Beers's description of the meeting with the CCSS organizers reveals a particular orientation toward institutional collaboration, one in which NCTE was grateful to be included but skeptical of having good results from collaboration. Unlike previous engagements in policy from decades past, wherein NCTE had lobbied for Congress's attention to needs in literacy education, this time NCTE was sought out for its disciplinary expertise by business leaders and professional organizations. NCTE provided feedback under the presumption that its members' expertise would be considered with the same good faith in which it was provided.

Doug Hesse wrote about his experiences at that August 10 meeting for the 2012 collection *Who Speaks for Writing: Stewardship in Writing Studies in the 21st Century*. Hesse notes that NCTE's partnership with the authors of the Common Core ELA standards was fütile from the very beginning, as "input from experts in writing was missing in the development stages, sought during the end game and pretty much after the fact, then ignored" (11). Hesse writes that NCTE's twenty-one-page response excoriated the July Draft for its shortsightedness in digital studies, multimodality, and the social and civic aspects of writing (12). Moreover, NCTE challenged the Common Core's insistent claims that the standards were "evidence-based," noting that "none of the evidence has been drawn from peer-reviewed research journals or similar sources" (12).

Two months later, at a daylong meeting where CCSS representatives discussed NCTE's feedback, there were "no revisions in major components of the document that had most troubled the NCTE review group." What is more, continues Hesse,

> to everyone's surprise . . . the governors' group had gone the next step of "backmapping." Confident in their graduation standards for reading and writing, the governors and chiefs had set up a process to establish specific grade-level standards from kindergarten on, thus dictating at the finest grain what ought to be taught when. We were stunned, and while we generated six objections to the draft standards, we realized that this matter was far down the road, pulled substantially by the horse of Race to the Top. (12)

In other words, even though NCTE had raised detailed objections to the Common Core in its report, it was clear to Hesse that the organization's role was merely to rubber-stamp standards that had *already been tied to Race to the Top funding* and then "backmapped" from college-readiness to learning outcomes beginning in kindergarten. As far as Hesse was concerned, NCTE's suggestions were unheeded by the authors of the Common Core.

In the next section, I try to account for this disregard by analyzing two documents: NCTE's response to the July Draft and the final draft of the ELA standards. In its response, NCTE made distinct appeals to disciplinary peer-reviewed research as the *more valuable* form of evidence, which it used to show the inadequacy of the ELA standards. NCTE's appeals to discipline-based evidence show how evidence functions not as an objective path to persuasion by plugging gaps with knowledge but as a discursive framing of values and way of seeing the world. The values NCTE asserted through evidence in this discursive exchange reflected a policy paradigm counter to the accountability policy paradigm, one that presumed the persuasiveness of disciplinary knowledge, a presumption not shared by those in the establishment groups. Moreover, the whole exchange illustrates that in any kind of institutional collaboration wherein values and ideologies are sure to clash, there is a heightened need, as Carolyn Miller writes, to rely on more than just "decision science" to facilitate dialogue ("Rhetoric of Decision Science"). Decision science is a narrowly defined approach to policy deliberations that "encourages submission to technical, knowledge-based solutions for what are social, value-based problems" (46). NCTE's failed appeals to traditionally authoritative grounds for persuasion reveal less about the futility of this specific partnership and more about the importance of fostering sustained collaborations for meaningful institutional engagement in the accountability era.

NCTE's Critique of the July Draft

The Common Core authors sent NCTE a draft of the ELA standards in the summer of 2009. NCTE's critique, written a month later, is separated into two parts: part one is a general critique, and part two is a specific critique organized in terms of scope, omissions, and language use.[4] Part one notes how new developments in language and literacy, which include new texts, composing practices, and the impact of globalization, require "innovation, creativity, and adaptability" in a literacy learning environment. The ELA standards in the July Draft, NCTE argues, do not reflect the accelerating rate of change in American public education; the standards apply more to "the schools of 1950" than they do "to the schools of this decade" (*Report of the NCTE Review Team* 3). While the apparent goal of the Common Core is to create standards that are "higher, clearer, and fewer," NCTE charges that the ELA standards are "articulated as individual, testable actions rather than as authentic performances in college classrooms or workplaces." In particular, NCTE fears that students from underprivileged groups, who are more likely to underperform in assessment, will be at a distinct disadvantage under the narrowly defined ELA standards. Teachers of these students, NCTE contends, "will be forced to attend narrowly to the standards." To back up this claim, NCTE notes how "research demonstrates that narrow and high-stake assessments reduce the scope of curriculum and decrease student engagement." Left dangling in parentheses are six separate academic citations (3).[5]

Next, NCTE notes how a decrease in student engagement disproportionately impacts those from underserved communities. This statement is followed by three more citations from academic sources (4).[6] The Common Core authors claim that the ELA standards are evidence-based, yet "none of the evidence has been drawn from peer-reviewed research journals or similar sources." Rather, the evidence offered in the July Draft "consists of surveys conducted by the testing companies that stand most immediately to gain from the testing of these standards" (4). This statement is followed by two more academic citations in support of the claim that peer-reviewed research into different literacy practices has been overlooked in the ELA standards.[7] To ameliorate this oversight, NCTE recommends that "those who are familiar with the relevant research and important practices" should be "invited to contribute their insights to the standards," and NCTE even goes so far as to suggest that the authors of the Common Core get rid of *any* "claims that these standards are based in valid evidence, since such claims will only invite skepticism and criticism that cannot be answered" (4). By having eleven citations in the first few paragraphs of its response, NCTE implicitly claims that *its* evidence—peer-reviewed research produced by scholars of writing and language—is the *more truthful* form of evidence to use in forming education policy. NCTE bolsters this claim by denouncing the CCSS authors' use of the word *evidence* at all, since what they cite is not a *valid* form of evidence.

The second part of NCTE's critique of the July Draft affirms the value of academic research by showing how the ELA standards are not based on current research. Notwithstanding the "few" things the standards do well, NCTE indicates important areas the standards do not address, such as the multiple purposes of writing, which go beyond college and career (5–6); writing as a process, which underscores the range of repertoires and practices students can harness in particular literacy situations (6); diversity, which would help twenty-first-century communicators understand cultural difference and "organized knowledge about cultural differences" (6); the social dimensions of learning, which highlight the "role of others in individuals' developments of [writing] skills (6); the varieties of writing quality, which help students understand that "what counts as an effective text varies immensely in terms of audience and purpose" (7); and twenty-first-century literacies, which would help students deal with the "real, substantive, and high-stakes" demands of an information society (7). The July Draft of the ELA standards, NCTE writes, omits the kinds of writing practices studied in academic research and focuses instead on the "ease of assessing," which has unfortunately "given rise to distortions in the drafted standards for teaching and learning" (6). Moreover, these distortions "misrepresent the nature of composition" and falsely advertise themselves as "standards for learning" instead of what they really are: "standards for assessment," a move that is "extremely costly for the nation" (6). NCTE's scathing estimation of the ELA standards positioned the organization in stark opposition to the

Common Core, a stance that undoubtedly served to increase the gulf between them.

NCTE continues to widen this gulf through line-by-line suggestions for revision. These revisions are

> grounded in NCTE policy, the peer-reviewed research base that underlies those policies, and the real-world experience of schools, districts, and states who have encountered unforeseen frustrations when the standards-based reforms they pursued didn't square with rapid changes in the practice of literacy and the conditions of schooling. (7)

NCTE's suggested revisions reflect its views on how academic research should be valued and incorporated into the standards. For example, in "Section 1.B, Required Range and Contexts, Complexity, Sentence," the original language apparently read,

> In college and careers, students will need to *extract knowledge* and information from reference materials, technical manuals, literature, and other texts (print and online) that are characterized by demanding and context-dependent vocabulary, subtle relationships among ideas and characters, a nuanced rhetorical style and tone, and often elaborate structures or formats. (10; my emphasis)

NCTE proposed to change the text to the following:

> In college and careers, students will need to *construct understandings* with reference materials, technical manuals, literature, and other texts (print and online) that are characterized by demanding and context-dependent vocabulary, subtle relationships among ideas and characters, a nuanced rhetorical style and tone, and often elaborate structures or formats. (10; my emphasis)

The phrase in the draft, "extracting knowledge and information," NCTE argues, is "outdated in reading and psychology (since the 1970s)" and needs to acknowledge more recent perspectives of a "constructive model of reading" as opposed to the "simple extraction of information." NCTE offers six more parenthetical citations to support its claim.[8]

Another suggested change comes in "Section 1.B, Required Range and Contexts, Quality." NCTE proposed that three new sentences be added to the end of the section:

> Students also build reading strength and engagement through highly motivated experience with a range of texts, and they must be provided with opportunities to develop independent reading agendas, favorite authors and topics, and habits that sustain a literate life. They must learn as well to discuss features of textual quality in reference to the everyday texts in their lives, such as songs, websites, and advertisements. Such transfer of notions of quality is essential to the practicalities of the workplace and to lifelong literacy. (12)

The proposed language here reflects research on the importance of "engagement and motivation" in developing habits of "lifelong literacy." Appealing to nine more citations, NCTE argues that adding this section would reflect how engagement and motivation are "of intrinsic value to a literate life, almost by definition" (12).[9] These proposed revisions and academic citations exemplify NCTE's strategies for engaging with the authors of the Common Core: NCTE made appeals to disciplinary expertise in asserting the value of multimodal and context-specific literacies.

The Final Draft of the ELA Standards

NCTE's critique of the July Draft was a clear, focused, and bold evaluation. NCTE was right to invoke the literature of its field when engaging with the organizations that composed the Common Core. Its critique was an attempt to do what Linda Adler-Kassner calls "reframing" in the standards debate. But when NCTE's critique is juxtaposed with the final ELA standards published later, we see a final document that reflects few, if any, of NCTE's suggestions. We see in the two groups' appeals to research how their value systems diverged even farther after collaborating. For instance, the introduction to the final draft of the ELA standards says that each standard is informed by the "best available research" that indicates whether a skill is "essential for college and career readiness in the twenty-first century" (*Common Core State Standards for English Language Arts* 3). Indeed, the appendix to the ELA standards contains 104 citations from the field of writing, language, literacy, and speech.

The standards do cite "surveys conducted by the testing companies," as NCTE had charged, but the final draft also cites a range of evidence in the field of literacy that illustrates the increasing complexity of texts that students face in the twenty-first century.[10] Appendix A catalogs this research as a way of bolstering the Common Core's quantitative method of grading text complexity with specific scales and correlating complexity with standards for each grade level. Elsewhere in the appendix, literacy scholar Gerald Graff is cited as evidence of the need for increased proficiency in argument (24), and the rhetorician Richard Fulkerson is cited to back up a claim about the social and public value of being able to argue well (25). In other words, both groups appealed to academic evidence in one way or another to bolster their claims and affirm their different sets of values.

The authors of the ELA standards clearly value accountability-based policy regimes of education reform, which hold that student success, and the well-worn concept of *equity*, can be fostered by prioritizing easy assessment, standardizing writing curricula across all grades, and gradually displacing "literary" texts in favor of teaching more *real world*, or "informational" texts, which supposedly better prepare students to enter the workforce. These values are apparent in the appeals to evidence throughout the document. The document is divided into three sections: "Standards for English Language Arts and Literacy in History/Social Studies, Science, and Technical Subjects K–5," "Standards for English Language Arts 6–12," and "Standards for Literacy in History/Social Studies, Science, and Technical Subjects." The beginning of each section features "college and career readiness anchor standards," which outline what students should be able to do by the end of each grade. After the anchor standards come grade-specific standards that elaborate on those objectives. For example, here are the ten anchor statements for writing standards in grades six to twelve:

> Text Types and Purposes
>
> 1. Write arguments to support claims in an analysis of substantive topics or texts, using valid reasoning and relevant and sufficient evidence.
> 2. Write informative/explanatory texts to examine and convey complex ideas and information clearly and accurately through the effective selection, organization, and analysis of content.

3. Write narratives to develop real or imagined experiences or events using effective technique, well-chosen details, and well-structured event sequences.

Production and Distribution of Writing

4. Produce clear and coherent writing in which the development, organization, and style are appropriate to task, purpose, and audience.
5. Develop and strengthen writing as needed by planning, revising, editing, rewriting, or trying a new approach.
6. Use technology, including the Internet, to produce and publish writing and to interact and collaborate with others.

Research to Build and Present Knowledge

7. Conduct short as well as more sustained research projects based on focused questions, demonstrating understanding of the subject under investigation.
8. Gather relevant information from multiple print and digital sources, assess the credibility and accuracy of each source, and integrate the information while avoiding plagiarism.
9. Draw evidence from literary or informational texts to support analysis, reflection, and research.

Range of Writing

10. Write routinely over extended time frames (time for research, reflection, and revision) and shorter time frames (a single sitting or a day or two) for a range of tasks, purposes, and audiences. (41)

After the anchor statements come grade-specific standards. For example, for grades eleven and twelve, the first anchor statement, "write arguments to support claims in an analysis of substantive topics or texts, using valid reasoning and relevant sufficient evidence," is supplemented by five grade-specific standards: incorporating counterevidence; developing claims "in a manner that anticipates the audience's knowledge level, concerns, values, and possible biases"; using appropriate syntax; establishing appropriate tone and style; and supporting arguments with concluding statements (45).[11]

What is obvious in the anchor statements is that none of NCTE's suggested language revisions—*constructing understandings* and cultivating *habits of mind* that sustain engagement with literacy—were incorporated. Instead, the anchor statements and outcomes for grades eleven and twelve correspond with the original definitions of *literary* and *informational* texts. The ELA standards define literature as stories, dramas, and poetry, and informational texts as literary nonfiction and its subgenres of "exposition, argument, and functional text in the form of personal essays, speeches, opinion pieces, essays about art or literature, biographies, memoirs, journalism, and historical, scientific, technical, or economic accounts (including digital sources) written for a broad audience" (57). This distinction between literary and informational texts is a key element of the ELA standards that clearly diverges from NCTE's feedback. "Most of the required reading in college and workforce training programs," the standards read, "is informational in structure and challenging in content" (4).

Following this logic, the standards deemphasize literary texts as students progress toward twelfth grade. The Common Core authors cite the 2009 "reading framework" of the National Assessment of Education Progress, which requires a "high and increasing proportion of informational text on its assessment as students advance through the grades" to support this deemphasis (4). The ELA standards recommend ratios of literary to informational texts by grade: in grade four, the recommended ratio is 50 percent and 50 percent; in grade eight, the ratio decreases to 45 and 55 percent; and in grade twelve, 30 and 70 percent (5). As the ratio of literary to informational texts skews toward informational, the distribution of students' "communicative purposes"—writing to persuade, to explain, or to convey real or imagined experiences—also changes as students progress through school (5). In grade four, for example, writing to persuade should be the purpose for 30 percent of all assignments, writing to explain for 35 percent, and writing to convey experiences for 35 percent. In grade eight, writing to persuade increases to 35 percent, while writing to explain stays at 35 percent and conveying personal experience decreases to 30 percent. By grade twelve, the standards recommend that writing to persuade should be assigned 40 percent of the time, writing to explain 40 percent of the time, and writing to convey personal experience only 20 percent of the time (5).

Clearly, the language offered by NCTE was ignored, and a difference in values is apparent in the ELA standards' insistence on apportioning literary and informational texts in ratios. "The dichotomy of literature/informational texts creates too restricted a set of purposes," NCTE had warned:

> The assertions about the nature of literary reading are not supported in research. The claim that literary reading has a causal relationship to success in other reading purposes has no basis in reading research beyond elementary school, and so it misstates the purposes of literary study in secondary and tertiary education. (*Report of the NCTE Review Team* 13)

NCTE's critique had also stated that even though "a significant amount of reading in college is "informational," an equally important amount is "persuasive" or "argumentative" or "reflective." As such, "much reading in the workplace occurs not simply to extract information but to evaluate recommendations or courses of action" (7). But despite NCTE's thorough appeals to scholarship in its field, the split between informational and literary texts remained in the final draft. In fact, many of NCTE's citations and suggestions for revision are unrecognizable in the final ELA standards, making cross-referencing difficult. But by and large, based on my analysis and on Hesse's testimonial, the final draft of the Common Core ELA standards does not incorporate any significant changes that NCTE's critique had recommended.

Negative Impact on Policy Deliberation

The research cited by the authors of the Common Core for dividing informational and literary texts evinces a particular value system that suggests equity and student success can be achieved by standardizing curricula to create more efficient tools for assessment. Diane Ravitch has argued, though, that the recommended ratios, such as the 70 to 30 percent split in grade twelve in favor of informational texts, are spurious percentages meant to be "instructions to test developers," not to teachers. In fact, she writes, the National Assessment of Educational Progress "never intended that these numbers would be converted into instructional mandates for teachers"; the arbitrary ratios are hard to enforce, are inaccurate representations of how knowledge is conveyed in college and the workplace, and are unfair to teachers. "Frankly," she writes, "I think that teachers are quite capable of making that decision for themselves. If they choose to teach a course devoted only to fiction or devoted only to non-fiction, that should be their choice, not a mandate imposed by a committee in 2009" (qtd. in Strauss). Nevertheless, the Common Core's ELA standards suggest that dividing informational and literary texts is a best practice, based on what the authors describe as "*extensive research* establishing the need for college and career ready students to be proficient in reading complex informational text independently in a variety of content areas" (*Common Core State Standards for English Language Arts* 4; my emphasis).

In a sense, though, it is not the research cited by both parties that matters but the gulf in values widened by these appeals to evidence without any presumption of partnership between the two groups. The Common Core authors used research in literacy to suggest that students' abilities to decipher texts are declining and that a new set of rigorous quantitative evaluations are necessary to increase student success and equity in American schools. NCTE, on the other hand, used research to suggest that narrowly defined and easily quantified standards do not take into account the multimodal nature of writing and will disproportionally impact at-risk communities. But at no point were the two groups able to cultivate a meaningful relationship and have a genuine intellectual exchange.

It could be argued that genuine intellectual exchange was never the goal of soliciting NCTE's feedback on the ELA standards, which is a fair point. However, if NCTE's goal was to participate meaningfully in effecting education policy, its strategy of excoriating the July Draft did the organization no favors. In fact, NCTE's appeals to the value of disciplinary knowledge represent the policy paradigm of the old regime, one in which disciplinary expertise was valued by stakeholders in education policy. But in the new regime, the policy paradigm prioritizes competition in a global marketplace, not the particulars of local classroom-based assessments or the protection of at-risk students and communities or the complexity of multiple literate environments.[12] NCTE's efforts to showcase this value system to the authors of the ELA standards through appeals to academic research, while laudable, actually exposed how important it is to foster sustained collaboration in addition to evidence-based policy work. As Hesse attests, the Common Core authors did not incorporate any of NCTE's critiques into their final document, which left him wondering whether NCTE's feedback made any difference at all.

Building and Sustaining Relationships

When considering a path forward for institutions like NCTE that want to effect education policy in the accountability regime, they need more *kairotic political engagement strategies.* Political science research might be helpful for crafting this new kind of institutional rhetoric. Research in public health and political science has been looking at the role of evidenced-based policymaking since the 1970s and by and large has found that the role of research in deliberating policy is limited at best.[13] Scholars in these fields have been making the case that evidence-based research has little impact in actual policy decisions—or rather that evidence-based research is only one of many available strategies in the formation of public policy. For example, public health researcher Nick Black writes that evidence-based policymaking often assumes a linear relationship between research and policy in which "research is used to fill an identified gap in knowledge" (275).

Despite trends to connect policy decisions with evidence in areas of public life from policing to defense to health care, "research has only a limited role because government policies are driven by ideology, value judgments, financial stringency, economic theory, political expediency, and intellectual fashion" (Black 276). Public health experts Greenhalgh and Russell describe evidence as serving a rhetorical function:

> Evidence for policy making is not sitting in journals ready to be harvested by assiduous systematic reviewers. Rather, it is dynamically created through the human interaction around the policy making table—and, probably more significantly, the lobbying, campaigning and interpersonal influencing going on in the back rooms and corridors leading up to official policy making meetings. (36)

Greenhalgh and Russell's emphasis on human interaction is reinforced in Wood et al.'s empirical study of behavioral patterns in medical patients in the United Kingdom. They found that

> scientific evidence is not a clear, accepted and bounded source. There is no such entity as "*the* body of evidence." There are

> simply (more or less competing) (re)constructions of evidence able to support almost any position. Much of what is called evidence is, in fact, a contested domain, constituted in the debates and controversies of opposing viewpoints in search of ever more compelling arguments. (1735)

The authors continue by arguing that evidence functions not as a way to *win* a debate but rather a way to *widen* it:

> The nature of evidence is ambivalent. It is constructed into debates and controversies, which are often equally supportive of opposing viewpoints. Such issues appear recursive and intractable *not* linear and incremental, so that a final resolution remains unlikely in many cases. The "progress" of science serves only to widen the debate. (1737)

In other words, policy decisions are not made based on which piece of evidence is the best; policy happens when groups commit to a *sustained engagement* by harnessing an array of interpersonal skills beyond making appeals to academic evidence. In his book *An Alternate Pragmatism for Going Public*, James Webber addresses this specifically in relation to the Common Core, noting that while *redirecting* narratives about education reform toward our own research is important, the policy paradigm of the accountability regime prioritizes different values. As a "means of authorizing our professional judgment," he recommends a kind of pragmatism for the current moment, one in which we find opportune moments to *make* our expertise competitive. It is a mistake, Webber warns, to participate in discussions about policy by forwarding our own "professionalism as *the* means of democratically representing our diverse publics" (29).

Rather than having a linear problem-solving understanding of policy in which research serves to plug perceived knowledge gaps, Elliott and Popay suggest other models for using research in policymaking. There is the interactive model, which relies on research as "one of several knowledge sources on which policy makers draw in an iterative process of decision making" (462), and the dialogic model, proposed by Giddens, which holds that social knowledge is created through the process of interaction: "the influence that research has on policy makers is most likely to come about through an *extended process* of communication between researchers, policy makers, and lay actors" (463; my italics). Through case studies, Elliott and Popay found that the factors of budget or time constraints are just as likely to influence policy and that "sustained dialogue between researchers and the users of research increases the use of research-based evidence in policy" (465). Moreover, research is often "shaped by the personal and professional values of the interpreter and by the social contexts within which research findings are to be applied" (467). The key phrases for Elliott and Popay are *extended process of communication* and *sustained dialogue*: two features that research has shown can impact policy decisions and two features that NCTE was unable to leverage in its dialogue with the authors of the ELA standards.

Additionally, there is a bit of unpredictability when different groups work together. In the case of NCTE and the Common Core authors, NCTE was almost entirely ignored. Black concludes that, in the formation of public policy, it is *usually* the case that researchers are ignored:

> researchers have to accept that their work may be ignored because policymakers have to take the full complexity of any situation into account. They need to consider that the other legitimate influences on policy (social, electoral, ethical, cultural, and economic) must be accommodated and that research is most likely to influence policymakers through an extended process of communication. (277)

Black's suggestion speaks to the kairotic ways that NCTE can influence establishment groups beyond invoking its own peer-reviewed publications. For example, a key component of collaboration is what Black calls an "extended process of communication," which allows for research and expertise to be wielded in a way that can make meaningful inroads in policy discussions.

While public policy research is a good place to find arguments about the function of research in policy decisions, rhetoricians have also made similar claims. In 1989, for example, Carolyn Miller critiqued the limits of "decision science," popular at the time in business, management, and economic journals. Decision science, she writes, is an instrumental approach to reason that "presupposes a dichotomy between fact and value, between procedure (which alone can be rational) and substance (which is always arbitrary), and prefers, in each case, the former" (*Rhetoric of Decision Science* 44). Miller argues that decision science "provides no room for audience and treats rationality as wholly procedural" (45); the rhetorical tradition formulates a better alternative. The rhetorical turn "challenges the assumption that intellectual and social progress demand the certainty sought by the instrumental reason of scientism" (46). In other words, the role of research in public policy has always been a rhetorical problem of forming relationships rather than *scientistic* statements of fact. Put another way, writing researchers do not have to stray too far away from their field to find scholarship on the function of evidence in policy debates.

Conclusion

It is clear from NCTE's critique of the July Draft and the final draft of the ELA standards that NCTE's appeals to the value of disciplinary knowledge had little impact on the formation of the ELA standards. It is also clear that the authors of the Common Core approached NCTE in bad faith, having already "backmapped" the standards for K–12 and even begun to pitch the standards to states for formal adoption (Hesse). In the exchange between NCTE and the Common Core, NCTE's appeals to the value of disciplinary knowledge represented the policy paradigm of an old regime based squarely on equity, a regime in which stakeholders relied on the disciplinary knowledge of experts to decide how and when to spend federal dollars to improve equity in education. But an accountability regime, while still claiming to value *evidence*, *equity*, *collaboration*, and *student success*, prioritizes evidence that serves the ideological function of supporting competition in a global marketplace. This contrasts with what NCTE espoused in its critique: the idiosyncrasies of local classroom-based assessments and institution-wide commitments to protecting at-risk students and communities.

Writing assessment scholarship generally expresses lingering unease with Common Core policies, which are designed mostly for large-scale assessment (Broad; Huot). This disciplinary unease with mass assessment places NCTE at a distinct disadvantage in its efforts to have its research taken seriously in policy formation and suggests an ethical dilemma as to whether it should have a role in this formation at all. However, the last chapter showed that working within prevailing policy paradigms can result in success, however fleeting. Recall how NCTE's Washington Task Force circulated relevant writing research to policymakers as a way to persuade them to support writing-based initiatives. This past effort of NCTE at effecting education policy reveals that developing sustained relationships with stakeholders is one way to ensure that values can align for a time.

In one regard, the ELA standards may have an upside for writing studies. As Kelly-Riley asserts, the ELA standards *do* give writing a higher priority in K–12 learning; the emphasis on writing in the ELA standards puts writing researchers and writing program administrators "in excellent positions to meaningfully contribute to the ongoing discussions and decisions related to the costs and benefits associated with standardization and assessment of writing" (194). By asking students to analyze not just literary texts but also "informational and nonfiction" texts, the ELA standards situate writing as a "skill worthy of overt instruction and evaluation whereas previous standards-based curricula emphasized reading and/or knowledge of grammar" (198). In other words, there might still be opportunities to participate in discussions about the Common Core ELA standards in ways that prioritize what we *want* writing policy to look like, discussions where NCTE and the CCSS can find common ground without our having to set aside disciplinary values. As Linda Adler-Kassner has shown, if institutions like NCTE want to participate in these discussions, it might help to "come up with what we *want* in response to these questions, not what we *don't want*" (135).

It is important to note that the role of evidence in policy debates still matters. In the interaction between the Common Core authors and NCTE, we see that each group made appeals to evidence in its attempt to craft policy. The accountability regime paradigm *does value* evidence, no doubt, but only insofar as that evidence aligns with its value system. Accountability regimes draw on a policy paradigm that values economic efficiency and high-stakes testing, and since most academic knowledge about writing and literacy does not logically lead to policy arrangements like school choice, efficiency, scale, speed, and workplace readiness, NCTE's critiques were unpersuasive for the Common Core authors. Without sustained collaboration and long-term relationships with these policy stakeholders, NCTE will be unable secure the ethos required for its own evidence to be taken seriously.

For this to happen in the future, institutions like NCTE need to consider a critical institutional rhetoric aimed at creating more kairotic political engagement strategies that actively put stress on prevailing policy paradigms. In other words, kairotic political engagement strategies, in which institutions seek out opportune moments to forge relationships with powerful policy stakeholders, do not just see policy engagement as "filling in the gaps" with *better* research but also take into consideration how policy is dynamically created through a range of rhetorical strategies beyond marshaling evidence. As policy regime theorists have shown, policy regimes can and do change, particularly when various *stressors* undermine the components that make a regime durable. For example, policy regimes weaken when policy paradigms lose credibility (Wilson 262–63) or when the public loses confidence in the ideologies justifying certain policies (264) or when new power arrangements emerge, either through political elections or through changing policy implementation procedures (264). Thinking of institutional political engagement as kairotic can help our professional organizations consider whether, when, and how to effect education policy. Our organizations might work to form sustained relationships with powerful policy stakeholders to gain the credibility needed to challenge prevailing policy paradigms in public debates about education, or they might choose to effect policy change through a range of more overt political actions in an attempt to change the power structures through which policy is enacted.

The Washington Task Force engaged in overt political action, consistent with the prevailing policy paradigm of equity, to win federal dollars for the support of English teachers. And the Task Force did succeed at it for a while. However, a new policy paradigm emerged that justified education policies in terms of their economic efficiency and their ability to be scaled up through high-stakes testing. By the time the authors of the Common Core solicited the advice of NCTE on the ELA standards, the notion that the authors might revamp the standards based on a thorough academic critique was a pipe dream. Scholars in public policy and public health have argued that, when deliberating about public policy, "the nature of evidence is ambivalent" and the way one employs evidence is largely contingent on the values of the audience in the rhetorical situation (Wood et al. 1737). From the research of writing studies, scholars Linda Adler-Kassner, Bob Broad, and Brian Huot suggest that, in order to make inroads with writing studies research in policy discussions in the accountability regime, we need to create new arguments for validity that would share in the values of the establishment groups behind the Common Core and would aid in the creation of a mutual discourse—that is, a more meaningful orientation from which action or change can emerge.

While establishing relationships with powerful groups is difficult and potentially ethically fraught, there are examples in our field of how such sustained relationships can play out. In another publication of mine, I interviewed several writing program administrators across the country about their involvement with establishment groups in other policy issues. They all told me that while the work was precarious, they valued the prospect of leading the charge in policies that were sure to impact them in the future. "Why not us rather than someone else?" one administrator told me (Branson 176). We should not "bury our heads in the sand," said another. We should not "discount something because it feels uncomfortable, political, or something about business and not about education" (181). In other words, a kairotic institutional rhetoric in which relationship building and value sharing are methods of political engagement might be a way to gain a seat at the table or to cultivate the ethos necessary to authorize our expertise on writing in policy-making discussions.

There is, however, no single *best* method of institutional action to effect policy change. Thinking kairotically calls for institutions to imagine diverse areas where they can put stress on accountability policy regimes. In the aftermath of the Common Core feedback interaction, for example, NCTE worked in conjunction with the Council of Writing Program Administrators and the National Writing Project to create the *Framework for Success in Postsecondary Writing*, a document that has applications for K–12 and college writing programs across the country (Behm et al.). This shows that even though writing studies research was ignored in the Common Core feedback interaction, professional organizations can still work to put stress on policy regimes in other ways, such as this instance when scholars in our field invented an alternative policy paradigm and worked to convince constituents to implement it in lieu of accountability policies.

Institutionalized kairotic policy engagement is different from the refrain of many scholars when it comes to effecting education policy. In Hesse's reflection on his involvement with the Common Core, one of the lessons he gleaned from it is that writing studies practitioners need to start communicating "with publics external to the field" in ways that are less "reactive" and more responsive to audiences beyond other experts (13).[14] Hesse's suggestion is apt, I think, but if we conceptualize engagement as publishing academic research for wider audiences, we would fail to take into consideration the kairotic possibilities for political engagement. I align more with Webber, who describes *going public* as a pragmatic function of "re-linking professional and public goods amid the neoliberal energy of reform" (5). The failed interaction between NCTE and the authors of the Common Core shows us that public engagement is just as much about cultivating sustained relationships in which values can be communicated as it is about the act of communicating those values. Working harder to become public intellectuals has the potential to devalue the work of individual teachers who work locally and micro-politically in their classrooms to bridge, partner, resist, or implement education policies and who might not have the time or rhetorical training to engage with broader publics. In the next chapter, I consider the policy arrangements that have brought programs of dual enrollment to many states in the country, and my case study concerns the dual enrollment program that operates today in Ohio.

CHAPTER 3

An Analysis of Dual Enrollment Policy from a Regime Perspective

Introduction

As mentioned at the outset of this book, in order to better understand the impact of education policy on writing and writing instruction, we need to consider not just education policies themselves but also the broader policy regimes that encompass all of the "ideas, interests, and institutions" associated with those policies, which often involves analysis over an extended period of time (McGuinn 19). The previous two chapters looked at an *institution* of writing studies from a regime perspective and considered how an institutional rhetoric centered on the concept of kairos might help the field find diverse ways of effecting education policies that impact the teaching of writing. This chapter, however, considers particular policy arrangements now impacting college writing: dual enrollment.

Dual enrollment is when secondary students take college-level courses for college credit. Dual enrollment epitomizes the accountability policy regime that prioritizes economic efficiency. Dual enrollment is varied, too, in having both federal and state components. Each state is now required to report to the federal government its efforts at establishing dual enrollment partnerships, yet each state also has its own funding structures, legislative aid packages, and transfer articulation guides dictating how dual enrollment operates. This variety makes any analysis of dual enrollment complicated. Therefore, in this chapter I analyze dual enrollment from a policy regime perspective to get a bird's-eye view of how a more recent accountability-based education policy impacts the teaching of college composition. A regime analysis encompasses dual enrollment's political arrangements as well as the ideological and structural features that provide dual enrollment with legitimacy and durability over time.

Because statewide dual enrollment policies are highly variable, most of the state-level examples in this analysis come from just one state, Ohio. To show how dual enrollment policies work as an extension of the accountability policy regime, the case study of this chapter is Ohio's dual enrollment legislation, College Credit Plus (CCP). Ohio is leading the way in legislative mandates, and accountability policy regimes are profoundly cemented in CCP, enacted in 2014. Policies like CCP are surprisingly common across the country, having been in place in Ohio and other states in one form or another since the 1970s, due in part to a paradigm touting such policies as cost-saving and workplace-readiness measures. Dual enrollment policies are strengthened thanks to the legislators and other local and state-level stakeholders who fiercely defend them.

It is important to note that while there are many accountability-style education policies that impact writing teachers, dual enrollment deserves a policy analysis for two reasons. First, dual enrollment is a formidable concern for writing studies practitioners of all stripes in many different institutional and regional contexts. Considering dual enrollment's rapid rise at the state and now federal levels over the past several decades, our field has not published enough studies on the impact of dual enrollment on freshman composition. Scholars Christine Denecker, Casie Moreland, Kristine Hansen, and Christine Farris, to name a few, are leading the way, but for a set of policies that are affecting millions of students across the country, we do not yet have as many perspectives as needed to understand dual enrollment's full impact on college composition.

Second, dual enrollment impacts students and teachers at the high school *and* college levels. At a time when accountability regime logics are prompting special-interest groups to cash in on the standards and assessment movement in K–16 (Addison), and when scholars in our field are responding by calling for increased collaboration across grade levels (Callahan et al.), dual enrollment is where all these interests converge. Whereas No Child Left Behind and the Common Core were policies designed primarily for K–12 contexts, dual enrollment brings institutions of higher learning under a K–16 umbrella of accountability. That is not to say that No Child Left Behind and the Common Core did not have an impact on college-level instruction and on writing studies in particular. Scholars in our field have shown that they did (McCarthey; Nichols and Berliner; Pence and Platt; Clark-Oates et al.). However, dual enrollment is the most recent manifestation of a singular K–16 accountability policy.

Therefore, in analyzing the governing arrangements of dual enrollment, I refer to three key aspects of dual enrollment policy. First, there are the power arrangements of the various stakeholders in dual enrollment policy, from national interest groups that represent dual enrollment programs, to deep-pocketed think tanks and philanthropic organizations that promote dual enrollment partnerships, and even individual teachers and administrators who broker these partnerships. Second, I consider the broader policy paradigm that governs dual enrollment partnerships: the narratives that circulate about dual enrollment that structure policy approaches to such partnerships. These narratives structure dual enrollment as a *reasonable* way for college students and their parents to save money, to *get through* entry-level college composition courses, and to *enter the workforce* more quickly, which will, proponents suggest, spur growth in the economy. And, third, I map out the policy arrangements of dual enrollment, that is, the legislative policies themselves: for example, there is federal legislation that defines the nature and scope of dual enrollment, Every Student Succeeds Act, but there is also legislation at the state level, such as the law that created the CCP program in Ohio.

I begin by situating dual enrollment as a policy problem. I discuss key pieces of legislation, national enrollment statistics, and the research literature on dual enrollment nationally, paying close attention to data that pertain to the teaching of college composition and untangling the power arrangements and policy paradigms that govern how dual enrollment is seen as a solution to perceived problems in education. Next, I analyze the State of Ohio's landmark dual enrollment legislation, CCP, which emerged out of these national conversations. By analyzing CCP's unique dual enrollment mandates, funding structure, participation rates, and policy history, I argue that Ohio represents a microcosm of how policy regimes of accountability can impact the teaching of college writing. Ohio's dual enrollment policies differ from those of other states, so I am not suggesting that we can generalize about policy solutions or effective policy interventions from a regime analysis of Ohio's policies. However, understanding the particulars of one state's manifestation of accountability regime logics—and the way a policy regime of accountability has worked in concert with powerful institutions, ideological paradigms of choice and efficiency, and bureaucratic mechanisms through which policy becomes entrenched in the day-to-day operations of schools—can be a fruitful way of understanding how policy regimes impact the durability and legitimacy of policies. In other words, dual enrollment is an extension of policy regimes of accountability and is part of a collection of ideas and arrangements within a particular policy regime that sees education as an economic good instead of a public good.

For readers not familiar with Ohio, my hope is that by delving into one state's education policies, I can highlight similarities in how policy regimes impact the experiences of teachers even when governing arrangements may vary from state to state. In this way, writing studies scholars and writing teachers can envision more variable, kairotic engagement strategies for putting stress on accountability regimes, whether by creating new power arrangements, conceiving of alternative policy paradigms, or even forging new policy approaches. As I argue at the end of the chapter, this work will involve teachers just as much as institutions.

Power Arrangements and Policy Paradigms of Dual Enrollment

Dual enrollment is an extension of accountability-based education reform initiatives that prioritize *student choice*, *time-to-degree*, and models of education seen to be *efficient* and *cost-effective*. Similar to the emergence of the Common Core, these terms and phrases correspond with a paradigm that logically connects education to economic efficiency. As I mentioned in previous chapters, the national conversation about the condition of public education shifted toward policy regimes of accountability in the 1970s and '80s through narratives that characterized the nation's schools as failing and that suggested policy solutions for "fixing" schools that would hold them *accountable* for failure. This policy paradigm also sees colleges and universities as broken institutions, with rising tuition costs and slashed budgets. A significant number of Americans—including 58 percent of Republicans—now view colleges and universities as having a negative impact on the country. One way that policymakers have sought to remedy this is by increasing efficiency in students' time-to-degree (Pew Research Center 17). Dual enrollment policies epitomize accountability logics because their proponents argue that they reduce cost for students and families, decrease time toward graduation, and offer a version of education that sees students as consumers and higher education as a commodity. At the same time, accountability regime paradigms are not explicitly *against* the values of equity and access. In fact, the main ideological work of the accountability regime is to define equity, access, and student success narrowly in economic terms so that the programs and initiatives that emerge from those paradigms *seem* to work.

When people talk about dual enrollment, they are usually referring to programs that allow high school students to earn college credit while still in high school. Other terms refer to similar arrangements: *concurrent enrollment*, *dual credit*, or *co-enrollment*. These different terms are sometimes used to refer to the same thing (Robertson et al.), which means that defining terminology is necessary. According to Tobolowsky and Allen, in a report for the Association for the Study of Higher Education, *dual credit* is an umbrella term for any "courses high school students take where they earn both high school and college credit simultaneously without having to take a standardized test to gain the credit" (19). The National Alliance of Concurrent Enrollment Partnerships (NACEP) maintains that *dual enrollment* is the broader term encompassing "partnerships [that] provide high school students the opportunity to take college credit–bearing courses" and that *concurrent enrollment* refers to a "subset of dual enrollment courses taught by college-approved high school teachers" ("What Is Concurrent Enrollment?"). While the terminology varies in educational scholarship, I adhere to NACEP's definitions. I use *dual enrollment* as the umbrella term for postsecondary enrollment partnerships, and I use *concurrent enrollment* to refer to college-level courses taught in high schools by so-called college-approved teachers in secondary education.

The accountability regime policies that support dual enrollment have persisted through the education agendas of six presidential administrations, both Republican and Democrat, beginning with Reagan and extending into the Trump administration with the appointment of Betsy DeVos as secretary of education. For the last forty years, dual enrollment partnerships have been defended as needed programs that serve students and families. Only within the last twenty years or so, though, have dual enrollment partnerships really taken off. In the 2010–2011 academic year, the National Center for Education Statistics reported that 82 percent of all high schools in the country had some kind of dual enrollment partnership with two- or four-year colleges, amounting to about two million enrollments (Thomas et al. 3). Moreover, dual enrollment partnerships saw an annual growth rate of 7 percent since the 2002–2003 academic year (NACEP). On the side of higher education, 46 percent of all institutions reported in the 2010–2011 academic year that high school students took a college course in a dual enrollment partnership, amounting to about 1.2 million high school students (Marken et al. 3). Of institutions that had dual enrollment partnerships with local high schools, 64 percent reported offering courses taught at the high schools (3). Alec Thomson writes in a post for the National Education Association's website that these numbers represent "a fundamental shift in the goals of dual enrollment and a realignment of the relationship between colleges and high schools."

Recognizing the growth of dual enrollment partnerships nationally, higher education researchers and practitioners have sought to influence how these partnerships are formed, assessed, and accredited so as to monitor and moderate the scaling up that occurs with accountability regime programs. Accrediting bodies demand *actual* accountability from partnering members. For example, NACEP formed in 1999 to offer consistency and curricular guidance to institutions of higher learning interested in either forging new dual enrollment partnerships or assessing existing ones. Today, NACEP boasts member institutions in forty-eight states with national standards, assessment criteria, and peer-reviewed accreditation ("NACEP History"). According to Hansen, NACEP has high accreditation standards. NACEP requires that courses of concurrent or dual enrollment be taught and assessed in the same way as traditional college courses. The standards "are so rigorous [that] they cannot be met quickly, writes Hansen; "a concurrent enrollment program must be in place for five years to gather assessment data before it even seeks accreditation" ("Composition Marketplace" 28). According to NACEP's website, for the 2017–2018 academic year, only 105 concurrent enrollment programs held NACEP accreditation. As the statistics I cited above show, NACEP-accredited programs represent only a *tiny fraction* of all concurrent enrollment partnerships, and we can expect spotty accreditation to increase as more states decide to pursue dual enrollment and scale the program up (28).

As I argued with the emergence of the Common Core English language arts standards, the governing arrangements in today's advanced accountability regime have granted power and political influence to interest groups and businesses as opposed to educators and researchers with content expertise. As Post et al. explain, education reform interest groups like the National Governors Association, the Bill and Melinda Gates Foundation, the Partnership for 21st Century Skills, Achieve Inc., and others have convinced powerful stakeholders that "a successful overhaul of secondary education includes establishing dual-enrollment programs between high schools and colleges . . . so that students can earn college credits in core subjects such as writing, science, and mathematics while still in high school" (167). These establishment groups have exerted significant influence on dual enrollment policy in recent decades.

As regime theorists have shown, the work of establishment groups serves not only to concretize power and make policies favor their interests, but they also serve to influence public opinion about policy by invoking ideologies of accountability. In the case of dual and concurrent enrollment partnerships, accountability policy regimes produce narratives that frame such partnerships as good, equitable, and commonsense ways for students to *get ahead*. These rationales have remained durable since at least the 1970s, although scholars are extending dual enrollment policies back even further. Casie Moreland, for example, traced some of the earliest dual enrollment partnerships back to at least the 1950s in her recent doctoral dissertation (*White Resistance*).

Proponents of dual enrollment generally cite research that focuses on dual enrollment's relationship to degree attainment and time-to-degree. From the logic of accountability, answering this kind of research question—does dual enrollment help students finish college faster?—seems like a reasonable way to measure success. And there certainly are studies that support that ideological perspective. For example, the Department of Education's What Works Clearinghouse conducted an extensive review of studies that included over 77,000 students across the country and found that dual enrollment programs "have positive effects on students' degree attainment (college), college access and enrollment, credit accumulation, completing high school, and general academic achievement (high school), with a medium to large extent of evidence" (*WWC Intervention*

Report 1). In 2013 Brian P. An's study in *Educational Evaluation and Policy Analysis* found that "dual enrollment participation increases the probability of attaining any postsecondary degree and a bachelor's degree by 8 percentage points and 7 percentage points, respectively" (62). The percentage is even greater for students whose parents never attended college (67). Joni Lynne Swanson, in her 2008 dissertation, found that dual enrollment students with twenty or more credit hours by their first year of college were "more likely to persist through the second year in college than were students who did not complete dual enrollment courses" (3). Other statewide studies, from Illinois (Blankenberger et al.) and Texas (Radunzel et al.), are similarly positive, showing that dual enrollment policies in their states increased the likelihood that students would earn a bachelor's degree. Moreover, as Allen found in his literature review, many studies, both qualitative and quantitative, appear to show the benefits of dual enrollment when benefits are understood in terms of accountability-based outcomes like degree attainment and cost reduction. According to Allen, some of the benefits of dual enrollment are "allowing students to complete a degree faster," "reducing costs for a college education," and even "freeing space on college campuses" (10).

However, if we view accountability policies through ideological lenses that do not prioritize market-based logics, then dual enrollment policies raise red flags. For example, according to Museus et al., white and affluent students are more likely to enroll in dual enrollment programs, which has "the potential to exacerbate persisting inequities in college access" (6). Another study analyzing community college dual enrollment programs in Oregon found that white, female, high-achieving students were overrepresented in the population of dual-credit students compared with their representation in the overall population of Oregon high schools (Pierson et al. 12). According to other data from the state of Texas, in 2018, the dual enrollment participation rate among Black students was a little over 10 percent while the white student participation rate was about 24.7 percent. Moreover, in Texas, researchers found that student outcomes were more positive for white, higher-income students than for underrepresented minorities (T. Miller et al. 3). With these alarming statistics in mind, Erik Gilbert, writing for the *Chronicle of Higher Education*, says that "for middle-class suburbanites, college is potentially one year shorter and thousands of dollars cheaper than it is for students of lesser means, who must spend more time in college and take on more debt to earn the same degree." Additionally, McClure et al. write that dual enrollment programs put a strain on resources, particularly in rural schools: "high school administrators who steward [dual enrollment] programs face magnified issues of school and curricular integrity, student safety, and transportation costs . . . which drain state funds away from high schools" (194).

McClure et al. argue that concurrent enrollment courses, in which high school students take college courses at their high school, are more equitable for rural schools, yet the data to support this claim are not certain. As high schools are mandated to move toward concurrent enrollment, these mandates present new challenges. "An English teacher teaching a junior-level AP [Advanced Placement] course in Arkansas," write Post et al.,

> has to prepare students for the AP exam, and that requires very specific to-the-test instruction. But that teacher also has to prepare students for the state's eleventh-grade literacy test, another exam with very different requirements. Now add to that load University of Central Arkansas's first-semester composition course, which stresses rhetorical flexibility rather than a specific writing style for test taking. . . . High school teachers have always had to listen to principals, school board members, and parents; now they have to deal with us [college faculty]! (181)

Thus, despite all the research touting the *success* of dual enrollment partnerships, when success is defined from an alternative policy paradigm that does not prioritize the values of accountability-based reform, dual enrollment fails on several fronts.

Moreover, as Speroni contends, despite the precipitous rise of research on dual enrollment partnerships, there are still few rigorous national statistics on their growth, nor are there many quantitative studies showing convincingly that dual enrollment is an effective policy even according to the accountability-based assumptions its proponents have. In other words, even taken *on its own terms,* dual enrollment still seems to fall short. Speroni argues that extensive literature reviews from Bailey and Karp (2003) and Lerner and Brand (2006) show that there is scant evidence of dual enrollment programs having a net positive impact on college success or increased college access, despite a vast amount of literature on the subject. The reason, Speroni says, is selection bias:

> Assessing the impact of dual enrollment is difficult because of the well-known problem of selection bias. The selection problem is twofold: high school students choose to take college courses based on their academic ability, motivation, and expected gains from participation; colleges are also allowed to set their own admission requirements to ensure the integrity of their academic programs. In addition, students who have already decided to go to college would likely consider dual enrollment an attractive way to obtain a head start on accumulating credits, causing a spurious correlation between participation and outcomes. (1–2)

Thus, attributing student success and college access to dual enrollment experiences is hard to do with certainty.

Research specifically on concurrent enrollment (dual enrollment courses taught in high schools by approved high school teachers) is less abundant. We do know that, according to the National Center for Education Statistics, of the surveyed institutions of higher learning that reported high school students taking their courses in dual enrollment programs in the 2010–2011 academic year, 64 percent of them offered concurrent enrollment courses (Marken et al. 7). As Hansen notes, while there are no definitive data for concurrent enrollment specific to college composition, it is generally understood that college-level writing is "one of the most frequently offered" dual enrollment courses, and "the most common model is . . . to train high school teachers to deliver the college course at the high school, with the colleges offering liaisons who make site visits to consult with teachers and supervise delivery of instruction" ("Composition Marketplace" 25). Indeed, my case study in the next chapter concerns a high school teacher and her concurrent enrollment class.

From the limited research available on concurrent enrollment partnerships, we know that, according to Edwards et al., they *might* make college courses less intimidating because the high school environment gives students a sense of "comfort and familiarity" (20). Bailey and Karp argue, however, that concurrent enrollment programs do not "recreate the college experience" or help students grow accustomed to the "expectations of postsecondary education" (8). Unlike dual enrollment programs in which students spend time on a college campus, concurrent enrollment programs may not give students a "realistic expectation of what college is like," so students may not "adjust more easily to college life upon high school graduation" (3). Tobolowsky and Allen cite one study from Florida (by Speroni, cited above) that showed concurrent enrollment students had a lower likelihood of enrolling in a college or university than did those who took dual enrollment courses on campus. Nevertheless, they write, "with so many variables at play (such as course content, instructor quality, and others) . . . it is hard to know how the location contributed (or did not contribute) to these students' success" (46–47). Future research on concurrent enrollment partnerships, they recommend, should explore ways that "instructor's training, the course subject, and other variables" impact student success (47).

Regardless of these uncertainties, from an accountability perspective, teaching first-year composition through concurrent enrollment is a viable method of dual enrollment instruction. For one, it is cheaper for institutions of higher education to outsource the teaching of composition to high school instructors because, in many cases, the institutions themselves do not compensate the high school teachers. The courses are instead paid for by the public school districts. For another, enrollment at the participating institutions of higher education is boosted by students who are actually taking courses off campus taught by their high school English teacher.

Dual Enrollment and College Composition

The first-year writing course is where the national conversation about dual enrollment—often invoking notions of cost-effectiveness and of "getting ahead"—fits into the discipline of writing studies. The first-year writing course is a general education course required of all incoming students. We know that composition is the most popular dual and concurrent enrollment course for high school students (Hansen, "Composition Marketplace" 25). The scholarship on dual enrollment's impact on college composition is growing, and it generally focuses on academic standards, cognitive demands, and writing abilities.

For instance, in her study "Transitioning Writers across the Composition Threshold," Christine Denecker argues that dual and concurrent enrollment students struggle to cross the threshold between high school and college writing because of significant differences in K–12 and postsecondary writing pedagogy. Kara Taczak and William H. Thelin's 2009 essay, "(Re)Envisioning the Divide: The Impact of College Courses on High School Students," builds on Denecker's essay by using a participant observation methodology to investigate the effects of a dual enrollment section of composition taught on a college campus to students in middle school and high school. The students had the opportunity to gain more knowledge than traditional high school students, and even described their positive experiences in the course to the researchers in interviews, yet the students in the course nevertheless struggled. They "appeared to have overlooked the larger mission of the writing course; they misunderstood the goal of the class, so the application to later courses, civic participation, and employment opportunities might be limited" (20). Taczak and Thelin attribute this lack of understanding to the students being unready for the cognitive demands of a college composition course: due to their young age, "we cannot reasonably expect the vast majority of them to respond to the challenges found in a progressive composition classroom" (20). Barbara Schneider, in the edited collection *College Credit for Writing in High School: The "Taking Care of" Business*, echoes this view:

> young students generally do not have the miles on their tires to have accumulated much experience on which to reflect. But even when young students have a rich background on which to draw, critically examining the values, opinions, and beliefs with which they have been raised while they are still in the home and in the process of being raised is enormously difficult. (157)

In addition to studies of the cognitive demands of first-year composition for dual and concurrent enrollment students, other studies have looked empirically at student success. For example, Kristine Hansen et al. gathered empirical data from a writing-intensive course at Brigham Young University; they compared the essay grades of students who had completed first-year composition in dual enrollment or concurrent enrollment classrooms with the grades of students who had either taken the institution's regular first-year composition course or had placed out the requirement owing to Advanced Placement credit. Whereas Taczak and Thelin cautioned that the cognitive demands of first-year composition may be too intense for younger students, Hansen et al. found "no significant differences between the scores of DC [dual credit]/concurrent enrollment students and those of other groups"; moreover, "it seems clear that, for the students whose writing we analyzed, taking a DC/concurrent enrollment course in high school prepared them as well for [their] writing assignments as other pre-college or college versions of FYW [first-year writing] did" (73). Proponents of dual enrollment policies might find these results promising, but Hansen et al. caution that the logic underpinning race-to-credit policies is still "economiz[ing] on the wrong things" and does not let students and parents see writing "as an iterative, open, and perpetually improving activity." All students, whether they received dual enrollment credit or not, "need to have opportunities to revisit and reapply their learning—whether in a sophomore course, linked courses, a WAC [writing across the curriculum] program, or all of these" (77).

From a policy perspective, the least persuasive critiques of dual enrollment in the literature are the ones that question the maturity level of high school students, doubt their cognitive capacity to grapple with college-level material, or compare the grades they make in dual enrollment courses with those of traditionally enrolled students. Student performance assessed by grades is not the *only* way of measuring the success of dual enrollment writing courses. Measuring student success in this way is how a policy paradigm of accountability tries to claim the success of dual enrollment policies. It creates a framework in which dual enrollment is a logical and natural way for parents and the state to save money, which, the theory goes, creates a more equitable (that is, more *competitive*) society. In other words, dual enrollment policies are "successful" if they are defined narrowly in terms of accountability-based policy paradigms. If we consider dual enrollment instead in terms of fairness or equity, for example, then rationales that define these policies as "effective" and "logical" may not hold up. In other words, when we analyze policies like dual enrollment from a regime perspective, we can see how policies function through ideological paradigms, and scholars and teachers of writing can thus imagine other approaches that do not pit K–12 and college-level instructors against one another, or worse, put writing scholars in the position of evaluating who is and who is not mentally prepared to handle college-level material. Hansen et al. are right to suggest that their findings do not rationalize the economic logics that favor getting college writing "out of the way" early. On the contrary, though, analyzing dual enrollment writing courses through a paradigm of accountability will only strengthen the regime by giving its policies more legitimacy among proponents.

Policy regime analyses might better respond to dual enrollment by viewing it as a policy problem. In a 2009 *CCC* Special Symposium on Exploring the Continuum between High School and College Writing, scholars began to consider a dynamic range of responses to dual enrollment, though not from a specific policy perspective. For example, Christine Farris argued that we need to create more bridges between high school and college writing policies (440); Gerald Graff and Cathy Birkenstein-Graff claimed that we need more shared principles of literacy instruction between high school and college writing (410). And in her piece, Denecker (cited above) writes that "the most powerful element for moving students from Point A to Point B as writers may lie not with the students themselves but with those who plan, oversee, and carry out dual enrollment composition instruction" (31). In other words, there are multiple ways we can respond to policy problems in writing studies. A policy regime framework, however, which May and Jochim argue includes analyses of the "institutional arrangements, interest alignments, and shared ideas" attached to a policy problem (428), reveals that policy problems in writing studies need kairotic responses: whether through building better relationships across K–16, engaging in dialogue with establishment groups through our institutions, or working in various ways to put stress on literacy policies that do not reflect an accurate version of what we know about literacy. In the words of Dennis Baron, "literacy is more than a skill that can be deployed in any circumstance and measured at will" (433).

Dual Enrollment and Its Policy Arrangements

If we want to see how dual enrollment functions as an extension of accountability-based policy regimes of education reform, we need to zoom out from writing studies and look at how dual enrollment policies work at the federal and state levels. Generally speaking, postsecondary enrollment partnerships were largely left to states to legislate until President Obama signed the Every Student Succeeds Act (ESSA) in 2015. In this act, we see for the first time a federal statute that defines dual enrollment. According to the legislation, dual enrollment requires a

> partnership between at least one institution of higher education and at least one local educational agency through which a secondary school student who has not graduated from high school with a regular high school diploma is able to enroll in one or more postsecondary courses and earn postsecondary credit that (a) is transferrable to the institutions of higher education in the partnership and (b) applies toward completion of a degree or recognized educational credential. (United States Code)

Absent from ESSA's definition is an arrangement where high school students take college-level coursework in their high schools taught by a "college-approved" high school teacher. Nevertheless, ESSA does guide administrators through the process of reporting. ESSA stipulates that schools need to detail their efforts to establish and assess dual enrollment partnerships as part of new mandatory reporting requirements for any schools seeking Title 1 funding—an apparent effort to incentivize schools to implement dual enrollment partnerships and to include them in their reporting. As Zachary Malter notes in a blog post for the American Youth Policy Forum, ESSA created new funding opportunities for dual enrollment:

> For the first time, dual enrollment can be covered by Title I grants for schools serving low-income students, Title II professional development grants, Title III grants for ELL [English language learners] and immigrant students, and Title IV grants for student support and academic enrichment.

ESSA was a game-changer for institutions that participate in dual enrollment partnerships because it created de facto dual enrollment mandates in the states, which will surely increase the number of partnerships throughout the country in the years to come.

As the number of dual and concurrent enrollment partnerships grows, the landscape of such partnerships on the state level remains highly variable. As Hansen has written about concurrent enrollment courses in particular, "it is difficult to generalize about concurrent enrollment because there isn't one national brand, just a lot of local and regional brands" ("Composition Marketplace" 26). As mentioned above, the National Center for Education Statistics reported that concurrent enrollment courses were offered in 64 percent of all dual enrollment partnerships in the 2010–2011 academic year (Marken et al). But a 2005 study by Karp et al. found that eighteen states had "mandatory" dual enrollment policies, which means that "high schools must inform students of program opportunities and accept credit"; nine states had "voluntary" policies, which makes participation by colleges and high schools optional; two had "mixed" policies, which means that "high schools have the option of whether to offer dual enrollment, but colleges cannot refuse to participate in dual enrollment"; and twenty-one states either had no policy or an unspecified policy on dual enrollment (qtd. in Hansen, "Composition Marketplace" 26). This mixed matrix of policy arrangements means that, across the fifty states, the governing arrangements that fund, admit, and broker partnerships between high schools and colleges are highly variable and subject to the policy preferences of state and local governments. This loose organization creates what Hansen describes as an "unregulated" marketplace for dual enrollment partnerships. According to Hansen, the idiosyncratic nature of concurrent enrollment courses across the country creates possibilities for a range of scenarios:

> In the worst-case scenario, some postsecondary institutions may be too loosely franchising their name to high school courses to increase tuition dollars, and such courses may be drawing high numbers of students looking for the easiest way to complete the required FYC [first-year composition] course before they arrive on a college campus. In this scenario, the common currency of the market, the credit hour, is seriously devalued as such institutions grant credit to students for courses that do not meet rigorous standards. In the best-case scenario, however, the relationship between the postsecondary and secondary institutions is less that of a loosely operated franchise and more like a cooperative, in which both partners view courses as jointly owned, and both have a stake in the turning out of students who write well. (30)

Given the mixed matrix of policy arrangements for dual and concurrent enrollment partnerships, and the potential for worse-case partnerships, there are two takeaways. First, there is a glaring need for an updated analysis of the current state of dual enrollment, including state-by-state comparisons of concurrent enrollment policies. The last comprehensive national portrait of dual enrollment came from the National Center for Education Statistics, based on data from 2010. The last state-by-state comparison was completed by Karp et al. in 2005. Writing program administrators and writing researchers might be able to collect more recent data about participation rates, longitudinal student success, and financial issues tied to dual enrollment, such as its relationship to revenue, retention, and persistence. The second key takeaway is that federal efforts to incentivize dual enrollment partnerships in the states will open the dual enrollment doors to millions of students over the next decade, and as writing researchers, program administrators, and instructors, we will be tasked with figuring out how best to serve these students in our classrooms and how best to make sense of what to do with these partnerships moving forward.

By framing dual enrollment as a policy problem and not a *student* problem or a *high school* problem, we can consider high school teachers, public school counselors, college and university administrators, writing program administrators, and writing instructors of all stripes and all credentials to be partners in dual enrollment policies. As I showed in the last chapter, accountability-based education policies may not consult the expertise of writing instructors. Therefore, thinking broadly about our roles in dual enrollment—whether we want to be part of it or not—as a function of policy reveals other ways we can imagine ourselves within these structures. For instance, how might we find new opportunities to draw on the expertise of the field to imagine and implement alternative paradigms that put stress on prevailing ideologies of accountability? How might we collaborate across academic contexts to collect, share, and leverage data with powerful policy stakeholders to make dual enrollment policies more equitable in our own local contexts?

Dual Enrollment Policies in Ohio

At the time I write this, it is difficult to generalize about dual enrollment policies since there are so many factors that dictate how they are designed and implemented and whether they are implemented effectively. But as an extension of the governing arrangements of accountability, dual enrollment, while variable at the micro-level, pursues a goal of subjecting higher education, and college writing in particular, to market-based economics. This common objective helps us think about dual enrollment structurally and ideologically, not just in terms of particular policy implementations.

I turn to Ohio to analyze one state's landmark dual enrollment legislation as part of a policy regime of accountability. To understand how Ohio arrived at its current dual enrollment program, it is important to note that the concept of dual enrollment emerged out of a national conversation about the government's role in education, and the reason that Ohio abandoned its old policy and adopted a new one in 2014 had much to do with making its program more *competitive* with other states, which falls in line with markers of success in the economy-based logics of accountability.

One of the first pieces of dual enrollment legislation in the United States was the Postsecondary Enrollment Opportunities Act passed by the Minnesota state legislature in 1985 (Boswell). This came on the heels of *A Nation at Risk*, which, many argue, jump-started the accountability movement. Two code words in accountability regimes are *rigor* and *options*, which harken back to the "school choice" debates of the 1960s. The goal of Minnesota's law was to "promote rigorous academic pursuits and to provide a wider variety of *options* to high school pupils by encouraging and enabling secondary pupils to enroll full-time or part-time in nonsectarian courses or programs in eligible post-secondary institutions" (Minnesota Statutes 1985, section 124D.09; my italics). Minnesota's law focused primarily on high school students taking courses on postsecondary campuses, although it did authorize concurrent enrollment courses "according to an agreement between a public school board and a governing body of an eligible public postsecondary system or an eligible private postsecondary institution" (qtd. in Henderson and Hodne). According to the Minnesota Office of Higher Education, participation in the program in the 1985–1986 school year was modest, at 3,528 students. But the number of participating students grew over the next three decades such that by the 2014–2015 academic year, participating students numbered more than 37,000, with over 27,000 of them taking concurrent enrollment courses in some form ("Minnesota High School Student").

According to Smith et al., the very first dual enrollment legislation in the state of Ohio was modeled on the work being done in Minnesota. Called the Postsecondary Enrollment Opportunities (PSEO) program, which was legislated through the Education Reform Act of 1989, Ohio's policy allowed eleventh- and twelfth-graders to enroll in colleges courses for free. As Mary Jo Geise and William E. Knight report, Ohio's dual enrollment law expanded in 1997 to include freshman and sophomores and then, eventually, only included students with a grade point average of 3.0 or higher. More amendments followed in 2008, when then governor Ted Strickland unveiled the Seniors to Sophomores Initiative, which gave high school seniors the option of earning college credit for their entire last year of high school. The goal of the program, according to its handbook, was to "provide expanded opportunities for appropriately qualified high school students to experience coursework at the college or university level" (Blanco et al. 2). As in Minnesota, Ohio's early dual enrollment legislation capitalized on narratives of providing "choice" and "options" and relied on a paradigm of expediency as a response to perceived faults in public education.

Ohio's dual enrollment law, both the old one and the revamped version (which I describe in more detail below), was funded through a redirection of funds from school districts to postsecondary institutions. For example, as Blanco et al. report, in 2004–2005, Ohio redirected 17.8 million dollars from school districts to colleges and universities to pay for public high school students to take college courses in the state. This meant that "funds that would have been expended at the high school [were] now going to support dual credit"; for colleges and universities, this transfer of funds did not "replace the total revenue postsecondary institutions usually generate," which left a shortage of about 9.3 million dollars in 2004–2005 (Blanco et al. 4). This funding structure was preserved in the revamped dual enrollment legislation of 2014 and is the keystone accountability measure that makes Ohio notable in how it passes down the cost of dual enrollment to public school districts.

One of the reasons the Ohio state legislature wanted to overhaul its dual enrollment program was its perception of a stagnating participation rate. Accountability regime policy paradigms hold that education policies are successful if they can scale up, and scale up fast, especially in comparison with other states. In Ohio's first dual enrollment program, student participation was mostly stable, increasing only modestly over a decade. As Geise and Knight write, the level of student participation in Ohio's first program was steady, with "6,859 students participating in 1998 and 12,195 students participating in 2007." Between 1998 and 2004, about 55,000 students in all earned credit through the program (5).

Another reason Ohio revamped its legislation owed to incompetent record keeping by the first program. Most of the studies cited above on Ohio's early dual enrollment program begin with data from 1998, despite the fact that the program began in 1989. Statistics for the early outcomes of the legislation are incredibly hard to find. In her dissertation, Larisa Harper writes that "from the beginning of PSEO in 1989 until 1998, no data are available and no research reports can be found" (19). Harper does cite a 2007 report by Blanco et al. (which I drew from above) that presented descriptive data from 1998–2004, but "no other research or data are publicly available"; moreover, she writes, "this lack of information leads one to believe that decision makers may be making policy changes about dual enrollment without adequate evidence" (20).

Despite the dearth of older data, it is possible from what we have to get a sense of where the trends were going before Ohio revamped its program in 2014. For example, Blanco et al. reported that, by at least 1998, ten years after the PSEO program was introduced, more than 6,500 students participated annually in the program. By 2004, there were around 10,000. From 1998 to 2004, enrollment in PSEO grew only about 48 percent, and the rate of participation remained steady. Participation in Ohio lagged behind several other states with greater increases in participation for their dual enrollment programs. Also notable is that the courses Ohio students took were mostly arts and humanities courses, which made up 37 percent of all courses taken. According to the Ohio Department of Education, the most frequently taken course in 2006 was composition.[1]

Blanco et al. were critical of these early numbers. Despite a steady increase in enrollment numbers, and some hints at successes, they charged the old program with poor data-keeping. "On almost every measure reviewed," they write, "data were incomplete or were not broken down in ways that allow for a comprehensive analysis" (3). The data they did uncover, though, were not encouraging for equity. Of high school students participating in the program in 2004–2005, "nearly 9 out of 10 PSEO participants are white and two out of three are female" (4). In Harper's dissertation, she describes the main problems with PSEO as a matter of "information gaps" and "funding issues." Information on PSEO since 2006, for instance, is also tough to find: "no information has been published focusing on the success and effectiveness of PSEO since the Blanco et al. publication of data up to the academic year of

2004–2005" (20). The funding model that redirects funds is also a significant concern as it resulted in a loss of 17.8 million dollars in 2004–2005. "This loss of funding," claims Harper, "creates a financial dilemma for high schools as they struggle to balance their budgets from year to year," and the colleges and universities that receive the redirected funds fare no better, as they are "not complete reimbursements equaling exact costs of tuition, books, and fees," which puts pressure on their budgets as well (21).

Blanco et al.'s critique of Ohio's PSEO program holds that education policies impacting tens of thousands of students are unsustainable without protocols for data-keeping because there is no way to ensure that the policy interventions are doing what they were designed to do. Harper's criticism of the so-called achievement gap in dual enrollment participation is also apt, not to mention her criticism of the financial pressure put on higher education institutions and on school districts. However, the state's response to these criticisms in 2014, with the creation of the College Credit Plus program, or CCP, was not anchored in the goals of equity or transparency. Instead, Ohio leaned even harder into a policy paradigm of choice and efficiency by creating a program based on legislative mandates that flooded the system with more students and more partnerships. The aim was to scale up participation massively, while also putting in place mandates for strict accountability-based data collection. This measure was a bureaucratic technique for avoiding future criticism or legal challenges as opposed to a way of ensuring meaningful change.

Case Study: College Credit Plus in Ohio

In 2013 the 130th Ohio General Assembly passed its biennium budget, House Bill 59. In section 363.590, the bill states that the chancellor of the Ohio Board of Regents shall make official recommendations "to establish the College Credit Plus program, whereby high school students may earn credits through Ohio institutions of higher education." Chancellor John Carey stated in his recommendations that PSEO, which had been running in the state for nearly twenty-five years, was "underutilized and is administered across the state with varying degrees of efficacy and quality." The new CCP program, Carey wrote, is "a great opportunity to transform this system into a highly effective and indispensable component of the state's education infrastructure" (5). According to

Carey, CCP would raise retention, lower costs for students and parents, and contribute to "diversifying the college-going population." Clearly, Carey's recommendations are couched in notions of equity and access, but CCP nevertheless would serve economic purposes. Citing the 2010 data from the National Center for Education Statistics, Carey stated that while the national average of dual enrollment participants grew nearly 60 percent over the previous eight years, Ohio's had stayed relatively stable, which was why a change was needed. Plus, CCP would remedy other problems of PSEO: a lack of transparency in how PSEO was funded, a lack of information for students and parents to make adequate decisions, an inadequate number of qualified instructors, and a lack of "complete data." CCP would remedy these problems by consolidating rules and procedures and by establishing streamlined data collection so that Ohio could match the growth in other states with "a larger percentage of their students" participating in dual enrollment (6).

Chancellor Carey's recommendations did not respond directly to the criticisms of Harper and Blanco et al.; rather, they responded to a broader policy problem that corresponds with the logics of efficiency. To Ohio's policymakers the problem was not the funding model itself but rather a lack of *transparency* about the funding model. The problem was not the lack of educational opportunities for Black and Brown students but was instead one of scaling up the total number of students enrolled to keep pace with other states. The problem was not that data either did not exist or did not show a tangible educational benefit, but rather the fault lay in having data not "complete" enough. The framing of the new dual enrollment legislation, in other words, corresponded with an accountability-based policy paradigm that sees public schools in crisis and holds schools, teachers, and educational partnerships *accountable* to the economic needs of society as a solution to that crisis. The creation of Ohio's CCP program to remedy these problems illustrates the durability of accountability-based policy regimes: without a fundamental shift in power arrangements or ideological paradigms that justify the need for these kinds of policy solutions in the first place, policies of accountability tend to re-create themselves no matter who is in charge. CCP, in other words, is different from its predecessor only in being its supercharged successor.

Let us consider Ohio's CCP legislation in more detail to see how it maps fairly neatly onto accountability regime logics. Through a series of selective mandates and competition-based configurations, CCP was pitched as a solution to economic problems instead of an educational initiative that serves the public good. Just like the old law, the new law was designed to "govern those arrangements where a student is engaged in nonsectarian, non-remedial educational coursework while in high school that automatically results in transcripted high school and college credit at the successful conclusion of that coursework" (Carey 9). CCP is still funded through a transfer of funds from a school district's budget to the partnering college or university. Where the new law differs from the old is in the *mandated participation* of institutions of higher learning (IHEs) and public school districts. And while participation is mandatory, "each IHE is permitted to determine its College Credit Plus admission requirements" (10). Moreover, IHEs are able to negotiate the cost of tuition with local school districts. According to Carey's recommendations, IHEs charge districts tuition according to a scale with a maximum per-credit charge, or *ceiling* on one end, and a minimum per-credit charge, or *floor* on the other; this arrangement allows school districts to "retain a portion of state funding in recognition of continuing costs of providing support for the education of the students regardless of delivery method" (12). Under CCP guidelines, IHEs negotiate with partnering school districts on an amount per credit hour between the ceiling and the floor.

At an institution like mine, the University of Toledo, which is essentially open access, we have to comply with the mandates and are thus absorbed into the accountability regime. In our local context, one way we can compete for dual enrollment students in the CCP era is by offering credit-hour charges that are closer to the floor than what our competitors offer. In the policy paradigm of accountability, this move makes sense insofar as the university is effectively competing for the most cost-effective and efficient model of educational partnership, which supposedly gives students and parents more *choice* in what schools they select for dual enrollment courses. The new mandates of CCP do not mandate equity, diversity, or pedagogies of democratic citizenship; what they create is a crude marketplace where IHEs negotiate with public school districts for an acceptable per-credit tuition cost.

Ohio's CCP program also mandates the transfer of course credit, communication, and data-collection mechanisms, effectively creating what sociologist George Ritzer calls "McDonaldization," or a set of organizing principles akin to what makes fast food restaurants successful: efficiency, quantification, standardization, and uniformity. These mandates open the floodgates for dual and concurrent enrollment students across the state. Regarding coursework, one of the main provisions of the law is that dual enrollment courses must be "the same as courses offered on campus." Moreover, each public high school needs to develop two "pathways" for students, one whereby a student can earn fifteen college credits and another whereby a student can earn thirty college credits, and the high school must develop these pathways "in coordination with at least one partnering IHE" (15). Chancellor Carey also called for "aggressive communication" about the new program, which includes the distribution of information packets to students and parents, mandated promotion of CCP on the websites of public schools and IHEs, required parent and student orientations, required communication with IHEs in a thirty-mile radius of a high school (or the nearest one if more than thirty miles), and a required advisor for each CCP student at all IHEs (16–17). Another important aspect of the mandatory participation requirement is that IHEs not only aid in promoting CCP in their communities, but they are also required to conduct at least one observation of each CCP section taught per year. And, finally, as an attempted corrective to the failed data collection of PSEO, CCP mandates that all secondary and postsecondary institutions "consistently collect, report, and track College Credit Plus data to identify the students enrolled, the courses offered and taken, credits earned, the instructor qualifications, student performances, and agreement innovations" (18).

Because all public IHEs and all school districts are mandated to participate in CCP, we should have a lot more data to consult in Ohio in the coming years, data with which we can analyze the benefits and challenges of dual enrollment in the state. As of the writing of this book, we have data from three years of CCP in operation. What writing studies scholars need to do is to interpret such data through alternative policy paradigms that privilege learning, equity, and community—those areas where quantification, uniformity, scale, and other principles of accountability education reform often come up short.

For example, in table 3.1, I present the first three years of data we have for CCP (*College Credit Plus Annual Report, 2017–2018*). These three years show a 400 percent increase in student participation from the numbers for PSEO. Blanco et al. reported that participants in PSEO amounted to about 14,000 in 2014. In 2015, the first year of CCP, there were more than 50,000 participating students. The next academic year, there were 68,000 students, and the year after that, over 70,000 students. Whereas dual enrollment numbers grew slowly and steadily from 2004 to 2014 in Ohio, at a rate of about 4 percent annually over a decade, since the CCP legislation took effect, the numbers have skyrocketed. Nevertheless, white students have consistently made up about 70 percent of all CCP participants since the program began, while Black student participation in CCP has gone up only one percentage point over three years, to 7.6 percent. This figure contrasts with the racial makeup of Ohio's ninth- to twelfth-graders. According to the Ohio Department of Education, the proportion of Black students in the state's public secondary schools is about 16 percent. In other words, CCP participation numbers do not seem

Table 3.1. Demographics of students enrolled in English courses in Ohio's CCP program (data source: *College Credit Plus Annual Report, 2017–2018*)[a]

Year	*Race*	*Coursework in English*	*Participation*	*Concurrent Enrollment*
2015–16	71.6% white 6.3% Black 2.6% Hispanic 15.0% unknown	18%	54,000	49.4%
2016–17	69.4% white 6.8% Black 2.7% Hispanic 16.4% unknown	23.9%	68,000	42.1%
2017–18	69.7% white 7.6% Black 1.6% Hispanic 13.8% unknown	23.7%	71,000	36.2%

[a]The number of students enrolled in English courses in Ohio's CCP program were initially reported as 18 percent in year one (2015–16), 23.9 percent in year two (2016–17), and 23.7 percent in year three (2017–18). However, as new data have come in, the numbers have changed, and participation rates are now seemingly more stable over time than they first appeared, with 24.4 percent in year one, 23.9 percent in year two, and 23.7 percent in year three (Larisa L. Harper, personal correspondence).

to confirm Carey's assertion about CCP "diversifying the college-going population." (This is a promise many other states make with regard to the equity of dual enrollment policies).

Moreover, nearly a quarter of all CCP participation comes from English composition, with even higher rates for concurrent enrollment. These numbers are striking, especially considering how little say English teachers and administrators had in setting the terms of a policy that is fundamentally changing enrollments throughout the state. However, as I have said before, in an accountability-based policy regime, expertise and content knowledge are not always persuasive to powerful policy stakeholders. When education reform is couched in neoliberal logics of the marketplace, the numbers cited above *seem* to prove its success, so the input of content experts is unnecessary.

According to the annual reports, for example, CCP participation rates are quantified in terms of "tuition savings," which refers to the amount of money students *would have paid* had they paid full price for tuition. These *savings* do not account for money lost from having been transferred *out of* state school districts, nor do they quantify the loss for IHEs that charged discounted tuition to local school districts. Nevertheless, these terms reflect a policy paradigm that, as McGuinn has shown, is a response to perceptions of a crisis in public education that understands the government's role in education to be a broad commitment to maintaining accountability. Moreover, as "global economic competition and the shift to a skills-based economy" has created power alignments in which elites see education as a way to fast-track human capital (McGuinn 188), we should expect this kind of dual enrollment program to persist because it encourages competition and mandates accountability-based data that measure success in terms of tuition savings or other metrics that belong to what Stenberg and Whealy describe as "efficiency models."

Conclusion

Similar to chapter 2, where I described NCTE's role in responding to a draft of the Common Core English language arts standards, the analysis in this chapter showed how power arrangements in accountability-based policy regimes work to deprofessionalize writing expertise. Dual enrollment policies frame general education requirements, and writing in particular, as something to *get out of the way*, a course to *take care of*, or "a set of low-level skills that can and should be fairly quickly mastered early in college, or even before, so that the skills can then be transported easily into new settings and efficiently applied over and over again" (Hansen, "Composition Marketplace" 2). As writing studies specialists, we have some tough choices to make in our positions vis-á-vis dual enrollment. From a regime perspective, we can see policy problems like dual enrollment as a confluence of broad power arrangements consisting of national organizations like NACEP, the Community College Research Center, and other think tanks that research, promote, or are otherwise invested in these policy problems; add to this governing arrangements of statewide policy that mandates participation in dual enrollment, federal law that incentivizes reporting of states' dual enrollment efforts, and local policy arrangements that compel high school teachers to obtain credentials to teach college composition at their high school. These forces, as May and Jochim write, "profoundly shape the legitimacy . . . coherence . . . and durability . . . of polices" (427).

In the state of Ohio, there are glaring racial and economic disparities in student participation in dual enrollment. In addition, over a third of all CCP students are taking courses in their high schools taught by a high school teacher. These issues should give writing studies researchers pause as they consider how accountability-based policy regimes are impacting writing classes in their own states. Furthermore, K–16 accountability-based policies like dual enrollment represent opportunities for writing studies researchers, teachers, and administrators working in different contexts to consider ways that we can put stress on the current policy regime given our institutional and local constraints.

Such a perspective makes room for questions like these: One, how might writing program administrators work locally to better serve, mentor, credential, and work with stakeholders, particularly high school teachers who are either already teaching dual-enrolled students or are seeking to do so in order to meet what is clearly a growing demand for dual enrollment courses in composition? Two, how might administrators make effective use of their time in forming coalitions with these stakeholders by lending their expertise and power, whether through observing, promoting, training, or working alongside public school districts to ensure that instruction is consistent with best practices in the field? Three, how might writing researchers understand concurrent enrollment specifically and dual enrollment generally as an under-researched area in the field? Four, what new research questions might we ask of education policy to better understand this phenomenon? These are potential questions to answer as we figure out how the field might effect education policy from a politically kairotic orientation. In the next chapter I zoom in on an individual teacher and her students who work as the levers of education policy, so as to analyze their individual kairotic strategies within accountability regimes.

CHAPTER 4

Experiencing Policy on the Ground: A Case Study of Midwest High

Introduction

In the previous chapter I analyzed the policy problem of dual enrollment and argued that a *regime framework* can help us see the dynamic ways that we as a field can respond to this and other policy problems. But merely to critique dual enrollment as an accountability-based policy is not enough. There is a human component to policy, so we also need to understand how policy regimes are experienced by those who are tasked with carrying out policies on the ground. As well, we need to know about the experiences of students, who are supposedly the beneficiaries of these policies. As Jim Webber writes in *An Alternate Pragmatism for Going Public*, this method of first investigating "institutional, community, state, and national reform discussions" and then "scaling down to local experience" can help researchers in writing studies answer calls to *go public* with our work, or as he puts it, "draw on the participatory energy of public inquiry to support the professional goal of improving the discourse of reform" (21). Micro-level engagements with policy often go unaccounted for in conversations about public engagement: "In efforts to make arguments at the policy level," Webber writes, "reformers and professionals tend to avoid emphasizing specific acts of teaching and learning" (33).

Therefore, what follows in this chapter are the results of my semester-long participant observation in a concurrent enrollment class at a high school participating in Ohio's dual enrollment program, College Credit

Plus. I refer to the high school by the pseudonym Midwest High. Located in a suburb of a large city in northwest Ohio, Midwest High serves mostly white middle-class students and has a dual enrollment partnership with my university. By observing in the classroom and conducting interviews with students, I sought to understand, qualitatively, what stakeholder experiences with dual enrollment reveal about how policy regimes of accountability affect the day-to-day operations of schools. The field of writing studies—from the discourses of truth produced by its institutions, all the way down to the classrooms where teachers and students function as levers of policy—is imbued with policy regimes. The key difference at the micro-level is that teachers and students interact with, interpret, individualize, and find ways to put stress on policy regimes. Here is where we see up close what establishing new power arrangements, alternative policy paradigms, and other possible policy arrangements might actually look like in practice.

Focusing on the experiences of one teacher and her students helps us see what policy regimes of accountability mean for those on the ground. Unlike previous chapters, which relied on archival research and policy analyses, the research site for this chapter was a space filled with people. The teacher in the classroom was a high school English teacher credentialed to teach college composition through my university. Her students, several of whom I interviewed after the semester was over, understood and experienced dual enrollment policy much more fluidly than do the legislators, administrators, and bureaucrats who extol the policy paradigm of choice and efficiency. In fact, their embodied experience as high school students changed the dynamic of instruction. The instructor, whom I call Ms. Elliot, experienced and navigated dual enrollment policy in ways that also belied the narrative of those who back dual enrollment policy in Ohio.

The main priority for Ms. Elliot was to help her juniors and seniors *transition* from high school to college. This involved leveraging the *liminal space* of the concurrent enrollment classroom to her advantage. She made a series of *micropolitical* pedagogical moves that helped her in this aim. At the individual level, a politically kairotic orientation to accountability regime policies was fundamental to her and her students' experiences. By documenting the lived experiences of a teacher and students impacted by our current policy regime, I emphasize two seemingly contradictory ideas. On the one hand, policy regimes, in their power arrangements, policy paradigms, and policy features, have profound effects on the durability and legitimacy of specific policies, no matter the facts and disciplinary expertise leveraged against them. But on the other hand, at the micro-level more than anywhere else, we see wiggle room for new formations and opportunities to make new connections and conceive of alterative paradigms with which we can conceptualize policy.

In this chapter I study the potential at the micro-level for developing new politically kairotic practices for policy engagement, yet a regime approach to policy necessarily involves analyzing broader arrangements. Therefore, to see the full picture of how policy regimes of accountability play out in one classroom, this chapter unfolds through three distinct views of Midwest High's concurrent enrollment composition course. First is the *macro*-level, or the perspective of my university, where a team of professionals forge partnerships with local school districts. Second is the *meso*-level, which is Midwest High and its school district. At the meso-level we see a pernicious issue that arises when we have critical conversations about equity in dual enrollment. The district in which Midwest High is located is mostly middle class and white, a student demographic that tends to benefit the most from dual enrollment policies. Surrounding districts with fewer dual enrollment students at my university have higher rates of poverty, more racial segregation, and lower rates of academic achievement at school. Third is the *micro*-level, which is Ms. Elliot's concurrent enrollment classroom, where both she and her students demonstrated kairotic rhetorical savvy in how they worked with, around, and sometimes put stress on dual enrollment policies. Taken as a whole, this multiscopic regime analysis of dual enrollment composition in Ohio showcases how dual enrollment is seen as a solution to a specific policy problem and how this policy solution—and others like it—fit into broader public discourse about education in America. But it also showcases how there is room for individuals—teachers, students, and writing program administrators across all educational contexts—to participate in effecting education policy.

A Brief Word on Method

Concurrent enrollment composition courses are likely the most common kind of dual enrollment partnership that exists throughout the country. Ironically, however, they are the least studied. Scholars point out the fundamental role that high school has always played for histories of rhetoric and composition pedagogy (Lueck; Addison and McGee). The concurrent enrollment class taught in a high school is thus an incredibly important site of convergence for high school and college pedagogies. Knowing more about how teachers and students in high school experience accountability policies can help us understand more broadly the ways that education policy shapes college composition teaching, research, and administration.

To study the lived experience of teachers and students in concurrent enrollment spaces, I performed *participant observation*, which is an ethnographic research technique common in studies of education systems. For instance, scholars have used participant observation to study school administrators (Wolcott), university registration processes (Hendricks), and even student life (Ahola and Lucas). Like Jorgenson, I used participant observation to understand the "practical and theoretical truths about human life grounded in the realities of daily existence" (14). Taking my cues from ethnographers Becker and Geer, I consider participant observation to be a "method in which the observer participates in the daily life of the people under study . . . observing things that happen, listening to what is said, and questioning people, over some length of time" (28). Scholars Lutz and Iannaccone define participant observers in three ways: (1) the participant *as* an observer, (2) the observer as a limited participant, and (3) the observer as a nonparticipant. At Midwest High I mostly used the second of these. Having limited participation means that the researcher becomes a "quasi member" of the class. Most of my interactions were conversations initiated by the students or the teacher that "focus[ed] on the research project, either demonstrating curiosity about the purpose of the study or asking about the progress of the research" (Ahola and Lucas 81). I made sure that my responses to the students and teacher were simply a way to "establish and maintain rapport," in my capacity as a participant observer, as Ahola and Lucas suggest (78).

I must admit, though, that the boundaries of my limited participation were tested by students' natural curiosity about the presence of a researcher in their classroom. I had students gaze at my observation journals and playfully exclaim, "One day I'm going to find out what you're writing in there," or turn to me in class to ask for help on their papers. I found that the warier I was in response to their inquisitiveness, the more awkward my presence became, which could have impacted the way the students engaged with their teacher and the course material. Thus, as the semester progressed, I found myself saying hello to the students each morning, chatting with them and Ms. Elliot before class began, and occasionally taking part in class discussion.

My data collection consisted of recording the classroom activities in extensive descriptive notes, including verbatim remarks when possible, which I subsequently narratized in my observation journals after each visit. I summarized my own thoughts, comments, feelings, and interpretations of the events of the day. In this way, I became familiar with classroom routines, course materials, school policies, learning activities, classroom dynamics, and student-teacher interactions, and I also described in my notes the learning process of college-level writing when taught in a high school classroom. I made ten site visits to Ms. Elliot's class in fall 2018 and conducted four post-semester interviews with students. These efforts at gathering data served my goal of describing how individuals carry out, enforce, or sometimes resist policies in their daily lives.

The Macro: Dual Enrollment Implementation by Institutions of Higher Learning

When writing studies scholars or education scholars talk about education reform, much of the conversation takes place at the level of secondary school. Conventional wisdom has it that accountability-based policies of education reform primarily impact elementary and high schools. No Child Left Behind was, after all, a reauthorization of the Elementary and Secondary Education Act, which was not targeted at the colleges and universities that some students attended after they graduated high school. However, as I argued in the previous chapter, accountability regime policies also affect institutions of higher learning through policies like dual enrollment that connect students, teachers, and administrators from K–16 in ways that other education reform policies do not.

Ohio's dual enrollment program, College Credit Plus (CCP), mandates not just that secondary schools offer students free college-level courses but also that public institutions of higher education (IHEs) negotiate partnerships with school districts and provide extra resources for their students and parents. These mandates impose new responsibilities on IHEs that put them in regular interaction with secondary schools in unprecedented ways. The accountability-based mandates of CCP, moreover, have resulted in new personnel at the university level, including enrollment management staff who broker partnerships; faculty, staff, and administrators who coordinate dual enrollment instruction; and staff in institutional research who collect and report dual enrollment data to the State of Ohio. These institutional resources for implementing dual enrollment are a fundamental component of how policy regimes are strengthened and legitimized.

Most policy implementation for dual enrollment at IHEs happens through enrollment management. A key feature of today's neoliberal university, enrollment management is an office staffed by higher education professionals who implement strategies for recruiting and retaining students in an effort to increase institutional revenue. As many state governments shift toward accountability-based education reform, wherein education is seen as an economic as opposed to a public good, public colleges and universities rely less and less on the state for their operating budgets and so must compete for revenue from tuition dollars. This creates the need for a dedicated team that can develop competitive enrollment strategies. Enrollment management is now a profession in its own right, with its own organizations, publications, conferences, and, to be sure, critics. Some critics have described enrollment management professionals as "faceless, pragmatic technocrats with too much power" (Hoover). Others, however, acknowledge the indispensability of their work, as Eric Stoller outlined in his *Inside Higher Ed* piece "Strategic Enrollment Management Keeps the Lights On." It is important, therefore, to acknowledge that those who work in enrollment management are dedicated individuals who care about access, inclusion, and diversity and whose jobs are crucial for public universities to function as they currently do. But it is also the case that, as a manifestation of managerial science, enrollment management reinforces accountability regime logics, as it produces what Donna Strickland has called a "managerial unconscious," a confluence of material conditions and cultural values by which economic logics of managerialism impact intellectual work at universities, including the day-to-day decisions that teachers and students make in writing classrooms.

Enrollment managers broker partnerships with secondary schools and secure contracts that set the terms for tuition rates, methods of instruction, and the number of sections offered. As mentioned in the previous chapter, Ohio's CCP is funded through a transfer of resources. Once a secondary school and a postsecondary institution agree to partner, money for tuition is transferred from the school district's budget to the university's budget. While CCP annual reports characterize this as *money saved* for parents, it comes by way of significant *money lost* for secondary school districts. Colleges and universities, since they often offer reduced tuition for dual enrollment courses, also experience this transfer as a revenue loss. In other words, while students and parents experience Ohio's CCP program as "free," their secondary school district foots the bill for books and tuition, and the participating university receives fewer tuition dollars than would come from traditionally enrolled students.

Higher education administrators in Ohio invoke the accountability policy paradigm of market-based education reform to defend these policies, noting that while secondary schools may experience CCP as a loss of funding, the *state* is still saving money. Since public universities continue to rely on state funding for a share of their operational expenses, the state calculates how much to fund universities based on "full-time equivalent" students. For a program like CCP, with more than 70,000 high school students participating, this significantly lowers the amount of funding received per full-time equivalent student at public universities since secondary school districts are now taking on that burden. University administrators are also inclined to see this as "profitable" since the seats that dual-enrolled students fill would have otherwise remained empty. And even with the subsidies the state pays to make up for the loss in tuition revenue (my university receives small subsidies from the state for CCP implementation), the State of Ohio still considers it a cost savings, as long as CCP partnerships are pursued and maintained by secondary school administrators and IHE enrollment managers.[1] Higher education administrators experience less costly CCP partnerships when a significant chunk of the courses are taught at the high school by high school instructors, since high school teachers receive no extra compensation for their labor and the only money paid by the university in this instance is a small stipend for university faculty to serve as mentors to the high school instructors. Enrollment management therefore plays a fundamental role in maintaining the durability of policy regimes, not just in the ways its offices implement the mandated policy, but also in the ways those implementation procedures serve to legitimize a paradigm of choice, efficiency, and market-based logics that define "successful" or "effective" policies as those that save money for the state even when those benefits are couched in equity terms of increasing access for students.

As Carter A. Wilson writes in "Policy Regimes and Policy Change," individuals and institutions charged with developing and maintaining a policy not only strengthen that policy's durability, but they also work to recruit others into the prevailing policy paradigm: "the organizational and bureaucratic literature is full of examples of public officials who become defenders and advocates of the policies they implement" (259). "The implementation process," writes Wilson, "operates to sustain the policy and becomes part of the policy regime" (259). Similarly, the work that enrollment management does to implement dual enrollment mandates in the state of Ohio is indispensable to the stability of the accountability regime. CCP's mandates create the need for personnel at IHEs to implement the policy, which in turn creates a complex chain of command wherein individuals work on behalf of that policy, with duties that require them to advocate for the policy in the process.

Another way that dual enrollment policy is implemented in the state of Ohio is through the administration of the courses themselves. At my home institution, data from fall 2019 show that 1,023 high school students enrolled in CCP courses across the university. That represents about 5 percent of the university's student body of 19,759. At the department level, chairs are tasked with overseeing, staffing, and attending to other details of dual enrollment policy implementation. Our department chair, for example, manages staffing for 444 dual-enrolled students in our freshman- and sophomore-level composition courses. Of those students, 135 of them, or about 30 percent, took composition through concurrent enrollment, that is, in courses taught at a high school by a credentialed high school teacher. Online students accounted for another 30 percent of CCP participants (133 students) who were taught by our own composition faculty, and the remaining 176 students, about 40 percent, took in-person composition courses on campus. And, as part of the state-legislated CCP mandate, the composition program's administrators (I and one other person) provided mentorship to nine high school teachers credentialed to teach our courses at their schools. This mentorship included providing workshops, traveling to the high schools to conduct teaching observations, and offering other professional development opportunities throughout the year. At my university, all of this represents a fundamental shift in the student makeup of our composition courses and in the job duties of department chairs, writing program administrators, and the composition faculty teaching dual enrollment students either online or on campus. The changing nature of labor for a university's writing program in Ohio is indicative, one can only assume, of what is to come in other states that pursue dual enrollment partnerships as aggressively as Ohio.

Another component at the macro-level of dual enrollment is an office of institutional research, which is required to report dual enrollment data to the Ohio Department of Higher Education. In his 2014 recommendations for the CCP program, John Carey, chancellor of the Ohio Board of Regents, asked that all secondary and postsecondary institutions keep track of "students enrolled, the courses offered and taken, credits earned, the instructor qualifications, student performances and agreement innovations" (18). The Office of Institutional Research at my university must submit meticulously organized CSV-formatted files to a web portal that tracks CCP students across six domains: student data, alternate funding, course outcomes, college readiness assessments, student demographics, and compliance ("College Credit Plus Data").

To be clear, data collection is valuable. We *need* to have a clear grasp on demographics, course outcomes, funding structures, and student success for all of our students and university initiatives, not just dual enrollment. Moreover, collecting these numbers improves on the previous dual enrollment program in Ohio, which was severely lacking in its data collection. Nevertheless, the data collection mandated by CCP puts the objectivity of data in service of the ideology of an accountability-based policy regime. From an accountability perspective, standardization is seen as a way of serving the public good. "Common outcomes," writes Webber, "allow states to measure public institutions' performance, performance data allows public choice among institutions, and public choice drives innovation in efficiency" (19). In other words, data collection in and of itself is not nefarious, but data are often deployed within a market-based framework of reform that reinforces accountability policy regimes.

Higher education data collection like that mandated in Ohio operates under the guise of objectivity. But there is also what Ben Williamson calls a "hidden architecture" of data collection that serves the interests of accountability regime policies with a goal to further *marketize* higher education and "align the work of the university with the logics of capitalist markets" (Komljenovic and Robertson qtd. in Williamson 1). In chapter 2, I argued that data are often leveraged not necessarily to "fill gaps" in knowledge but rather to reflect values. Williamson concludes that accountability-based data mandates work through paradigms that aim to reform the university through new tools, analytics, and other platforms for data collection. And the reporting platforms currently used by IHE administrators and policymakers are "going to be plugged into the architecture of the university in ways that will impose new modes of quantification and standardization while also bringing new actors and priorities from across the public and private sectors into contemporary" higher education (24).

The Meso: Midwest High and Its Surrounding District

The macro-level context showed us that even before students took Ms. Elliot's concurrent enrollment class, governing policy arrangements were jockeying for economic leverage. Efforts to recruit students for dual enrollment frame recruitment as a viable economic solution for parents, teachers, students, and administrators. This creates a compelling ideological narrative that says dual enrollment saves money and allows students to enter the workforce more quickly, which is necessary and good for a productive and competitive economy.

It is important to point out, however, that dual enrollment at the meso-level tends to complicate the narratives that institutions and the state offer about the policy as a solution to education. Even though CCP is couched in equity buzzwords like *access*, the program falls short. Chancellor Carey's 2014 recommendations mentioned equity as one of the program's key concerns (though if you look closely at CCP literature, the word *equity* is rarely used); he wrote that CCP would provide "seamless and equitable pathways . . . across all demographic populations" (3). However, CCP has consistently benefited mostly white high school students in Ohio. The CCP annual report for year three boasted of having 71,000 participants, or more than 12 percent of Ohio's ninth- to twelfth-graders. Nearly 70 percent of those participants, however, were white. This figure makes it clear that Ohio high school students of color are systematically left out of this statewide education policy (*College Credit Plus Annual Report, 2017–2018* 9). At my university, our dual enrollment numbers pretty much mirror those statewide, with white students making up around 65 percent of participants and Black students making up only 7.1 percent of participants.

Midwest High is located in a suburb just outside the city. This is typical of the active dual enrollment partnerships at my university. Of the top-ten area schools where dual enrollment courses were taught in 2019, only one of them is in the district where my university is situated. The rest of the schools are on the outskirts of town, where more students are white and districts tend to fare better on annual report cards.[2] According to the National Center for Education Statistics, of Midwest High's student population of around 400, over 80 percent are white. There are only seven Asian American students, six African American students, thirty-nine Hispanic students, and eleven students identified as multiracial. The district that includes Midwest High is predominately white as well, with only twenty-five Black students district-wide, or about 1.6 percent of the district's students. Hispanic and multiracial students make up only 11 percent of the district's student body. Per-pupil spending at Midwest High is far above average, too, at about $13,000 per student in 2016–2017, compared with an average of about $9,000 for the state of Ohio.[3]

The demographics of Midwest High are typical of the high schools that my university partners with to fulfill the mandates of CCP. Half of the top schools my university partnered with in 2019 were composed of white student populations of 90 percent or higher. Several of the partner high schools had no Black students at all, and only one school had a Black student population above 10 percent. In the case of my university, the so-called "equitable pathways" on which CCP is predicated have not come to bear on the demographics of the students enrolled in dual enrollment courses. The facts are that, when pursuing CCP partnerships, institutions operating within accountability-based policy regimes tend to favor high schools that fare better on their annual report card because that means they potentially have more "college-ready" students. Considering that high schools in the urban districts close to my university are nearly all rated as "failing," dual enrollment students tend mostly to come from suburban districts, where performance indicators are higher and the student population is whiter.

Midwest High is a "successful" dual enrollment partnership—if success is defined in terms of accountability. Performance indicators at Midwest High show that most of its students passed statewide tests, doing particularly well in the subject of US government, where nearly 90 percent of students passed. The students did not perform as well in algebra and English language arts, where a little over 50 percent passed state tests. But 96 percent of students graduated, and most of the student body made progress at or above the rate expected by the state.

This performance contrasts with that of the school district surrounding my university, where a majority of students are minorities and nearly 87 percent of the student body is considered economically disadvantaged. Students in the district's high schools failed to meet performance indicators in *every* subject. A little over half of the students passed US government, 29 percent passed algebra, and 46 percent passed English. The four-year graduation rate district-wide was 71 percent, but there are high-poverty schools in the district with lower rates of graduation. That such disparity exists between two districts less than ten miles apart is a hallmark of public education in America, where fault lines of race and socioeconomic status divide city from suburb.[4] And it also shows how the market-based logics of accountability policy regimes incentivize institutions to give access to more white and economically privileged high school students, despite their official narratives of equity and access for "all."

Midwest High is not the only school in the area whose budget and racial makeup reveal the fault lines of race and socioeconomic status. In another affluent district near Midwest High, barely outside the city, its elementary school received the grade of A for most of its statewide performance indicators. Yet an elementary school just five miles to the east, in the middle of the city and in a different district, had some of the lowest performance indicators in the entire state. Ninety percent of its student body lives in poverty. Such inequalities are not unique to Ohio, of course. According to the *New York Times*, districts with the most students of color receive nearly 15 percent less per student than the whitest districts (Yin). According to the 2015 National Assessment of Educational Progress, the average reading score of white students was twenty-six points higher than that of Black students, and 7 percent of Black students were deemed proficient in math in 2015, compared with 32 percent of white students ("K–12 Disparity"). Across the country there is a glaring disparity in academic performance relative to race and class, with white students in majority white districts receiving more school funding and scoring higher on nearly all performance indicators. Midwest High is no exception.

Unsurprisingly, educational inequality also reveals itself in most studies of dual enrollment statistics. For example, the US Department of Education's February 2019 report on dual enrollment participation showed that African American and Hispanic students were around 30 percent less likely to take dual enrollment courses than were white students (*Dual Enrollment*). Other studies found that affluent students too were overrepresented in dual enrollment participation (Zinth and Barnett). The systemic problems in equity and access for accountability regime policies impact all students' experiences before they even enter a dual enrollment classroom.

The Micro: Case Study of Ms. Elliot's Concurrent Enrollment Classroom

As Ms. Elliot's students trickled into the classroom in the morning for their English composition course at Midwest High, policy regimes of accountability were already shaping the experience. For example, their experiences had been shaped by institutional partnerships, forged primarily by universities' offices of enrollment management, which bureaucratize dual enrollment policies. These policies are then administered by department chairs and writing program administrators, in consultation with high school principals and college enrollment management teams, and later they are surveilled by teams in offices of institutional research. Moreover, student demographics, performance indicators, and glaring educational inequalities that marginalize Black and Brown students further shape the perspectives of students in CCP courses and may influence whether they buy into the policy paradigm that frames these courses as good, equitable, and cost-effective.

Not surprisingly, Ms. Elliot and her students fared exceptionally well that semester. All of the students I interviewed after the semester had ended spoke highly of Ms. Elliot, their high school, and CCP as an educational policy. The temptation here is to surmise that dual enrollment at Midwest High is a *good* policy given the positive experience for this group. But what sticks out the most from my observations is that both the students and their teacher navigated accountability regime policies of dual enrollment in strategic ways, regardless of whether they felt like they had benefited from the policy. When we consider whether dual enrollment is *good* policy from a paradigm of access as opposed to accountability, the question then becomes, good for *whom*? The teaching and learning practices I identify below give us something to consider when we carry out, navigate, or resist accountability regime policies like dual enrollment at our home institutions. If dual enrollment is on the rise for the foreseeable future, then the classroom practices exemplified below might help administrators consider what ethical questions to ask when we pursue dual enrollment partnerships and consider how we might forge different kinds of political arrangements where partnerships with schools in less academically successful (and less white) districts could be seen as successful.

Midwest High's dual enrollment composition course had five distinct features: (1) the embodied experience of *being in high school* markedly changed the dynamic of the college composition course, despite the students' intellectual capacity to engage with the material in most cases; (2) in addition to meeting the learning outcomes of traditional first-year composition, which, for the most part, did happen, instructor-student interactions often took the form of pedagogical efforts to help students *transition from high school to college*; (3) although course content resembled that of traditional first-year composition, the instructor's efforts to transition students created a space of *liminality* where prospective college students studied college-level writing under the auspices of a college-affiliated mentor; (4) the instructor made micropolitical moves in choosing how and when to enforce policy in order to take advantage of the liminality of the course to meet the needs of her students, and the students made micropolitical choices of their own in their motives for taking the class; (5) the class's racial and socioeconomic homogeneity—every student who finished the class was white and college-bound—reflected the troubling statistics on race, class, and academic achievement found in dual enrollment and in public education generally. This is a major issue that our field needs to consider when we evaluate, implement, partner with, or resist dual enrollment policies at our home institutions. In the subsections below, I expand on each of my five research findings.

College Composition Was a Different Experience in High School

Although state policy in Ohio mandates that dual enrollment courses should be the same as those taught on campus, and that dual enrollment students should be treated no differently from anyone else, I observed that the embodied classroom experience is one of being in high school, and cannot be otherwise, and the social world of high school fundamentally changes the way that dual enrollment composition courses are taught. Concurrent enrollment composition courses occur in a familiar environment and are taught by a teacher whom most of the students already know. These courses do not *feel* like college, even though the legislation governing dual enrollment partnerships in Ohio specifies that these experiences are supposed to *be* college in every way. From the spatial arrangements of high schools and the physical artifacts inside them, to the strict focus on routine, structure, and student safety in high school—the experience of concurrent enrollment is fundamentally different from what one might consider to be a typical college experience.

Midwest High operates with the regimented pace one would expect of a mid-size high school: a bell rings to start first period promptly at 7:30 a.m. The weekly schedule alternates between *blue* and *red* days, with different schedules each day. Students wear school IDs on lanyards as they stop by their lockers before hurrying to class. Teachers and administrators patrol the halls, ensuring student safety and making sure nobody is wandering around after the bell rings. Security at Midwest High is a high priority. After being questioned and waved on by a security guard in the parking lot, all guests sign in at the front office and obtain temporary passes to enter the building. On my first day observing, the principal himself escorted me to Ms. Elliot's room and knocked on the door, which was locked from the outside.

When I was let into the room, Ms. Elliot, a veteran teacher with a master's degree in curriculum development, pointed to a seat in the back where she had made a name tent that read, "Dr. Branson." Around the room were artifacts that signified the space as *high school*. On the days that I observed, for example, Ms. Elliot's classroom was a university-level English composition course. On other days, though, it was an Advanced Placement literature or drama classroom. After school, the room became a meeting place for the Midwest High Chess Club. The walls of Ms. Elliot's room reflected these differing purposes: posters of MLA style, examples of student work, chess trophies, bookshelves holding Norton anthologies of literature, and a laminated handmade sign above Ms. Elliot's desk that read, "No whining." The spatial arrangements, the emphasis on student safety, the distribution of power and authority, and the artifacts—all these felt different from what one might consider the typical college experience. For all intents and purposes, it *felt* like high school.

The embodied experience in Ms. Elliot's classroom impacted teacher-student interactions. For example, on the first day, groups of students were arranged around the room: Five male students in football jerseys sat together. One female student with pink hair and a black sweater sat by herself. Another male student in a tie-dye shirt and headphones sat in the opposite corner of the room. Another male in the back slept on a hoodie. Two others sat in the middle of the room, one on her phone and the other fastidiously writing in her planner. When Ms. Elliot introduced students to the course, it was immediately clear that most of them were familiar with her, as they had taken her courses over their years at Midwest High, some for beginning English, some for drama, and some for other literature electives. At least one student knew her as the sponsor of the chess club.

As Ms. Elliot introduced the course assignments, which included a research paper on the intersection of poverty with an issue of their choosing, students immediately began asking questions. Many of them struggled with the very concept of a syllabus. "So these are organized by week and not by day?" one student asked about the course calendar. About the reading list on the syllabus, one asked, "So are the readings things we have to read as homework *for next time* or what we need to have read before class?" The equivalent composition course taught on campus ended when the high school students still had several weeks left in their semester, so questions about the calendar dominated the first few discussions. "What are we going to be doing those last few weeks of school?" they asked.

Other similar moments underscored how college writing at Midwest High was a different embodied experience from the instruction students typically receive on my college campus. For example, during my second observation in September, the day started, like most, with announcements read to the class. Ms. Elliot informed students that homecoming tickets were finally on sale. There was no school on Friday because of a teacher in-service day, and Ms. Elliot said that this year she was in charge of the "crush candygrams," which meant that students could anonymously send candy and a message to their crush. *But*, she continued, her tone changing to stern admonition: inappropriate or explicit messages would not be tolerated this year. Later in the semester, these morning announcements concerned where students could purchase their caps and gowns for commencement and what time they needed to show up to rehearsals. These characteristics that designated the space a *high school* did not preclude delivering course content at a college level, though. Ms. Elliot demonstrated that she was a more-than-competent first-year writing instructor. And the students, for the most part, seemed intellectually capable of handling the material. Still, the sights, sounds, and embodied experience of dual enrollment at Midwest High revealed a discrepancy between Ohio's policy of dual enrollment, which stipulates that dual enrollment courses should have *the same* educational *rigor as regular sections* and that the students enrolled should be treated *no differently* from college students on campus, and the reality of Ms. Elliot's concurrent enrollment classroom, where the experience was markedly different from courses taken at the university.

The social world that students inhabited at Midwest High fundamentally changed the way college composition was taught. In late October, for example, Ms. Elliot conducted a whole-class rhetorical analysis of a college student's paper. In the paper, written for a writing class a decade prior, the writer was arguing against conscientious objectors in the military. As students unpacked the essay line by line with Ms. Elliot, they interjected periodically to ask her what a word meant, how to pronounce a word, or whether it was appropriate to use a citation in some way. There was an element of trust they had in Ms. Elliot as their guide. They were not embarrassed about asking her questions, and they looked up to her as a role model, especially since many of them had known her for years. This intimate classroom environment showcases just how important high school teachers are to the lives of their students, developmentally and intellectually. While traditional college composition instructors also play an important role in the intellectual lives of their students, the student-teacher dynamic in high school is more trusting and nurturing. And while many on-campus college students are young, some are veterans, parents, professionals, or other older students who have accumulated life experience, or what Barbara Schneider calls "miles on the tires" (157). This embodied element of the concurrent enrollment classroom at Midwest High made the learning fundamentally different, which belies the policy that mandates sameness.

Pedagogy Was Often Aimed at Transitioning Students from High School to College

Ms. Elliot's classroom at Midwest High was a space in which a group of college-bound high school students worked closely with a talented college-writing mentor who helped them transition from high school to college. On the first day, for example, Ms. Elliot assigned the essay "Bam," by Amanda Winalski, from the book *What Is College-Level Writing?* edited by Patrick Sullivan and Howard Tinberg. The essay relates a firsthand perspective on transitioning from high school to college-level writing. Ms. Elliot pointed out a sentence in the essay where the author realized that, in college, "What I wrote was more important than *how* I wrote." She asked the students to unpack what Winalski meant. One student, Nick, said the author was saying that, in college, it is a matter of "function over form." Nick went on to say that, in high school, writing is mostly about "making six words out of two" to meet a word count and gussying up a text to make it "seem smart." Another student agreed and said that, in high school, writing a paper is a matter of making sure the beginning thesis and concluding thesis aligned, and it did not really matter what was in the middle. Then Ms. Elliot steered the conversation toward the main idea of Winalski's essay, which is that transitioning to college-level writing means considering *argument* as opposed to the veneer of correctness that characterizes high school writing instruction. This move got the students talking about their fears and expectations for transitioning to college-level writing. One student, Ricky, said that the essay made her feel better because it gave her a map of things "to look out for" once she got to college. Ms. Elliot reiterated that transitioning to college-level writing is less about memorizing rules and more about developing tools to apply concepts to learning and revising your writing. A student in the back agreed and said that, in college, writing is not a "a step-by-step process." Yes, Ms. Elliot said, "Our writing process can't be this straight line anymore."

Realizing the "straight line" of writing instruction is actually circular in college came up again in my third observation, when Ms. Elliot was working with handouts from the textbook *They Say / I Say* by Gerald Graff and Cathy Birkenstein. Ms. Elliot copied some of the authors' appendices for students to use as a reference as they polished their writing for the current assignment, a rhetorical analysis. Ms. Elliot described how templates like these can help students achieve college-level quality in their writing. She provided other handouts as well: an example of a college-level paper and a set of questions about rhetorical strategies. One student, Corey, asked Ms. Elliot about the phrase *rhetorical strategies*. He had never heard it before. Another student began reading the sample paper and exclaimed, "Whoa, this is what they write like in college?" Even though everyone in the room was technically *already* in college, this student apparently saw the course he was taking as a prelude to the "real thing." Ms. Elliott told the students to think of rhetoric as an investigation of the claims and evidence of arguments. As the students praised the college-level paper because it "wasn't biased" and "had a good hook," Ms. Elliot pushed back and asked them whether it looked too formulaic: "Doesn't this look like a five-paragraph essay, though?" She continued, "How many more ideas could be broken up and expanded further?" She wanted her students to transition from the five-paragraph essay to which they had grown accustomed in high school to seeing the writing process in a new way. By allowing them to critique a college student's essay, she was helping her students develop their own vocabularies for giving sophisticated feedback on one another's writing. Eventually, one student, Karlie, said of the essay, "this person's ideas are all lumped together, and it's confusing." Another student, Brian, said that the "introduction was abrupt." Dan commented on logic and cohesion: "The conclusion is not the final knockout blow it should be."

This pedagogical move, aimed at helping students bridge the gap between high school and college, was repeated throughout the semester. On the last day of my observations, the class was brainstorming about their multimodal presentations the following week. From one of their textbooks, *The Call to Write*, Ms. Elliot pointed to a section called "The Do's and Don'ts of PowerPoint." She asked the class, "What are some mistakes you make in high school with PowerPoints?" The students said that having slides with too much text, including images that do not correspond to the message, and using too many slides were *high school* mistakes. Joel chimed in to say that, for him, good slideshows are ones that fulfill whatever the rubric says makes for a good slideshow. While part of Ms. Elliot's goal with this assignment was to meet my university's freshman composition outcomes, her pedagogy was frequently dedicated to ensuring a smooth transition for her students from dual enrollment composition to "the real thing" down the line. So the discussion about slideshows turned into how to use these tips for PowerPoint presentations once they "got to college."

Transitioning to college-level writing was one of the primary but unstated goals of dual enrollment composition at Midwest High. A significant hurdle in that transition was getting students to meet one of the most important outcomes of my university's composition course: critical thinking. For example, around midterm, Ms. Elliot introduced the research paper assignment, for which students had to pick an issue that interested them, research how that issue intersected with poverty, and eventually make an argument derived from their research. After she had the students do some free-writing, she asked them what problems they were encountering with the assignment. Karlie immediately raised her hand and said that her topic, poverty and Ohio, was going poorly. She could find only *two sources* related to her topic. Other students also expressed frustration over finding sources. These exchanges revealed that students in Ms. Elliot's class faced significant barriers in conducting academic research. Ms. Elliot, an experienced high school teacher with a graduate degree and training in rhetoric and composition, patiently listened to her students' concerns and gave tips for what to search for. While the students' struggles with research were not all that different from those that students have in traditional first-year composition, the main difference was that, at Midwest High, the students who did struggle had the safety net of a high school to fall back on—in this case a ten-student classroom community and a teacher who was willing and able to work with them line by line, day by day, and help them use research databases. Traditionally enrolled college composition students who face similar struggles often lack such a safety net.

An example of students having a hard time thinking critically comes from their discussion of a chapter from *Understanding Rhetoric: A Graphic Guide to Writing*, by Elizabeth Losh, Jonathan Alexander, Kevin Cannon, and Zander Cannon. Ms. Elliot told her students that, in college-level writing, a writer cannot make claims without offering evidence. "Why would people make claims without evidence?" she asked. Ms. Elliot wanted her students to consider how it is manipulative and unethical to make arguments without offering any support. Ms. Elliot elaborated on her question: "Sometimes people don't offer any evidence when they argue; they just say whatever. Why would they do that?" The students' responses were less than ideal. "To just get their thoughts out there?" one student said with the intonation of a question. "Maybe they do it because they don't think they need evidence because it's common knowledge," another said. And this answer from another student: "They assume their audience is too dumb to understand the evidence." The students in Ms. Elliot's high school classroom were unable to fully engage with the idea of arguments and evidence beyond their application in the classroom or beyond the scope of a paper written for school. That arguments and evidence also function outside school apparently did not match their experiences. The students were so trusting of institutions, authority, and things they read that when presented with the notion that an author would purposefully issue a claim without providing evidence, they considered a situation in which the author might be altruistically shielding the audience from complicated material. Ms. Elliot's attempts to push her students to consider how rhetoric can work insidiously to manipulate an audience, or how crafting arguments has ethical dimensions, revealed some significant gaps in their understanding.

The fact that students struggled with this is not unique to high school, but it does show that in the concurrent enrollment classroom, Ms. Elliot's students had the benefit of learning in a small, intimate space and working one-on-one with a dedicated mentor who could guide them through the process of critique as well as the social, cultural, and ethical transition from writing in high school to writing in college. This is a benefit that few students in traditional college writing classrooms have and is something not yet addressed in the literature on dual enrollment composition.

Concurrent Enrollment Functioned as a Liminal Space

Another finding from this case study is that the dual enrollment classroom at Midwest High resembled neither a high school nor a college classroom but instead a *liminal* space where students worked on problems in college writing. Anthropologists began using the term *liminality*, from the Latin word for threshold, to describe rites of passage in different cultures, particularly the transitional stage between one possibility and another. Victor Turner famously called liminality a "realm of pure possibility whence novel configurations of ideas and relations may arise" (236). In this transitional stage, which Turner also calls "betwixt and between" or a period of "fruitful darkness" (243), traditional boundaries and rules can dissolve, creating a kind of uncertainty where new possibilities are imagined. In the social and political sciences, Horváth et al. use the term to understand broader political transformations, arguing that in our contemporary globalized society, "liminal situations can facilitate understanding of the technologies used to shape identities and institutions" (2). Organizational theorists have explored how instances of liminality in institutional settings function as opportunities for new kinds of institutions to be formed (Tagliaventi). Accountability-based policies such as dual enrollment can also create pockets of liminality like these scholars have described. In a classroom setting that is *supposed to be college* but is *essentially high school*, the actual experience of learning is something not quite one or the other. This liminal space creates unique opportunities for teachers and students to put stress on accountability regimes.

Ms. Elliot's dual enrollment classroom resembled Turner's liminal world of "fruitful darkness," and it gave her wiggle room to think more kairotically about the needs of individual students and to question or even test the boundaries between college and high school when opportunities arose. Some of the best examples of this liminality are from the students' one-on-one conferencing sessions with Ms. Elliot, juxtaposed with the underlife of the students in the back of the room. In their first conferencing session early in the semester, for example, Ms. Elliot conferred with students about their first assignment, a literacy narrative. The conferencing sessions were done *in class*, and Ms. Elliot would simply call on each student to conference with her in the front of the room, while the other students worked on their papers in the back. The first student she met with was Joel. Ms. Elliot asked, "What are three questions, and what are three concerns?" But Joel did not have any response. Instead, he wanted to know what he needed to do to pass, and he did not seem interested in taking ownership of his essay. So Ms. Elliot asked him to read his paper out loud so that she could "interrupt" when needed. Periodically, she did interrupt, more than once asking him to "show, not tell" in his narrative. She guided Joel through structure and coherence, saying things like "You mention this here, but further down the page I don't see this again." Or "I thought you were talking about Harry Potter in the beginning, but now it seems you've switched to a different book." Other times she helped him with his ideas. "What idea are you trying to convey here?" she asked. "What's the goal of this paragraph?"

Next up was Dan. Ms. Elliot worked with Dan just as she had with Joel, interrupting as he read aloud to say things like "What do you want people to take from this part?" Or "How do you incorporate this idea into the body paragraphs later on?" Later, with Brian, Ms. Elliot said, "Some people don't know what this term is, so you need to spell it out." For Avery, who was one of the only students with questions about his paper (he wanted help getting "unstuck"), Ms. Elliot helped him open up a very traditional-looking five-paragraph essay about the ways that compulsory schooling stifles creativity. Ms. Elliot said to him, "you're starting off too general; you need to make it about *you*."

Meanwhile, at the other end of the room, students Corey and Karlie were reviewing each other's papers, and so were Ricky and Sara. I overheard Karlie say, "I need to redo my whole paper because I just found out what I'm going to write about!" Later I overheard Ricky say, "I need to put this on my blog—not my paper." And then Corey: "What can I do to make my paper better, Ricky?" After a while I heard a frustrated Karlie say, "I think I just don't have good ideas." At the front of the room, Nick, conferencing with Ms. Elliot, said, "I think mine is a mess, Ms. Elliot."

One-on-one conferences continued throughout the semester as the assignments progressed from narrative to argument to multimodal projects. Ms. Elliot's pedagogy was the kind that most composition instructors strive for: intensive written and oral feedback on student writing for every assignment. The students seemed to benefit from conferencing, but some struggled with this kind of attention. At one point during a revision session, Brian and Ms. Elliot conferenced over an argument paper. Brian's thesis was that lowering the unemployment rate will lower poverty. Rather than a claim about a problem backed with evidence, Brian's position was too simplistic, and he needed to go deeper. Dejected, Brian said, "So I have to start over?" Ms. Elliot responded that whatever he did, he would need to figure out how to make his claim more specific. She asked him, "What do you *want* to argue?" He responded timidly: "That we need to bring jobs back to America?" Ms. Elliot asked, "How? You need to argue how we make that happen." Brian did not say anything. As Ms. Elliot moved on to someone else's paper, Brian muttered to himself, "I want to go back to fifth-grade writing," and he got up and threw his draft into the trash can by the door.

The conferences just described reveal the complex ways that dual enrollment composition functioned at Midwest High as a liminal space. Ms. Elliot's one-on-one conferences with students were much like other first-year composition conferences. But doing it *in class*, for *every assignment*, was a pedagogical tool she could use thanks in large part to the kairos of the setting: the structure of the high school allowed for more one-on-one teaching opportunities. For high-achieving students like Nick, who needed help with idea development, to frustrated students like Karlie, who needed confidence, or struggling students like Brian, who lacked motivation, Ms. Elliot dedicated a lot of time to meeting their individual needs, while also granting significant downtime to non-conferencing students—time that led to meaningful investment in writing. Karlie, for example, who once said her paper "sucked," was able to read what her peers had written and discovered a paper topic in the process.

Ms. Elliot was not the only one who recognized the liminality of dual enrollment composition at Midwest High. Unconfident as a writer, Karlie nevertheless had a stellar high school transcript and list of extracurricular activities. She told me during our interview that she worked with Ms. Elliot one-on-one *all the time*: during class, at lunchtime, during study hall, and any other opportunities Ms. Elliot offered. "For one of the assignments," she said, "I did come to [Ms. Elliot] almost every day, and we reviewed it." Since Karlie was a senior who would be starting college in the fall, I asked her if she would feel comfortable next year going to her professors during office hours every day the way she went to see Ms. Elliot. She responded,

> Honestly, I [wouldn't]. I think it'll be different because I'm here [in high school] all day. Like, I would've seen [Ms. Elliot] in . . . study hall. But like, in college I'm sure I'll have my things going on, and [my professors] will have things going on, and I don't know if I'll go [to office hours] that often. But I'm hoping that this class is helping me to figure it out, and I won't need to do that.

Here, Karlie recognized the liminal space of dual enrollment composition. She knew Ms. Elliott would be around in study hall or in class to work one-on-one on her writing. She also speculated that once she got to the *real thing*, her professors might be too busy or too time constrained for such frequent meetings. So she saw Ms. Elliot's class as a kairotic opportunity to work on her writing so that she "won't need" to go to office hours once she gets to college. The concurrent enrollment classroom was a unique space for students like Karlie to learn *in between* high school and college. The students recognized this and tailored their educational experience in this composition class to help them work through stages of liminality.

Teacher and Students Made Micropolitical Decisions

To say that Ms. Elliot and her students recognized liminality and took advantage of it in how they approached the course is to imply that they were using dual enrollment policies *micropolitically*. In "The Micropolitics of Pathways: Teacher Education, Writing Assessment, and the Common Core," J. W. Hammond and Merideth Garcia document the "micropolitical work" of teachers, that is, the moves that educators make as they engage with various education reform initiatives in the classroom, particularly with regard to the Common Core State Standards (CCSS). Through in-depth interviews with nine high school teachers, Hammond and Garcia found that while their participants used the CCSS in their course planning, none used the standards in the same way, nor did they see the standards as a determining factor in shaping student pathways. "Instead," they write, "participants reported micropolitically interpreting and repurposing the CCSS—drawing strategically on the standards to supplement and support the local pathways they already had in mind for students." Just like Hammond and Garcia's participants, Ms. Elliot strategically interpreted dual enrollment policies to benefit her students in ways that she saw fit.

During my last observation, for example, Ms. Elliot introduced a multimodal rhetorical analysis assignment and showed Childish Gambino's music video for the song "This Is America" as an example of visual rhetoric. The video, which calls attention to issues of race and racial violence in America, is graphic but well suited for visual analysis in a college composition course. Later I asked Ms. Elliot if her principal might object to her showing the video in class since most of her students were still minors and some of the video was violent and graphic. She said no, because "this is a college classroom, not a high school classroom." Ms. Elliot decided that her role as a college instructor in this instance superseded her position as a high school teacher. And since Gambino's video *was* suitable for college-level student writers, she felt no qualms about showing it to the class. In her essay "Finding Freedom at the Composition Threshold: Learning from the Experiences of Dual Enrollment Teachers," Katie McWain describes concurrent enrollment high school teachers like Ms. Elliot as occupying a "liminal institutional positionality" where they are "hailed simultaneously as members of high school and college faculty accountable to both sides of the partnership"

(406). Ms. Elliot took advantage of this liminality to make pedagogical decisions on a micropolitical level—which undermines the prevailing policy arrangements of accountability regime policies like Ohio's CCP program, which demands sameness and efficient pathways through general education courses such as first-year composition.

During an observation before Thanksgiving break, Ms. Elliot used media again in a micropolitical way. She began class by discussing the students' final multimodal presentations and then showed a clip from HBO's political show *Last Week Tonight with John Oliver*. The clip was from one of his in-depth segments on income inequality, and in it he explains how American economic policies disproportionately benefit the richest people in America. The clip was educational but adult in nature, complete with curse words and off-color jokes—not something you often see in a high school class. After the clip ended, Ms. Elliot asked the students what they thought of it. Nick said it was "depressing." Dan said he was surprised to learn that so many Americans struggle economically while a few increase their obscene wealth. Ms. Elliot asked what the "call to action" was at the end of the segment. After a brief discussion Ms. Elliot then transitioned into a discussion of multimodality. Oliver's scripted delivery, interspersed with graphics, images, and video clips that enhanced his jokes, created an opportunity to discuss the role of images in argumentation. Here again Ms. Elliot was strategically harnessing the dual enrollment policy of Ohio. While in other instances she had used the high school setting to help her students transition from high school to college, here she leveraged dual enrollment policy to experiment with a pedagogical activity that would not suit traditional high school classrooms.

My interviews with students revealed that they too had made micropolitical decisions in navigating dual enrollment policies. For example, the students had varying motivations for signing up for dual enrollment and used the course for their own micropolitical needs. As Post et al. have written, powerful education reform interest groups, such as the National Governors Association, the Bill and Melinda Gates Foundation, the Partnership for 21st Century Skills, Achieve Inc., and others, all advocate for dual enrollment as a cost-saving mechanism for students and parents (167). But Ms. Elliot's students said that they took the class because they were "bored" with the traditional classes offered at the high school. Karlie told me that she took the class because she was "running out of classes to take here" and that dual enrollment was her only option. "I didn't want to just have a bunch of emptiness in my schedule," she said. "If I didn't want to take all electives, or just really show up for only what I need—then CCP was the [only] option." Andy told me that he took the class to challenge himself. For him, dual enrollment was "basically just an honors class. . . . That's why I like it." The fact that he would get college credit at the end was "just the cherry on top," he said. "I'm not taking it for college credit in high school. I'm taking it because it's a challenge for me." Nick said that he took the class because it was "good to get the experience of a college class before being thrown into [one]." In fact, he said, "I didn't even know it was worth college credit until like halfway through the semester. I'm just like, wait, this goes to my college degree?" Dan told me that he enrolled in dual enrollment to challenge himself because he had already taken all the advanced classes he could and felt bored in traditional English courses. Dual enrollment, though, despite the rule that it should be no different from a college classroom, was something unique: "I feel like with a CCP class it's still a high school class, just with the college credit, and it has slightly more [expectations], but I wouldn't say that it's overwhelming."

Two students I interviewed, Karlie and Dan, mentioned that getting college credit *was* something they considered. Karlie told me that her parents attended an informational seminar on earning college credit and factored that into their decision to enroll her in the course. Dan told me that he remembered a presentation on CCP in the auditorium one fall. For Dan, getting college credit while in high school was one motivating factor; he wanted to "get these lower-level classes out of the way and then take something more geared toward what I want to do with the semester hours that I get for free there."

The students' replies reveal that they were taking a dual enrollment course for different reasons. Dan and Karlie's interest in earning college credit aligns with the commonsense policy paradigms touted by dual enrollment policymakers in Ohio. Others, however, expressed ambivalence toward getting college credit. The students' varying attitudes show us that the accountability regime policy paradigms that justify education reform initiatives like dual enrollment are *not stable*, and students who experience these policies bend them to fit their own needs, which sometimes differ, even if ambivalently, from the educational reform rationale.

Midwest High's Concurrent Enrollment Composition Class Consisted of High-Achieving White Students

The policy paradigm of dual enrollment in Ohio has it that the policy is good for everyone, that it fast-tracks students to the workforce and saves them money on college, and that the program is equitable because it is free and open to students across all demographics. As I mentioned earlier in the chapter, this is not the reality, however. In 2019, of the top high schools partnered with my university for CCP courses, only one of them was located in our local public school district. A majority of our partnerships are in the suburbs, where student demographics skew whiter, per-pupil spending is higher, and student achievement scores are better. Relying on policy paradigms that focus on cost-effectiveness and expediency thus comes at the expense of equity, access, and inclusion.

As an example, all of the students I interviewed at Midwest High were white and involved in multiple clubs, sports, and volunteering opportunities. Andy played football and belonged to multiple clubs and organizations. Nick was involved in drama, choir, and art lessons outside school. Dan was part of the International Club, football team, baseball team, basketball team, and he coached Little League. Karlie played volleyball, ran track, led a club that made care packages for veterans overseas, wrote for the newspaper and yearbook, met regularly with the National Honors Society and the International Club, and worked as the treasurer for Student Council. These impressive students were also all receiving college scholarships of some kind, and each reported that they received "good" grades. There were no students of color in Ms. Elliot's class, in keeping with student demographics at Midwest High. Schools nearer to my university with higher proportions of Black and Hispanic students have fewer dual enrollment opportunities with my university, thus limiting my university's interaction with more marginalized public school districts.

The students in Ms. Elliot's class may not be cognizant of these racial considerations in dual enrollment's policy arrangements. They have the privilege of seeing the policy as an opportunity to *get ahead.* Dan told me, for instance, that one of the reasons he signed up for the class was "to experience [college]." When faced with a choice between CCP and a traditional English class, he decided that dual enrollment was the better option because of his academic aptitude. "I know from my one normal class that I have," he said. "I'm just . . . a step above, and then I just sit there and I don't do anything." Dan felt that he was not being challenged in his "normal" English courses. The dual enrollment course taught by Ms. Elliot was a great opportunity to do something *advanced*. Nick gave a similar answer about wanting to challenge himself. As a high school writer, Nick said, "I knew how to write well . . . I could always write my papers in one go, no rough draft needed . . . because I knew everything a high school teacher was looking for." However, Nick said, "What [Ms. Elliot's class] is teaching me is what college professors are looking for when you write a paper, and that's going to be really useful, and it'll help my writing process later." For high-achieving white students at Midwest High, dual enrollment is a liminal space where they can work closely with a college mentor to transition from high school to college writing and where they can challenge themselves by going beyond traditional high school English coursework. For school districts closer to my university with higher proportions of Black and Brown students, though, there is no liminality because there are fewer opportunities.

This case study illustrates what the literature suggests: that dual enrollment policies primarily attract and benefit high-achieving white students, and, at least in Ohio, universities are economically incentivized to exclude districts with higher proportions of Black and Brown students. While it is true that my case study concerned one small class of students and their teacher, the specter of institutional racism overshadows the entire conversation about dual enrollment. It shapes the perceptions of students and teachers at Midwest High before they even sign up for the course.

Conclusion

"Why Wait for Your Future?" This is a question on some promotional literature for CCP in Ohio and represents how insidiously policy regimes of accountability are couched in commonsense rationalizations. When dual enrollment partnerships are interpreted through an accountability paradigm, it seems inevitable and natural to see them as a way to provide more options to students from all demographics, to reduce students' time and money spent attending college, and to better prepare them for their future (which means their ability to earn income after college). These rationalizations also reflect changing attitudes about the purpose of higher education—which is no longer a public good but an economic good, where things like choice, efficiency, and profit are markers of success, bolstered by a set of governing arrangements that bureaucratize policies on the ground and legitimize them in public discourse.

However, the way dual enrollment is experienced at Midwest High reveals that some teachers and students strategically interpret accountability regime policies in ways not bound to accountability logics, and they work in politically kairotic ways to put stress on the regime. First, the dynamic of college composition is fundamentally impacted by the embodied experience of *being in high school*, despite students' intellectual capacity to succeed in the course. Second, in addition to meeting first-year composition learning outcomes, the instructor used the high school setting to fashion pedagogical activities that helped students transition from high school to college. Third, these distinct efforts at *transition* were made possible thanks to the liminality of dual enrollment when the courses are taught in high schools. Ms. Elliot's class was neither high school nor college but was a space in between, where high-achieving college-bound students could practice college-level writing with a dedicated mentor. Fourth, the liminality was furthered thanks to Ms. Elliot's use of strategic micropolitical decisions regarding course content, which took advantage of the liminality of the course to meet student needs. And fifth, racial and socioeconomic homogeneity, both at Midwest High and in dual enrollment nationwide, are crucial factors to consider as we evaluate, implement, partner with, or put stress on dual enrollment policies at our home institutions. My participant observation research helps us see how one teacher grappled with accountability regime policies in her classroom and made kairotic choices to either implement or resist certain aspects of dual enrollment ideology and its policy arrangements as she saw fit.

My observations at Midwest High revealed a privileged space. The conferencing that Ms. Elliot did with her students, for example, while not all that different from how conferencing works at the college level, was nevertheless supported in a different way: frequent, in-class, one-on-one mentorship is a luxury of a concurrent enrollment partnership, a luxury that many college composition instructors with a four-four teaching load simply do not have. Also, for the students who struggled with the course at Midwest High, the concurrent enrollment space functioned as a safety net. Having a ten-person class and a familiar teacher deeply invested in the students' success was an asset to them. Moreover, the students saw dual enrollment as a unique opportunity to challenge themselves and to work intensely on their writing with a familiar teacher a year or two before they actually enrolled in college.

The experiences of Ms. Elliot's students contrast with those of students going to school in the racially segregated city a few miles away. Education policies like dual enrollment cater to and disproportionally benefit white students who are already high achievers. There are disproportionally fewer opportunities for dual enrollment in the majority Black and Brown schools closer to my university. These blatant disparities in our public education system need to factor significantly in how college composition instructors and administrators think about the partnerships they forge with secondary schools. In Ohio's accountability regime, which demands sameness and efficiency, couched in neoliberal narratives of cost savings and competition, schools with lower per-pupil spending and higher percentages of Black and Brown students get left out. How might their teachers and students benefit from the strategies that Ms. Elliot used in her dual enrollment classroom? What kinds of rhetorical strategies are their teachers and students *already using* to navigate accountability-based education reform initiatives? On the other hand, how might dual enrollment partnerships, if pursued at these schools, further marginalize and discriminate against more vulnerable student populations? More studies of the racial implications of accountability-based policies like dual enrollment need to be done in order to arrive at a better answer to these questions.

The case study of Midwest High illustrates that accountability-based policy regimes of education reform can be reshaped not just at an ideological level but also at a bureaucratic level. Writing studies has traditionally participated in policy discussions through its professional organizations. NCTE, as described in chapter 1, created a special Washington Task Force during the Carter and Reagan administrations to engage policy at the ideological level. The Task Force had some success in making a case to stakeholders for the value of English studies. Several decades later, NCTE worked in a similar way to attempt to participate in discussions about the Common Core's English language arts standards. NCTE's efforts there took the form of pushing back against ideologies of high-stakes testing by making consistent appeals to disciplinary expertise. At the classroom level, though, writing practitioners—and here I include high school English teachers such as Ms. Elliot—engage in the same kinds of fights but do so on a bureaucratic front. On its surface,

Ms. Elliot's work may not seem compatible with NCTE's efforts at effecting education policy, yet Ms. Elliot's classroom pedagogy is still a significant part of what policy engagement looks like in our field. Our institutions, and our individual teachers, can and do work in politically kairotic ways by finding right times, opportunities, and spaces to chip away at prevailing paradigms, imagine new possibilities, or forge new political arrangements. Taking stock of these factors is necessary for writing studies to imagine newer, more creative ways to put stress on policy regimes of accountability.

This case study could help the field better understand how to collaborate with dual enrollment instructors like Ms. Elliot, who engages with policy regimes of accountability on the ground every day. It might also help us consider how concepts like liminality and micropolitical pedagogies could play out in other kinds of classrooms, the ones now left out of dual enrollment partnerships in Ohio. As administrators, part of our future efforts should be making connections with students, teachers, and administrators in the most vulnerable school districts, to see what kinds of partnerships work best for their students, whether dual enrollment or otherwise. That is not to say that if dual enrollment in Ohio were more equitable across racial demographics, then it would be good policy. Ohio's current version of dual enrollment would still be bad policy. To argue that we should consider districts left out of accountability-based dual enrollment mandates in Ohio is also to argue that we should work harder to be more inclusive in how we deal with and experience policy; we should constantly search for apt times, places, and spaces to put stress on oppressive policy regimes. Sometimes this might take the form of forging coalitions with secondary teachers to understand the impacts of policy at our schools and universities. Other times it might mean considering how and when it is appropriate to lend expertise or power to advocate for our shared interests, or even observing, promoting, training, or working alongside a range of public school districts, not just ones that have more "college-ready" or high-achieving white students. From this angle, here on the ground, we see the intersections of education policy and college composition more clearly, especially the kairotic ways that teachers and students across all levels of education work with, question, or resist policy regimes.

CHAPTER 5

Politically Kairotic Approaches to Effecting Accountability-Based Literacy Policies

As I write today in the summer of 2019, Betsy DeVos is secretary of education. Currently, she, along with the current presidential administration, is working to advance one of the most conservative education agendas ever seen in the United States. Her appointment to the cabinet is in line with the power arrangements of accountability regime policy that were put in place over the past several decades. These power arrangements give billionaires, businesspeople, philanthropists, and political donors more and more ethos to make policy decisions, all while giving academic experts in disciplines less and less. However, DeVos is unique, Kaplan and Owings point out, in that she never served in government before her current post, nor did she ever work as a school administrator or teacher. What is more, neither she nor her children attended public schools (58). DeVos was also a controversial appointment to the position because of her vocal commitment to so-called school choice, which plays on conservative talking points from the 1950s and '60s about parents needing to have the *choice* of whether to send their children to integrated schools. For DeVos, the choice is cast differently—whether or not children must attend the public school in the district where they reside—but the racial connotations remain (Epps-Robertson; Suitts).

DeVos holds other controversial stances as well. In the past she has vocalized her support for massive cuts to education (Meckler), for bigger incentives to charter schools (Green, "DeVos Backs $5 Billion"), for deregulation of for-profit colleges (Green, "DeVos Ends Obama-Era Safeguards"), and for lessening restrictions on student loan companies (Stratford). Due to extensive conflicts of interest, some speculate that she personally profits from these policy positions (Schwartz and Schoen). DeVos's positions tend to accord with accountability regime paradigms that frame public education, and public discourse about public education, as broken. As Kaplan and Owings write, these policy paradigms infiltrate the public imagination through "conservative think tanks and foundations' well resourced, skillful, and persistent criticisms of 'big government' and the public schools' 'establishment' in op-ed columns and research reports that champion school choice"; this discourse ultimately persuades "editorial boards, citizens and policy makers of school choice's benefits" (59). As Wilson reminds us, policy regimes are perpetuated thanks to policy paradigms that ideologically frame policy solutions as natural and inevitable, much like the proponents of school choice do. Policy paradigms—in their images and the public circulation of discourse in books, magazines, journal articles, and research reports—frame "ways of seeing, talking, and defining" education policy, which in turn "shape policy solutions" (258).

However, DeVos's education agenda, and her place in the policy arrangements of the current regime, resembles something a little different from the accountability regime politics of prior administrations. In this late-stage political arrangement of the accountability regime, DeVos's education agenda, in its ardent support of school vouchers, school choice, and defunding initiatives, is more concretely focused on *deregulation* than on accountability (Zeppos and Wallach). And as sympathetic states like Alaska follow DeVos's leadership with shocking maneuvers like that of Governor Mike Dunleavy, who once proposed slashing the state's education budget by 41 percent (Hazelrigg), we begin to see a fuller picture of the ways a *deregulatory* accountability regime might impact secondary and postsecondary education for generations to come.

Reflecting on the path charted from the outset of this book, readers may wonder how considering education policy problems in writing studies from a regime perspective can be most useful to writing studies scholars, teachers, and administrators in the era of accountability and deregulatory education politics. How can we use regime theory to do something new or think differently about how to effect education policies related to literacy, writing, and writing instruction? What I have tried to make clear through each case study—whether in analyzing NCTE's work in early 1980s to lobby Congress or its efforts decades later to provide feedback on the Common Core or in analyzing the current policies of dual enrollment in Ohio—is that we need a politically *kairotic orientation* toward accountability regime policies. Kairotic political engagement strategies, whereby institutions and individuals take stock of the policy arrangements, power arrangements, and policy paradigms in their own contexts, can help teachers and professional organizations find opportune moments to put *stress* on regime structures. As Wilson tells us, stressors are factors that enable change within a policy regime by weakening the regime over time: they can work through discourse to challenge the credibility of prevailing policy paradigms so that the public loses trust in their legitimacy (260–63); stressors can also take the form of shifts in the power arrangements or even changes in the people who implement policy (264). Analyzing our professional institutions that represent the interests of writing studies or the individual teachers who implement writing policy on the ground are helpful ways to imagine new kairotic orientations toward accountability regime policies in our own contexts.

Taking a look at the changing role of the federal government in education, starting with the Reagan administration, which gradually supplanted the equity regime of the 1950s and '60s with a new policy regime centered on accountability, shows us just how durable accountability regime policies have been over time. The Reagan administration's policies outlasted Reagan himself, and we can trace the policies promoted by *A Nation at Risk* in 1983 straight to No Child Left Behind Act in 2001, straight to the Common Core, straight to dual enrollment, and finally to Secretary DeVos's office, which couches dual enrollment in terms of school choice and steers competitive grants to schools that expand their dual enrollment programs (Klein). Policy regimes are not bound by presidential administrations, nor do they impact only the students and teachers in one particular social and political context. A policy regime can shape the educational experiences of their children, and their children's children. And more than that, the varying scopic levels of analysis in this book—from the ways that NCTE worked institutionally to engage in policy work to the ways that Ms. Elliot worked micropolitically in her concurrent enrollment classroom to navigate policy—all shed light on the diverse ways that policy shapes the disciplinary work of writing studies, as well as the ways that institutions and individuals can effect education policy. Now, thirty-six years after *A Nation at Risk*, we see that Reagan's policy is alive and well, and policy regimes of education reform still structure how the government sees its role in education and whether it values the disciplinary knowledge of writing experts.

Understanding how the field *has been* and *could be* working to put stress on accountability regimes in a range of politically kairotic ways is something our field needs to take incredibly seriously if we want to effect education policy moving forward. At this point one pressing question is how we might grapple with the lessons of accountability and take stock of the ways *deregulation* will impact education policies for the foreseeable future. How can writing studies, a discipline primarily interested in writing's "production, its circulation, its uses, its role in the development of individuals, societies, and cultures" (Bazerman 32), put stress on this policy regime's governing arrangements?

This is a big question, and answering it depends on the context of power, privilege, and politics in which each of us works. Instead of suggesting specific strategies, I have identified key moments of kairotic political engagement within a policy regime framework to show how institutions and individuals have attempted to put stress on accountability regimes at different times with varying degrees of success—and sometimes failure, though even failure can be productive. This book, in other words, is a meditation on the ways that policy regimes of education reform have impacted those of us concerned with writing and literacy, from the institutional perspective of our professional organizations to the individual experiences of instructors tasked with carrying out policies of reform in their classrooms. A kairotic political orientation, and the examples of others in our field's history, might help us better anticipate new problems before they arise or seek out new ways to collaborate in K–16 education as we research, teach, and administer writing programs in today's political climate.

One key takeaway is that *policy regime* studies offer useful theoretical and methodological perspectives for examining the policies that impact writing. Moving beyond merely studying the implementation of policies, or critiquing an individual policy, regime theory helps us think more broadly about how policies are shaped by a variety of governing arrangements, such as the power alignments of stakeholders, the policy paradigm that justifies policies ideologically, and the bureaucratic arrangements of a particular policy. This approach to policy is concerned not only with getting a seat at the table or becoming public intellectuals but also with purposeful, multiscopic interventions, from the institutional level to individual classrooms.

As a second takeaway from an institutional perspective, I argued that academic disciplines can play a key role in effecting education policies through their professional organizations. However, in an accountability regime, especially in the current phase favoring deregulation, the contributions that professional organizations have historically made may not be as effective as they once were. As I showed through a study of NCTE's policy engagement activities historically, the 1950s and '60s were the era of an equity regime, which comprised a variety of governing arrangements that saw the government's role in education as providing equal opportunities to students in poverty. Primarily, the government promoted equity by distributing funding to districts designated the most *in need*, and groups like NCTE contributed to policy by lobbying Congress for a portion of those funds, often, as Mason has shown, by framing the government's interests as being in line with NCTE's own. Starting in the late 1970s, NCTE's Washington Task Force continued advocating for the importance of English as the federal government's role in education intensified. Task Force members testified at congressional hearings, collaborated with other education reform stakeholders, and courted Senator George McGovern and others.

But by the end of President Carter's only term in office, the rise of the New Right ushered in a regime change to education policies, which drew on a rhetoric of crisis to assert that the government should ensure equity in education not simply by doling out money but by holding schools and teachers accountable for the material their students learn. Holding them accountable, the argument goes, will increase student achievement, train future workers who are competent, and allow America to compete with economies across the globe. This was a new approach to education, one that completely changed how an institution like NCTE was seen by those in power. As I showed in chapter 1, by 1984 the Washington Task Force, once a fairly prominent group of literacy lobbyists, was unable to cultivate relationships like they had grown accustomed to, and they eventually disbanded when Reagan secured his second term. This tells us that how institutions engage in policy formation is bound up in the prevailing policy regimes of education reform. What used to be an effective way to participate in education policy formation during the equity regime was no longer a serviceable strategy. If we want our institutions to participate in effecting education policy in any meaningful way, then NCTE needs to find engagement strategies that are consistent with the current governing arrangements. NCTE had perhaps once taken for granted that its disciplinary expertise was valued by those in power when determining appropriate funding. In the accountability regime, despite NCTE's critique of high-stakes standardized testing, school takeovers, and policies of efficiency, its efforts have often been ignored by powerful stakeholders.[1]

A third takeaway stems from the second: presuming that disciplinary expertise "fills in the gaps" for policymakers misunderstands that policy regimes are bound up as much in ideology as they are in nuts-and-bolts policy conversations. As I showed in chapter 2, almost three decades after the Washington Task Force dissolved, authors of the Common Core, one of the most important accountability reform initiatives since No Child Left Behind, asked NCTE for feedback on a draft of their English language arts standards. NCTE boldly came to the table with a scathing indictment of the standards, complete with an extensive reference list to display its scholarly ethos. But these negotiations, it seemed, were not conducted in good faith, and the Common Core authors did not take the advice of NCTE, even though they used NCTE's participation as a rubber-stamped endorsement of the standards and thus left a sour taste in the mouths of many who participated. From a policy regime perspective, this case reveals that in an equity regime, such tactics *may* have worked (since the government generally relied on institutions like NCTE for guidance on how to spend the Department of Education's money). But in an accountability regime, not only is disciplinary knowledge undervalued; it is often seen as irrelevant to the decision-making process. Where NCTE primarily came up short was its inability to cultivate the ethos necessary for maintaining a relationship with powerful policy stakeholders in order to gain influence in policy discussions. Or, to quote from Webber, in a paradigm where *competition* is the policymaking currency, NCTE was unable to "*make* our expertise competitive" (12).

A fourth takeaway: as we grapple with education policies right now that stand to change the way we teach writing and administer writing programs, policy regime theory can help us disentangle the power arrangements, unpack the ideological elements that are seen as natural and inevitable, and decide for ourselves what resources we have at our disposal and where the rhetorical windows open up from time to time that allow us to play a role in effecting policy. In chapter 3, I analyzed the rise of dual enrollment policies nationwide and specifically in the state of Ohio, which is a hotbed for accountability policies in the country. I argued that we have to look at the ideological narratives that frame dual enrollment policies as natural and inevitable answers to policy problems in order to better understand both how dual enrollment works and how it fits into a policy regime—and to learn where we can find the kairotic moments to put stress on the regime's legitimacy. So, for instance, narratives circulating about dual enrollment hold that it is a commonsense way to reduce students' and parents' costs for education, decrease time-to-degree, and grant students a choice in where they transfer their credits. This boils down to a fundamental principle of the accountability regime: that education is an economic good. The policy paradigm undergirding dual enrollment is hard to shake: How could you be against saving money? Why would you not want more choice in how our nation's students attain their degrees? Why would you not want students to get ahead?

My analysis made clear that the ideology of accountability attends to facts and evidence selectively and partially. Studies calling into question the efficacy of dual enrollment—such as Moreland's questioning of whether "'all students' [have] an opportunity to advance in DE [dual enrollment] courses regardless of race, gender, socioeconomic class, language backgrounds, and other widely varied subjectivities" ("Chasing Transparency" 194)—are unpersuasive to the powerful stakeholders advocating these policies. In Ohio, for instance, despite the lack of rigorous empirical evidence of dual enrollment's success, we went from roughly 14,000 dual-enrolled students in 2014 to more than 70,000 in 2018. The express goal for College Credit Plus was growing the dual enrollment population, almost as if it were a company whose main goals are growth and scale at the expense of making a quality product. But students are not shareholders. Schools are not companies. Powerful interest groups like the Bill and Melinda Gates Foundation and testing companies that tout the economic benefits of dual enrollment neglect to mention that, in places like Ohio, these policies work to *deprofessionalize* so-called low-level courses such as college writing. It will come as no surprise when we begin to see fewer sections of composition and lower enrollments in our departments as dual enrollment grows, especially if other states adopt Ohio's model of using mandates to open up dual enrollment to more and more high school students.

One mistaken conclusion we in writing studies might take from this analysis is to set up a false dichotomy between equity and accountability. The accountability regime pervades public education in the United States, and we have no choice but to comply with its legislative mandates, or at the very least we are compelled, whether we like it or not, to work within its structures. But we can put stress on areas that do not align with our values as a discipline. It is important also to point out that accountability logics do not reject equity. In fact, what makes accountability policy paradigms so insidious is the way they characterize economic policies as natural and inevitable means to realizing equity. Legislative mandates that ensure transparency and require data-collection protocols that monitor whether the policy is being implemented correctly are couched in terms of achieving greater *access* for students and achieving more *fairness* for participants in the program. In these ways, we are recruited into implementing accountability regime policy. Data collection in and of itself is not a bad thing—in fact, I believe that the more data writing program administrators can wield in their collaborations with K–12 instructors, principals, deans, provosts, or even policymakers at the state and federal levels, the better we can understand how our own contexts fit into the broader political discourse. Nevertheless, mandatory managerial imperatives to collect and report data serve the interests of the political arrangements of an accountability policy paradigm. As I argued in chapter 2, data as a concept is not necessarily an objective means for filling knowledge gaps. Data can be wielded rhetorically and in specific ideological ways.

Another mistake we should avoid making from a regime perspective is to set up an antagonistic relationship between scholars and teachers of college writing and teachers of writing in high schools. In chapter 4, I described the participant observation research I conducted over a semester in a concurrent enrollment classroom. By sitting in on Ms. Elliot's first-year composition course, I sought to bring the research for this book full circle: to move from questions about what the field does institutionally to participate in policy discussions, to how folks who experience policies directly work with them in class. Ms. Elliot was a great teacher who dutifully worked with her students to meet my institution's composition learning outcomes. While her graduate degree was not in rhetoric and composition, she received some training in my university's composition program and works with my department on continuing education and professional development, and I am confident in her abilities as an instructor. I consider her a valued colleague. The students were great, too. Inquisitive, dedicated, and ambitious, they seemed like any other college composition student any number of us encounter in our sections each semester.

However, I did find that the concurrent enrollment composition classroom differed dramatically from how composition is normally taught on my campus. From the embodied experience of this course when taught in a high school, to the curricular orientation toward transitioning students from high school to college, to the liminality that the transition created in the classroom, to Ms. Elliot's micropolitical moves as she navigated policy mandates, and to the racial and socioeconomic homogeneity of the class—these issues show us that, at least in this instance, there is something different going on in college writing taught in dual enrollment courses. And while many of those differences are not bad *per se*, they are nevertheless things we have not been paying enough attention to as a field, and they matter when we are discussing the kairotic ways we can collaborate with K–12 leaders to effect education policy.

How might we better pay attention to how concurrent enrollment classes differ from traditionally enrolled composition courses? For one, each of the characteristics I mentioned above needs to be taken into consideration in the context of the vast educational inequality that pervades our nation's K–12 schools. Whether in terms of academic achievement, graduation rates, punitive sanctions, or even the rate at which students of color are recommended for gifted programs compared with their white peers (Weir), a mountain of evidence shows how truly discriminatory current K–12 educational policies are for Black and Brown students. In fact, educational researchers are beginning to identify a "new racism" in K–12 policies that are couched in "racism-neutral" or "racism-evasive" rhetoric (Kohli et al.). And these disparities certainly do not go away when students enter college-level writing classrooms (Sanchez and Branson). As I argued at the end of chapter 4, students at Midwest High seem to be doing fine, and the education they receive in concurrent enrollment seems more or less to meet the goals of the composition program at my university.

But Midwest High is over 80 percent white and more or less middle class. In schools with lower per-pupil funding, or higher turnover rates for instructors, or more Black and Brown students, how might accountability logics that demand sameness and efficiency impact students' day-to-day experiences with policy? In Ohio, where funding for dual enrollment involves moving funds from public schools to public universities at a discounted rate, how might that impact districts already struggling with strained budgets? Moreover, as high-achieving concurrent enrollment students are siphoned off more and more from their high school classmates thanks to dual enrollment mandates, how might that affect district report cards and teacher experiences with English language arts in K–12? As our field continues to research how policy regimes of accountability impact the day-to-day experiences of teachers and students, these kinds of questions are going to be crucial as we decide on the best opportunities—the when, how, and the reasoning for—forging partnerships with secondary school districts. And in states like Ohio where dual enrollment partnerships are mandated, the question is how to forge ahead, often against our best interests, with integrity and according to best practices.

Finally, we need to value and learn from the histories and experiences of writing in K–12 contexts, where the work of bridging, partnering, advocating, and responding to policy is most visible. More and more scholars in our field are taking this route, adopting what some call a K–16 approach to studying rhetorics of education reform. The collection edited by Patricia L. Stock, *Composition's Roots in English Education*, which includes Cathy Fleischer's "A Case for Collaboration," pushes the field to consider the ways writing studies is embedded in the intersections of secondary and postsecondary education. More recently, Amy Lueck, in *A Shared History: Writing in the High School, College, and University*, argues for the historical significance of high school for rhetoric and composition pedagogy. Candice Epps-Robertson, in *Resisting Brown: Race, Literacy, and Citizenship in the Heart of Virginia*, draws from archival research to show how K–12 Black educators in Virginia's Prince Edward County established the Prince Edward County Free School Association after the county's board of supervisors opted to close all of their public schools rather than integrate after *Brown v. Board of Education.* In a similar vein, Carmen Kynard's book *Vernacular Insurrections: Race, Black Protest, and the New Century in Composition-Literacies Studies* describes various Black freedom movements as a series of "vernacular insurrections" of crucial importance to the field of composition. Kynard frames her work to include secondary and postsecondary contexts; "if you are serious about the research related to the histories, language policies, social contexts, and critical literacies and lives of students of color," she writes, "then you cannot afford to rest yourself solely in the scholarship and theories of college classrooms" (12). And, as I have cited elsewhere in this book, Joanne Addison and Sharon James McGee have written eloquently in *Writing and School Reform: Writing Instruction in the Age of Common Core and Standardized Testing* about how testing and accountability have impacted the way writing is taught from high school to college. In edited collections, Lori Ostergaard and Henrietta Rix Wood's *In the Archives of Composition: Writing and Rhetoric in High Schools and Normal Schools* and Thomas C. Thompson's *Teaching Writing in High Schools and College: Conversations and Collaborations*, contributors analyze the influence of secondary schooling on the history of rhetoric and composition and offer examples of effective secondary-postsecondary partnerships. Considering our current political climate, in which accountability-based policy regimes continue to shape the ideological prism through which education reform is viewed, this kind of work is the future of the field of writing studies.

But we need more analyses of how individual teachers enact policy in their classrooms and more narratives of teachers resisting policy regimes. We need more studies of how students transition from high school writing to college writing in the accountability era. We need more histories that situate the role of the high school in the field of writing studies. We need more archival work that uncovers how political forces impact the ways our institutions effect education policies. We need more studies of how accountability-based literacy policies affect school districts with majority Black and Brown students and more work from the perspective of writing program administrators on programmatic approaches to antiracist writing policies. In this book, my goal was to understand how our institutions participated in policy discussions historically and how teachers deal with accountability policies in their classrooms. While I chose as case studies the Washington Task Force, the Common Core, and dual enrollment in Ohio, there are other avenues to highlight. Ryan Skinnell's work on accreditation and federal funding, or Scott Wible's work on CCCC's language policies such as "Students' Right to Their Own Language," represent other places to study how policy regimes produce consequences for our institutions and classrooms.

I hope my book revealed that NCTE *has* at times played a key role in the deliberation on and formation of education policy. Contrary to complaints about our field not having a seat at the table, in actuality, English studies has been active in literacy policies for more than a hundred years. At other times, though, particularly since the ascendance of the accountability regime, NCTE has not been as consequential to those discussions as we in writing studies had hoped, particularly as the disciplinary expertise of writing studies is valued less and less, in favor of business leaders and education think tanks that push the perspective of the accountability policy regime.

However, I argue that a politically kairotic approach, using a regime framework to disentangle the governing arrangements of policy problems in writing studies, can help us effect education policy across a range of situations. What I am suggesting is a new kind of institutional rhetoric that understands the impact of policy regimes on the various governing arrangements of policy problems. Whether it is learning more ethical ways to align our interests with the prevailing policy paradigm, inserting ourselves into power arrangements that matter in policy discussions through sustained relationship building, or working *the beat* by lobbying or crafting policies ourselves—our own institutions have to find new ways to bring our disciplinary knowledge to bear on policy problems that impact writing teachers.

And I also argue that we will not be able to accomplish this task without looking at how individual teachers navigate policy. Accountability policies directly impacted Ms. Elliot's work as a writing instructor, yet she nevertheless asserted agency in her classroom when the right moment arose. And a fruitful postsecondary partnership with my composition program supports and guides Ms. Elliot in her work at helping students cross the threshold into college. This leads me to wonder whether there are ways we can provide the same opportunities for *all of our students*, not just high-achieving white students in suburban high schools. Teachers' experiences, in addition to the experiences of their students, matter. They are the ones who navigate the policy decisions made by bureaucrats and think tanks, and their tactics on the ground can help us imagine best practices at the institutional level. Students and teachers put human faces on policy discussions, which is vital in an accountability regime obsessed with metrics of success and not with faces of student writers. I hope that by coordinating the institutional and the experiential components of policy, our field can use these insights to effect education policy in more creative ways and better represent our disciplinary knowledge, whether in front of Congress or in front of a class.

NOTES

WORKS CITED

INDEX

NOTES

1. Regime Change: An Overview of NCTE's Policy Advocacy from ESEA to A Nation at Risk

1. Unlike MLA, which was concerned with training its members in linguistics and textual analysis, Lindemann writes, NCTE had to deal with state licensure requirements that control the certification of public school teachers. As the federal government began to oversee more and more state and local education policies, public school teachers found themselves "resisting and attempting to work with agencies over which they have little influence" in order to have a stake in defining "the K–12 curriculum and how it should be taught" (523).
2. I had wanted to spend much longer in the archives, but the archivist pointed out that many records pertaining to recent education initiatives like the Common Core, the subject of chapter 2, still lie in desk drawers and in three-ring binders or in email inboxes and on thumb drives, yet to be donated or even viewed as worthy of archival preservation.

2. NCTE's Critique of the Draft of the Common Core English Language Arts Standards

1. Joanne Addison's thorough history of the CCSS maps out the vast professional networks responsible for drafting and implementing the standards. Of particular importance were two players: Gene Wilhoit, former executive director of the Council of Chief State School Officers, and David Coleman, current head of the College Board, the company responsible for writing and administering the SAT. In 2008, Addison says, the two men pitched the idea of a common set of standards for all K–12 students to philanthropist Bill Gates, who then agreed to become a primary investor through his Gates Foundation. The Council of Chief State School Officers, which describes itself as a "nonpartisan, nationwide, nonprofit organization of public officials who head departments of

elementary and secondary education in the United States" ("About Us"), accepted over $14.6 million from the Gates Foundation between 2009 and 2013 to develop the Common Core standards ("Awarded Grants" [CCSSO]). The National Governors Association, which, according to its mission statement, is a "bipartisan organization of the nation's governors [who] share best practices, speak with a collective voice on national policy and develop innovative solutions that improve state government and support the principles of federalism" ("About"), received $2.1 million from the Gates Foundation to develop the Common Core standards between and 2009 and 2013 ("Awarded Grants" [NGA]).

2. Minnesota formally adopted the ELA standards but not the mathematics standards. Many other states have voted to delay the implementation of the standards and/or have legislation pending that delays, repeals, or otherwise defunds the standards, although technically they are still counted among the states having formally adopted the Common Core.
3. Achieve Inc. describes itself as "an independent, nonpartisan, nonprofit education reform organization dedicated to working with states to raise academic standards and graduation requirements, improve assessments, and strengthen accountability" ("About Us"). The Gates Foundation has given a total of $23 million to Achieve since its inception in 1996 ("Awarded Grants" [Achieve Inc.). The chairs of Achieve, a handful of CEOs and governors, served on several Common Core feedback groups in addition to serving as project managers for the Partnership for Assessment of Readiness for College and Careers, one of two assessment firms in charge of administering assessment for the Common Core standards. For more information, Truthout published an illuminating article and infographic detailing the Common Core's myriad corporate connections (Bernd).
4. NCTE's critique of the July Draft was actually published in September 2009 due to an embargo on the early draft of the ELA standards. This means that all I have to analyze is NCTE's critique of the July Draft and the final version of the ELA standards, which came out in fall 2009. Although I cannot look at the early draft itself, I can compare the critique of that draft to the final version sent to the states.
5. The citations in NCTE's critique all refer to prestigious scholarly journals or books: *Education Policy Analysis Archives* (Amrein and Berliner); *Research in the Teaching of English* (Anagnostopoulos; Ketter and Pool); *Anthropology and Education Quarterly* (Valli and Chambliss); George Hillocks's 2002 influential monograph *The Testing Trap: How State Writing Assessments Control Learning*; and Linda McNeil's 2000

monograph *Contradictions of School Reform: Educational Costs of Standardized Testing.*

6. Here the academic evidence comes from the *American Educational Research Journal* (Booher-Jennings); *Educational Evaluation and Policy Analysis* (Roderick, Jacob, and Bryk); and Angela Valenzuela's scholarly monograph *Leaving Children Behind: How "Texas-Style" Accountability Fails Latino Youth.*
7. Here the academic evidence comes from Kathleen Blake Yancey's "Literacy Demands of Entering the University" and Ann Beaufort's "Preparing Adolescents for the Literacy Demands of the 21st-Century Workplace," both from the *Handbook of Adolescent Literacy.*
8. The citations in this section come from prestigious journals and respected books: *Reading Research Quarterly* (Lee); *Scientific Studies of Reading* (Schraw and Bruning); a chapter from Alvermann, Unrau, and Ruddell's edited collection *Theoretical Models and Processes of Reading* (Rumelhart); and monographs like Paulo Freire and Donaldo Macedo's *Literacy: Reading the Word and the World*; Louise M. Rosenblatt's *The Reader, the Text, the Poem: The Transactional Theory of the Literary Work*; and Teun A. van Dijk and Walker Kintsch's *Strategies of Discourse Comprehension.*
9. NCTE's critiques continue line by line: rejecting the dichotomy of informational and literary texts, offering to change the phrase "determine the main idea" to "interpret for main ideas" (8), critiquing the fiction/nonfiction divide (8); challenging a characterization of writing as a solitary activity (9), and faulting the lack of attention paid to multiple modalities and genres (14).
10. In an appendix titled "Research Supporting Key Elements of the Standards," the authors cite Marilyn Jager Adams's "The Challenge of Advanced Texts" from the edited collection *Reading More, Reading Better: Are American Students Reading Enough of the Right Stuff?* and a study on the decline of SAT verbal scores from the *American Educational Research Journal* (Hayes, Wolfer, and Wolfe).
11. Also, grades nine to ten and eleven to twelve are coupled together as "bands," whereas the other grades are outlined specifically in the ELA standards.
12. This concern is seen in many NCTE position statements, notably in "NCTE Definition of 21st Century Literacies," which defines literacy as "multiple, dynamic, and malleable."
13. See Carol Weiss's work in public policy: "Research for Policy's Sake: The Enlightenment Function of Social Research" in *Policy Analysis* and

"The Many Meanings of Research Utilization" in *Public Administration Review*.

14. Hesse's other suggestion is that writing studies scholars should start publishing more empirical research (13), which aligns with Huot's call for better validity arguments. My own view is that empirical research would allow for more sustained engagement with establishment groups.

3. An Analysis of Dual Enrollment Policy from a Regime Perspective

1. Though Blanco et al. are using mostly information from 1998–2004, they do have limited data from 2003–2006 pieced together from the Ohio Department of Education and the Ohio Board of Regents (18).

4. Experiencing Policy on the Ground: A Case Study of Midwest High

1. I should mention that the State of Ohio distributes payments to universities participating in CCP. In fiscal year 2020, my university received over $420,000 in payments. But these payments do not guarantee that universities will offset their revenue losses or maintain ongoing profits because budgets and the "State Share of Instruction" numbers change from year to year ("FY2020 College Credit Plus Payment Report").
2. This is not to say that my university does not have a partnership with the public school district nearest the university. A formal partnership, though, does not necessarily mean there are always going to be dual enrollment courses taught at any of the district's public schools. In 2019, only one high school in the district had students enrolled in my university's dual enrollment courses.
3. I have refrained from citing the exact source of data for Midwest High in the interest of masking the school's identity; however, the website Ohio School Report Cards provides publicly available data about districts and individual schools across the state of Ohio.
4. For a moving portrayal of the starkness of these fault lines, see Johnathan Kozol's famous book *Savage Inequalities.*

5. Politically Kairotic Approaches to Effecting Accountability-Based Literacy Policies

1. This is not to imply that NCTE's policy advocacy simply stopped in 1984. On the contrary, NCTE remains involved in policy work today. The NCTE Executive Committee's 2019 policy recommendations have several important objectives at the federal and state levels for promoting

equity for all students in reading, writing, and literature ("2019 Policy Recommendations"). NCTE also holds its annual Virtual Leadership and Advocacy Summit in Washington, DC, where members can advocate for NCTE's recommended actions. NCTE also has a wealth of resources for educators interested in policy implementation and analysis state by state.

WORKS CITED

"About." *National Governors Association*, https://www.nga.org/about/. Accessed 16 Sept. 2019.

"About Achieve." *Achieve*, 20 Dec. 2011, https://www.achieve.org/about-us.

"About the Standards." *Common Core State Standards Initiative*, www.corestandards.org/about-the-standards.

"About Us." *Council of Chief State School Officers*, https://ccsso.org/about. Accessed 16 Sept. 2019.

"About Us." *NCTE*, https://www2.ncte.org/about/. Accessed 11 Sept. 2019.

Addison, Joanne. "Shifting the Locus of Control: Why the Common Core State Standards and Emerging Standardized Tests May Reshape College Writing Classrooms." *Journal of Writing Assessment*, vol. 8, no. 1, 2015.

Addison, Joanne, and Sharon James McGee. *Writing and School Reform: Writing Instruction in the Age of Common Core and Standardized Testing*. WAC Clearinghouse / UP of Colorado, 2017.

Adler-Kassner, Linda. *The Activist WPA: Changing Stories about Writing and Writers*. Utah State UP, 2008.

———. "The Companies We Keep *or* The Companies We Would Like to Try to Keep: Strategies and Tactics in Challenging Times." *WPA: Writing Program Administration*, vol. 36, no. 1, pp. 119–40.

Adler-Kassner, Linda, and Susanmarie Harrington. "Responsibility and Composition's Future in the Twenty-First Century: Reframing 'Accountability.'" *College Composition and Communication*, vol. 62, no. 1, 2010, pp. 73–99.

Adler-Kassner, Linda, and Peggy O'Neill. *Reframing Writing Assessment to Improve Teaching and Learning*. Utah State UP, 2010.

Adler-Kassner, Linda, and Elizabeth A. Wardle, editors. *Naming What We Know: Threshold Concepts of Writing Studies*. Utah State UP, 2015.

Ahola, Janice, and Barry G. Lucas. "Participant Observation in Educational Research: Dynamics of Role Adjustment in a High School Setting." *McGill Journal of Education*, vol. 16, no. 1, 1981, http://mje.mcgill.ca/article/view/7382.

Allen, Drew. *Dual Enrollment: A Comprehensive Literature Review and Bibliography*. CUNY Collaborative Programs Office of Academic Affairs, 2010, https://nacep.org/docs/briefs/Allen%20(2010).pdf.

An, Brian P. "The Impact of Dual Enrollment on College Degree Attainment: Do Low-SES Students Benefit?" *Educational Evaluation and Policy Analysis*, vol. 35, no. 1, Mar. 2013, pp. 57–75, doi:10.3102/0162373712461933.

Annual Report 1964. NCTE Archives, Record Series 15/70/2, Box 2.

Annual Report 1981. NCTE Archives, Record Series 15/70/2, Box 2.

Annual Report 1982. NCTE Archives, Record Series 15/70/2, Box 2.

Applebee, Arthur N. "Common Core State Standards: The Promise and the Peril in a National Palimpsest." *English Journal*, vol. 103, no. 1, 2013, pp. 25–33.

"Attainment Goal 2025." *Ohio Department of Higher Education*, 2017, https://www.ohiohighered.org/attainment.

Aulbach, Carol. "The Committee of Ten: Ghosts Who Still Haunt Us." *English Journal*, vol. 83, no. 3, 1994, pp. 16–17.

"Awarded Grants" [Achieve Inc.]. *Bill & Melinda Gates Foundation*, https://www.gatesfoundation.org/about/committed-grants?q=%22achieve%2C%20inc.%22#jump-nav-anchor0.

"Awarded Grants" [CCSSO]. *Bill & Melinda Gates Foundation*, https://www.gatesfoundation.org/How-We-Work/Quick-Links/Grants-Database#q/k=council%200f%20chief%20state%20school%200fficers.

"Awarded Grants" [NGA]. *Bill & Melinda Gates Foundation*, https://www.gatesfoundation.org/How-We-Work/Quick-Links/Grants-Database#q/k=national%20governors%20association.

"Awards" [Race to the Top Fund]. *US Department of Education*, 17 May 2016, https://www2.ed.gov/programs/racetothetop/awards.html.

Bailey, Thomas, and Melinda Mechur Karp. *Promoting College Access and Success: A Review of Credit-Based Transition Programs*. US Department of Education, Office of Adult and Vocational Education, Nov. 2003.

Baron, Dennis. "No Students Left Behind: Why Reports on the Literacy Crisis from the Spellings Commission, the ACT, and the ETS Just Don't Read America's Literacy Right." *College Composition and Communication*, vol. 61, no. 1, 2009, pp. W424–35.

Bazerman, Charles. "The Case for Writing Studies as a Major Discipline." *Rhetoric and Composition as Intellectual Work*, edited by Gary A. Olson, Southern Illinois UP, 2002, pp. 32–38.

Becker, Howard S., and Blanche Geer. "Participant Observation and Interviewing: A Comparison." *Human Organization*, vol. 16, no. 3, 1957, pp. 28–32.

Beers, Kylene. *An Open Letter to NCTE Members about the Common Core State Standards. NCTE*, 17 Aug. 2009.

Behm, Nicholas N., et al., editors. *The Framework for Success in Postsecondary Writing: Scholarship and Applications*. Parlor Press, 2017.

Berlin, James A. *Rhetoric and Reality*. Southern Illinois UP, 1987.

Berliner, David C., and Bruce J. Biddle. *The Manufactured Crisis: Myths, Fraud, and the Attack on America's Public Schools*. Addison-Wesley, 1995.

Bernd, Candice. "Flow Chart Exposes Common Core's Myriad Corporate Connections." *Truthout*, 6 Sept. 2013, https://truthout.org/articles/flow-chart-exposes-common-cores-myriad-corporate-connections/.

Black, Nick. "Evidence Based Policy: Proceed with Care." *BMJ: British Medical Journal*, vol. 323, no. 7307, 2001, pp. 275–78.

Blanco, Cheryl, et al. *The Promise of Dual Enrollment: Assessing Ohio's Early College Access Policy*. Western Interstate Commission for Higher Education / KnowledgeWorks Foundation, 2007.

Blankenberger, Bob, et al. "Diverse Students, High School Factors, and Completion Agenda Goals: An Analysis of the Illinois Class of 2003." *Education and Urban Society*, vol. 49, no. 5, 2017, pp. 518–45.

Bomer, Randy, et al. *A Report of the NCTE Review Team on the July 2009 Draft of the Common Core English Language Arts State Standards. NCTE*, Sept. 2009.

Bordelon, Suzanne. *A Feminist Legacy: The Rhetoric and Pedagogy of Gertrude Buck*. Southern Illinois UP, 2007.

Boswell, Katherine. "State Policy and Postsecondary Enrollment Options: Creating Seamless Systems." *New Directions for Community Colleges*, vol. 2001, no. 113, pp. 7–14, doi:10.1002/cc.3.

Branson, Tyler S. "Problematic Partnerships: An Analysis of Three Composition MOOCs Funded by the Gates Foundation." *Handbook of Research on Writing and Composing in the Age of MOOCs*, edited by Elizabeth A. Monske and Kristine Blair, IGI Global, 2017.

Brass, Jory. "English, Literacy and Neoliberal Policies: Mapping a Contested Moment in the United States." *English Teaching: Practice and Critique*, vol. 13, no. 1, 2014, pp. 112–33.

Brathwaite, Jessica. "Neoliberal Education Reform and the Perpetuation of Inequality." *Critical Sociology*, vol. 43, no. 3, May 2017, pp. 429–48, doi:10.1177/0896920516649418.

Brief Minutes of the Washington Task Force Meeting. 1 Feb. 1981. *NCTE Archives*, Record Series 15/71/9, Box 7.

Broad, Bob. *What We Really Value: Beyond Rubrics in Teaching and Assessing Writing*. Utah State UP, 2003.

Burns, Leslie David. "On Being Unreasonable: NCTE, CEE, and Political Action." *English Education*, vol. 39, no. 2, 2007, pp. 120–45.

Callahan, Diana, et al. "Crossing Levels: The Dynamics of K–16 Teachers' Collaboration." *Teaching Writing in High School and College: Conversations and Collaborations*, edited by Thomas C. Thompson, National Council of Teachers of English, 2002, pp. 201–13.

Caputo, John D., and Mark Yount. *Foucault and the Critique of Institutions*. Pennsylvania State UP, 1993.

Carey, John. *College Credit Plus: Chancellor John Carey's Recommendations for Ohio's Dual Credit System*. Ohio Board of Regents, University System of Ohio, 2014, https://www.ohiohighered.org/sites/ohiohighered.org/files/uploads/board/NewCCPlusReport.pdf.

Caro, Robert A. *The Years of Lyndon Johnson: Master of the Senate*. Alfred A. Knopf, 1982.

———. *The Years of Lyndon Johnson: The Passage of Power*. Vintage Books, 2013

"CCSSI Development Teams." *Truth in American Education*, https://truthinamericaneducation.com/common-core-state-standards/ccssi-development-teams/.

Clabaugh, Gary K. "The Cutting Edge: The Educational Legacy of Ronald Reagan." *Educational Horizons*, vol. 82, no. 4, 2004, pp. 256–59.

Clark-Oates, Angela, et al. "Moving beyond the Common Core to Develop Rhetorically Based and Contextually Sensitive Assessment Practices." *Journal of Writing Assessment*, vol. 8, no. 1, 2015.

Cody, Anthony. "Common Core Standards: Ten Colossal Errors." *EducationWeek (opinion)*, 16 Nov. 2013, https://www.edweek.org/teaching-learning/opinion-common-core-standards-ten-colossal-errors/2013/11.

———. "The Secret Sixty Prepare to Write Standards for 50 Million." *EducationWeek (opinion)*, 6 July 2009, https://www.edweek.org/policy-politics/opinion-the-secret-sixty-prepare-to-write-standards-for-50-million/2009/07.

College Credit Plus Annual Report, 2017–2018. Ohio Department of Education / Ohio Department of Higher Education, 2018, https://www.ohiohighered.org/sites/default/files/uploads/CCP/CCP%20 2018%20Report%20-%20Print%20Version%28c%29.pdf.

College Credit Plus Annual Report: Year Two of the College Credit Plus Program, 2016–17. Ohio Department of Education / Ohio Department of Higher Education, 2017.

"College Credit Plus Data." *Ohio Higher Ed*, https://www.ohiohighered.org/content/college_credit_plus_ccp_data.

College Credit Plus: Highlights of Ohio's Dual Enrollment Program. Ohio Department of Higher Education, 2015, https://www.ohiohighered.org/sites/ohiohighered.org/files/uploads/CCP/College%20Credit%20Plus%20guidance%20document%282%29.pdf.

College Credit Plus: Overview of Year One, 2015–16. Ohio Department of Education / Ohio Department of Higher Education, 2016.

Common Core State Standards Initiative. *Common Core State Standards for English Language Arts and Literacy in History/Social Studies, Science, and Technical Subjects*. 2009.

"Conference Report Filed in House (10/10/1978)." H.R. 15 – Education Amendments. 95th Congress, https://www.congress.gov/bill/95th-congress/house-bill/15.

Connors, Robert. "Dreams and Play: Historical Method and Methodology." *Methods and Methodology in Composition Research*, edited by Gesa Kirsch and Patricia A. Sullivan, Southern Illinois UP, 1992, pp. 15–36.

Constitution of the National Council of Teachers of English. *NCTE*, Jan. 2013, https://cdn.ncte.org/nctefiles/governance/constitution_2013.pdf.

Darling-Hammond, Linda. *The Flat World and Education: How America's Commitment to Equity Will Determine Our Future*. Teachers College Press, 2010.

Denecker, Christine. "Transitioning Writers across the Composition Threshold: What We Can Learn from Dual Enrollment Partnerships." *Composition Studies*, vol. 41, no. 1, 2013, pp. 27–50.

"Development Process." *Common Core State Standards Initiative*, http://www.corestandards.org/about-the-standards/development-process/.

Dual Enrollment: Participation and Characteristics. US Department of Education, Feb. 2019, https://nces.ed.gov/pubs2019/2019176.pdf.

Edwards, Lindsey, et al. *Different Approaches to Dual Enrollment: Understanding Program Features and Their Implications.* James Irvin Foundation / Community College Research Center, 2011.

Elliott, Heather, and Jennie Popay. "How Are Policy Makers Using Evidence? Models of Research Utilisation and Local NHS Policy Making." *Journal of Epidemiology and Community Health*, vol. 54, no. 6, 2000, pp. 461–68.

Enoch, Jessica. *Refiguring Rhetorical Education: Women Teaching African American, Native American, and Chicano/a Students, 1865–1911.* Southern Illinois UP, 2008.

Enos, Richard Leo. "Recovering the Lost Art of Researching the History of Rhetoric." *Rhetoric Society Quarterly*, vol. 29, no. 4, 1999, pp. 7–20.

Epps-Robertson, Candace. *Resisting Brown: Race, Literacy, and Citizenship in the Heart of Virginia.* U of Pittsburgh P, 2018.

Ericsson, Patricia Freitag. *Beyond the Laments, Beyond the Boundaries: Communicating about Composition.* 2003. Michigan Technological U, PhD dissertation.

Espinosa-Aguilar, Amanda. "The (Empty?) Promise of Dual-Enrollment." *NCTE*, 2017. https://ncte.org/report/the-empty-promise-of-dual-enrollment/.

The Essentials of Education: A Call for Dialogue and Action. National Council of Teachers of English, 31 July 1981.

Farris, Christine. "Inventing the University in High School." *College Composition and Communication*, vol. 61, no. 1, 2009, p. 190.

"Fast Facts about Dual and Concurrent Enrollment." *National Alliance of Concurrent Enrollment Partnerships*, https://www.nacep.org/resource-center/fast-fact-on-dual-and-concurrent-enrollment/. Accessed 16 Sept. 2019.

Flowers, Katherine S. "Resisting and Rewriting English-Only Policies: Navigating Multilingual, Raciolinguistic, and Translingual Approaches to Language Advocacy." *Literacy in Composition Studies*, vol. 7, no. 1, 2019, http://licsjournal.org/OJS/index.php/LiCS/article/view/209.

Foucault, Michel. *Discipline and Punish: The Birth of the Prison.* Vintage Books, 1995.

———. "Truth and Power." *The Foucault Reader*, edited by Paul Rainbow, Pantheon Books, 1984, pp. 51–75.

"FY2020 College Credit Plus Payment Report" *Ohio.gov*, http://webapp2.ode.state.oh.us/school_finance/data/2020/CCP/f2020_ccp_college.asp.

Gallagher, Chris W. "At the Precipice of Speech: English Studies, Science, and Policy (Ir)relevancy." *College English*, vol. 73, no. 1, 2010, pp. 73–90.

———. *Reclaiming Assessment: A Better Alternative to the Accountability Agenda*. Heinemann, 2007.

Geise, Mary Jo, and William Knight. "A Longitudinal Analysis of Outcomes Associated with Ohio's Postsecondary Enrollment Options Program." Annual Forum of the Association for Institutional Research, 21–25 May 2011, Toronto. *ERIC*, https://eric.ed.gov/?q=source%3a%22Association+for+Institutional+Research%22&ff1=autKnight%2c+William+E.&id=ED531714.

Gilbert, Erik. "How Dual Enrollment Contributes to Inequality." *Chronicle of Higher Education*, 5 Nov. 2017, https://www.chronicle.com/article/How-Dual-Enrollment/241668.

Gilman, Holly. "Are We Whom We Claim to Be? A Case Study of Language Policy in Community College Writing Placement Practices." *Journal of Writing Assessment*, vol. 12, no. 1, 2019, http://journalofwritingassessment.org/article.php?article=137.

Graff, Gerald, and Cathy Birkenstein. *They Say / I Say: The Moves That Matter in Academic Writing*. 2nd ed., W. W. Norton, 2010.

Graff, Gerald, and Cathy Birkenstein-Graff. "An Immodest Proposal for Connecting High School and College." *College Composition and Communication*, vol. 61, no. 1, 2009, pp. W409–16.

Green, Erica L. "Betsy DeVos Backs $5 Billion in Tax Credits for School Choice." *New York Times*, 28 Feb. 2019, *NYTimes.com*, https://www.nytimes.com/2019/02/28/us/politics/devos-tax-credit-school-choice.html.

———. "DeVos Ends Obama-Era Safeguards Aimed at Abuses by For-Profit Colleges." *New York Times*, 10 Aug. 2018. *NYTimes.com*, https://www.nytimes.com/2018/08/10/us/politics/betsy-devos-for-profit-colleges.html.

Greenhalgh, Trisha, and Jill Russell. "Reframing Evidence Synthesis as Rhetorical Action in the Policy Making Drama." *Healthcare Policy*, vol. 1, no. 2, 2006, pp. 1729–38.

Hammond, J. W., and Merideth Garcia. "The Micropolitics of Pathways: Teacher Education, Writing Assessment, and the Common Core."

Journal of Writing Assessment, vol. 10, no. 1, 2017, http://journalofwritingassessment.org/article.php?article=114.

Hansen, Kristine. "The Composition Marketplace: Shopping for Credit versus Learning to Write." *College Credit for Writing in High School: The "Taking Care of" Business*, edited by Kristine Hansen and Christine Farris, National Council of Teachers of English, 2010, pp. 1–42.

———. "The 'Framework for Success in Postsecondary Writing': Better Than the Competition, Still Not All We Need." *College English*, vol. 74, no. 6, 2012, pp. 540–43.

Hansen, Kristine, and Christine Farris, editors. *College Credit for Writing in High School: The "Taking Care of" Business.* National Council of Teachers of English, 2010.

Hansen, Kristine, et al. "How Do Dual Credit Students Perform on College Writing Tasks after They Arrive on Campus? Empirical Data from a Large-Scale Study." *WPA: Writing Program Administration*, vol. 38, no. 2, 2015, pp. 56–92.

Harper, Larisa L. *Dual Enrollment in Ohio: Participation, Performance, Perceptions, and Potential.* 2015. Ohio U, PhD dissertation.

Hazelrigg, Nick. "Imminent Massive Cuts Could Force Faculty, Staff Layoffs at University of Alaska System." *Insider Higher Ed*, 1 July 2019, https://www.insidehighered.com/news/2019/07/01/imminent-massive-cuts-could-force-faculty-staff-layoffs-university-alaska-system.

Henderson, Susan, and Barbara D. Hodne. "College in the Schools: University of Minnesota–Twin Cities." *Bridging the High School–College Gap: The Role of Concurrent Enrollment Programs*, edited by Gerald S. Edmonds and Tiffany M. Squires, Syracuse UP, 2016, pp. 18–23, http://www.jstor.org/stable/j.ctt1j1nwch.

Hendricks, Glenn. "University Registration Systems: A Study of Social Process." *Human Organization*, vol. 34, no. 2, 1975, 173–81.

Hesse, Doug. "Who Speaks for Writing? Expertise, Ownership, and Stewardship." *Who Speaks for Writing: Stewardship in Writing Studies in the 21st Century*, edited by Jennifer Rich and Ethna D. Lay, Peter Lang, 2012, pp. 9–22.

Hook, J. N. *A Long Way Together: A Personal View of NCTE's First Sixty-Seven Years.* National Council of Teachers of English, 1979.

Hoover, Eric. "The Enrollment Manager as Bogeyman." *Chronicle of Higher Education*, 28 July 2016, https://www.chronicle.com/article/The-Enrollment-Manager-as/237280.

Horváth, Ágnes, et al., editors. *Breaking Boundaries: Varieties of Liminality*. Berghahn Books, 2015.

Huot, Brian A. *(Re)Articulating Writing Assessment for Teaching and Learning*. Utah State UP, 2002.

Jeffrey, Julie Roy. *Education for Children of the Poor: A Study of the Origins and Implementation of the Elementary and Secondary Education Act of 1965*. Ohio State UP, 1978.

Jorgensen, Danny L. *Participant Observation: A Methodology for Human Studies*. Sage Publications, 1989.

"K–12 Disparity Facts and Statistics." *UNCF*, https://UNCF.org/pages/k-12-disparity-facts-and-stats. Accessed 17 Sept. 2019.

Kaplan, Leslie S., and William A. Owings. "Betsy DeVos's Education Reform Agenda: What Principals—and Their Publics—Need to Know." *NASSP Bulletin*, vol. 102, no. 1, 2018, pp. 58–84.

Karp, Melinda Mechur, et al. *State Dual Enrollment Policies: Addressing Access and Quality*. *Community College Research Center*, 2004, https://ccrc.tc.columbia.edu/publications/state-dual-enrollment-policies.html.

Katz, M. S. *A History of Compulsory Laws*. Phi Delta Kappa Educational Foundation, 1976.

Kelly-Riley, Diane. "Common Core State Standards: A Policy Review for WPAs." *WPA: Writing Program Administration*, vol. 40, no. 2, 2017, pp. 193–220.

Kirkland, David E. *A Search Past Silence: The Literacy of Young Black Men*. Teachers College Press, 2013.

Kirsch, Gesa E. "Being on Location: Serendipity, Place, and Archival Research." *Beyond the Archives: Research as a Lived Practice*, edited by Gesa E. Kirsch et al. Southern Illinois UP, 2008, pp. 20–27.

Klein, Alyson. "Could Betsy DeVos' Pitch to Expand School Choice Help Dual Enrollment?" *Education Week, Politics K–12* [blog], http://blogs.edweek.org/edweek/campaign-k-12/2017/10/betsy_devos_school_choice_pitch_help_dual_enrollment.html?cmp=SOC-SHR-FB.

Kohli, Rita, et al. "The 'New Racism' of K–12 Schools: Centering Critical Research on Racism." *Review of Research in Education*, vol. 41, no. 1, Mar. 2017, pp. 182–202, doi:10.3102/0091732X16686949.

Kozol, Jonathan. *Savage Inequalities: Children in America's Schools*. Broadway Paperbacks, 2012.

Kynard, Carmen. *Vernacular Insurrections: Race, Black Protest, and the New Century in Composition-Literacies Studies*. State U of New York P, 2014.

Larson, Joanne. "Foreword: Operationalizing the Neoliberal Common Good." *Closer Readings of the Common Core: Asking Big Questions about the English Language Arts Standards*, edited by Patrick Shannon, Heinemann, 2013, pp. ix–xv.

Lakoff, George. *Moral Politics: How Liberals and Conservatives Think.* U of Chicago P, 2002.

L'Eplattenier, Barbara E. "An Argument for Archival Research Methods: Thinking beyond Methodology." *College English*, vol. 72, no. 1, 2009, pp. 67–69.

Lerner, Jennifer Brown, and Betsy Brand. *The College Ladder: Linking Secondary and Postsecondary Education for Success for All Students.* American Youth Policy Forum, 2006.

Lindemann, Erika. "How Well Are We Listening? Lessons from the Founding of NCTE and CCCC." *College Composition and Communication*, vol. 62, no. 3, 2011, pp. 504–39.

Logan, Shirley W. *Liberating Language: Sites of Rhetorical Education in Nineteenth-Century Black America.* Southern Illinois UP, 2008.

Losh, Elizabeth M., et al. *Understanding Rhetoric: A Graphic Guide to Writing.* 2nd ed., Bedford / St. Martin's, 2017.

Lueck, Amy J. *A Shared History: Writing in the High School, College, and University, 1856–1886.* Southern Illinois UP, 2019.

Lutz, Frank W., and Laurence Iannaccone. *Understanding Educational Organizations: A Field Study Approach.* C. E. Merrill Publishing, 1969.

Malter, Zachary. "ESSA Strengthens Dual Enrollment, but Who Wins?" *American Youth Policy Forum*, 2016, https://www.aypf.org/blog/essa-strengthens-dual-enrollment-but-who-wins/.

Marken, Stephanie, et al. *Dual Enrollment Programs and Courses for High School Students at Postsecondary Institutions: 2010–11.* NCES 2013-002, US Department of Education, 2013, https://nces.ed.gov/pubs2013/2013002.pdf.

Mason, Curtis. *The National Council of Teachers of English and Federal Education Policy, 1958–1966.* 2011. Loyola U Chicago, PhD dissertation.

Maxwell, John C. Letter from Maxwell to Bob Hogan and Charles Suhor. 3 Aug. 1980. NCTE Archives, Record Series 15/71/9, Box 7.

———. Letter from Maxwell to Charlotte Brooks. 5 Feb. 1980. NCTE Archives, Record Series 15/71/9, Box 7.

———. Letter from Maxwell to Charlotte Brooks. 27 Sept. 1983. NCTE Archives, Record Series 15/71/9, Box 7.

———. Letter from Maxwell to James Alatis. 18 Dec. 1980. NCTE Archives, Record Series 15/71/9, Box 7.

———. Letter from Maxwell to James Slevin. 16 Feb. 1983. NCTE Archives, Record Series 15/71/9, Box 7.

———. Letter from Maxwell to Joan Mary Gibbons. 10 Dec. 1981. NCTE Archives, Record Series 15/71/9, Box 7.

———. Letter from Maxwell to Ralph Staiger. 17 Oct. 1980. NCTE Archives, Record Series 15/71/9, Box 7.

———. Letter from Maxwell to Richard Lloyd-Jones. 3 Jan. 1984. NCTE Archives, Record Series 15/71/9, Box 7.

———. Letter from Maxwell to Shirley Hufstedler. 11 Dec. 1979. NCTE Archives, Record Series 15/71/9, Box 7.

———. Letter from Maxwell to Zola Sullivan. 16 Mar. 1981. NCTE Archives, Record Series 15/71/9, Box 7.

———. Memo to Slate Representatives and SLATE Steering Committee. 22 June 1979. NCTE Archives, Record Series 15/71/9, Box 7.

———. Memo to the Washington Task Force. 26 Feb. 1979. NCTE Archives, Record Series 15/71/9, Box 7.

———. Memo to Washington Task Force. 30 Mar. 1979. NCTE Archives, Record Series 15/71/9. Box 7.

———. Memo to Washington Task Force. 16 Apr. 1979. NCTE Archives, Record Series 15/71/9, Box 7.

———. Memo to Washington Task Force. June 1979. NCTE Archives, Record Series 15/71/9, Box 7.

———. Memo to Washington Task Force. 11 Oct. 1979. NCTE Archives, Record Series 15/71/9, Box 7.

———. Memo to Washington Task Force. 17 Oct. 1979. NCTE Archives, Record Series 15/71/9, Box 7.

———. Memo to Washington Task Force. 17 Apr. 1980. NCTE Archives, Record Series 15/71/9, Box 7.

———. Memo to Washington Task Force. 15 Dec. 1980. NCTE Archives, Record Series 15/71/9, Box 7.

———. Memo to Washington Task Force. 15 Dec. 1980. NCTE Archives, Record Series 15/71/9, Box 7.

———. Memo to Washington Task Force. 5 Nov. 1981. NCTE Archives, Record Series 15/71/9, Box 7.

———. Memo to Washington Task Force. 10 Dec. 1981. NCTE Archives, Record Series 15/71/9, Box 7.

———. Memo to Washington Task Force. 21 Oct. 1982. NCTE Archives, Record Series 15/71/9, Box 7.

———. Memo to Washington Task Force. 14 Feb. 1983. NCTE Archives, Record Series 15/71/9, Box 7.

———. Memo to Washington Task Force. 6 June 1983. NCTE Archives, Record Series 15/71/9, Box 7.

———. Memo to Washington Task Force. 8 Sept. 1983. NCTE Archives, Record Series 15/71/9, Box 7.

———. Memo to Washington Task Force and Geraldine LaRocque from John Maxwell. 18 Sept. 1979. NCTE Archives, Record Series 15/71/9, Box 7.

———. Report on National Relations. May 1980. NCTE Archives, Record Series 15/71/9, Box 7.

———. "Taking Action: A Report on NCTE's National Relations Program." *English Journal*, vol. 68, no. 7, 1979, pp. 9–11.

May, Peter J., and Ashley Jochim E. "Policy Regime Perspectives: Policies, Politics, and Governing." *Policy Studies Journal*, vol. 41, no. 3, 2013, pp. 426–52.

Mayr, Andrea. *Language and Power: An Introduction to Institutional Discourse.* Continuum, 2008.

McCarthey, Sarah J. "The Impact of No Child Left Behind on Teachers' Writing Instruction." *Written Communication*, vol. 25, no. 4, 2008, pp. 462–505.

McClure, Randall, et al. "Concurrent Enrollment in Rural Minnesota: Addressing the Needs Caused by Shifting Demographics, Economics, and Academics." *College Credit for Writing in High School: The "Taking Care of" Business*, edited by Kristine Hansen and Christine Farris, National Council of Teachers of English, 2010, pp. 189–207.

McComiskey, Bruce, editor. *Microhistories of Composition.* UP of Colorado, 2016.

McGuinn, Patrick J. *No Child Left Behind and the Transformation of Federal Education Policy, 1965–2005.* UP of Kansas, 2006.

McNeil, Linda M. *Contradictions of School Reform: Educational Costs of Standardized Testing.* Routledge, 2000.

McWain, Katie. "Finding Freedom at the Composition Threshold: Learning from the Experiences of Dual Enrollment Teachers." *Teaching English in the Two-Year College*, vol. 45, no. 4, 2018, pp. 406–24.

Meckler, Laura. "DeVos Defends Billions in Education-Spending Cuts to Skeptical House Democrats." *Washington Post*, 26 Mar. 2019, https://www.washingtonpost.com/local/education/devos-defends-billions-in-education-spending-cuts-to-skeptical-house-democrats/2019/03/26/9a0c7a38-4ff3-11e9-88a1-ed346f0ec94f_story.html.

Miller, Carolyn R. "Opportunity, Opportunism, and Progress: Kairos in the Rhetoric of Technology." *Argumentation*, vol. 8, 1994, pp. 81–96.

———. "The Rhetoric of Decision Science, or Herbert A. Simon Says." *The Rhetorical Turn: Invention and Persuasion in the Conduct of Inquiry*, edited by Herbert W. Simons, U Chicago P, 1990, pp. 162–84.

Miller, Trey, et al. *Dual Credit Education in Texas: Interim Report.* RAND Corporation, 2017, doi:10.7249/RR2043.

"Minnesota High School Student PSEO and Concurrent Enrollment Activity." *Minnesota Office of Higher Education*, https://www.ohe.state.mn.us/mPg.cfm?pageID=797.

Minnesota Statutes. Postsecondary Enrollment Options Act. 1985, https://www.revisor.mn.gov/statutes/?id=124D.09.

Moreland, Casie. "Chasing Transparency: Using Disparate Impact Analysis to Assess the (In)Accessibility of Dual Enrollment Composition." *Writing Assessment, Social Justice, and the Advancement of Opportunity*, edited by Mya Poe et al., WAC Clearinghouse / UP of Colorado, 2018, pp. 171–99.

———. *White Resistance, White Complacency: The Absent-Presence of Race in the Development of Dual Enrollment Programs.* 2018. Arizona State U, PhD dissertation.

Mortensen, Peter. "Interview: Peter Mortensen—'I Had a Hunch.'" *Working in the Archives: Practical Research Methods for Rhetoric and Composition*, edited by Alexis E. Ramsey et al., Southern Illinois UP, 2009, pp. 45–50.

Museus, Samuel D., et al. "Access and Equity in Dual Enrollment Programs: Implications for Policy Formation." *Higher Education in Review*, vol. 4, 2007, pp. 1–19.

"NACEP History." *National Alliance of Concurrent Enrollment Partnerships*, http://www.nacep.org/about-nacep/history/.

National Governors Association and the Council of Chief State School Officers. *Common Core State Standards Initiative Validation Committee Announced* [press release]. Sept. 2009, www.nga.org/cms/home/news-room/news-releases/page_2009/c0112-content/main-content-list/title_common-core-state-standards-initiative-validation-committee-announced.html.

"NCTE Position Profile," *Council of Writing Program Administrators*, http://wpacouncil.org/files/NCTE%20Postion%20Profile%20FINAL.pdf.

Nichols, Sharon Lynn, and David C. Berliner. *Collateral Damage: How High-Stakes Testing Corrupts America's Schools*. Harvard Education Press, 2007.

Ostergaard, Lori, and Henrietta Rix Wood, editors. *In the Archives of Composition: Writing and Rhetoric in High Schools and Normal Schools*. U of Pittsburgh P, 2015.

Park, J. Charles. "Preachers, Politics, and Public Education: A Review of Right-Wing Pressures against Public Schooling in America." *Phi Delta Kappan*, vol. 61, no. 9 (1980): 608–12.

Parks, Stephen. *Class Politics: The Movement for the Students' Right to Their Own Language*. 2nd ed., Parlor Press, 2013.

Pence, Lucretia, and Linda Jordan Platt. "Evidence-Based Education Policies: Beyond the Yellow Brick Road." *Blurring Boundaries: Developing Writers, Researchers and Teachers: A Tribute to William L. Smith*, edited by Peggy O'Neill and William L. Smith, Hampton Press, 2007, pp. 329–42.

Perez-Pena, Richard. "Waivers for 8 More States from 'No Child Left Behind.'" *New York Times*, 29 May 2012, https://www.nytimes.com/2012/05/30/education/eight-more-states-get-waiver-from-no-child-law.html.

Pew Research Center. *Sharp Partisan Divisions in Views of National Institutions: Republicans Increasingly Say Colleges Have Negative Impact on US*. 2017, https://www.pewresearch.org/politics/2017/07/10/sharp-partisan-divisions-in-views-of-national-institutions/.

Pierson, Ashley, et al. *Earning College Credits in High School: Options, Participation, and Outcomes for Oregon Students*. REL 2017-216, US Department of Education, Institute of Education Sciences, National Center for Education Evaluation and Regional Assistance, Regional Education Laboratory Northwest, 2017, https://ies.ed.gov/ncee/edlabs/projects/project.asp?projectID=433.

Piper, Heather, and Pat Sikes. "Education, Neoliberalism, and 'Truths.'" *Power and Education*, vol. 7, no. 1, 2015, pp. 3–6.

Porter, James, et al. "Institutional Critique: A Rhetorical Methodology for Change." *College Composition and Communication*, vol. 51, no. 4, 2000, pp. 610–42.

Post, Joanna Castner, et al. "Round Up the Horses—The Carts Are Racing Downhill! Programmatic Catch-up to a Quickly Growing Concurrent Enrollment Program." *College Credit for Writing in High School: The "Taking Care of" Business*, edited by Kristine Hansen and

Christine Farris, National Council of Teachers of English, 2010, pp. 165–88.

Preliminary Agenda, Washington Task Force. 24 Mar. 1983. NCTE Archives, Record Series 15/71/9, Box 7.

Purveys, Alan. Letter from Alan Purveys to Sec. Shirley Hufstedler. 18 Jan. 1980. NCTE Archives, Record Series 15/71/9, Box 7.

Race to the Top Program: Executive Summary. US Department of Education, Nov. 2009, https://www2.ed.gov/programs/racetothetop/executive-summary.pdf.

Radunzel, Justine, et al. *Dual-Credit/Dual-Enrollment Coursework and Long-Term College Success in Texas*. ACT Research and Policy: Issue Brief. *ACT.org*, 2014, https://www.act.org/content/dam/act/unsecured/documents/DualCreditTexasReport.pdf.

Ravitch, Diane. *The Death and Life of the Great American School System: How Testing and Choice Are Undermining Education*. Rev. and expanded ed., Basic Books, 2011.

———. "The Lost Purpose of School Reform." *New York Review of Books*, 2015, http://www.nybooks.com/daily/2015/04/02/lost-purpose-no-child-left-behind/.

Renshaw, Betty. Letter from Betty Renshaw to Maxwell. 27 Jan. 1980. NCTE Archives, Record Series 15/71/9, Box 7.

A Report of the NCTE Review Team on the July 2009 Draft of the Common Core English Language Arts State Standards. National Council of Teachers of English, https://cdn.ncte.org/nctefiles/resources/standards/report_corestds_9-09.pdf.

Ritter, Kelly. *To Know Her Own History: Writing at the Woman's College, 1943–1963*. U of Pittsburgh P, 2012.

Ritzer, George. *The McDonaldization of Society*. Sage, 2013.

Robertson, Piedad F., editor. *Systems for Offering Concurrent Enrollment at High Schools and Community Colleges*. Jossey-Bass, 2001.

Ross, E. Wayne, and Rich J. Gibson. "Introduction." *Neoliberalism and Education Reform*, edited by Wayne and Gibson, Hampton Press, 2007, pp. 1–14.

Royster, Jacqueline Jones. *Traces of a Stream: Literacy and Social Change among African American Women*. U of Pittsburgh P, 2000.

Sanchez, James Chase, and Tyler S. Branson. "The Role of Composition Programs in De-Normalizing Whiteness in the University: Programmatic Approaches to Anti-Racist Pedagogies." *WPA: Writing Program Administration*, vol. 39, no. 2, 2016, pp. 47–52.

Schneider, Barbara. "Early College in High Schools: Double Time." *College Credit for Writing in High School: The "Taking Care of" Business*, edited by Kristine Hansen and Christine Farris, National Council of Teachers of English, 2010, pp. 141–64.

Schwartz, Brian, and John W. Schoen. "Betsy DeVos and Family See Profits Soar after Trump Tax Reform Bill, Deregulation Efforts." *CNBC*, 22 July 2019, https://www.cnbc.com/2019/07/22/betsy-devos-profits-after-trump-tax-bill-and-deregulation.html.

Scott, Jerrie Cobb, et al., editors. *Affirming Students' Right to Their Own Language: Bridging Language Policies and Pedagogical Practices.* Routledge / National Council of Teachers of English, 2008.

Shuy, Roger. Letter from Roger Shuy to Maxwell. 23 Jan. 1980. NCTE Archives, Record Series 15/71/9, Box 7.

Skinnell, Ryan. *Conceding Composition*. UP of Colorado, 2016, http://www.jstor.org/stable/j.ctt1d4tzt5.

Smith, Marc A., et al. "The Ohio Postsecondary Enrollment Opportunities (PSEO) Program: Understanding Its Under-Utilization." *Journal of Educational Research and Policy Studies*, vol. 7, no. 2, 2007, pp. 80–114.

Speroni, Cecilia. *High School Dual Enrollment Programs: Are We Fast-Tracking Students Too Fast?* Working paper, National Center for Postsecondary Research, 2011.

Squires, Robert. Letter from Robert Squires to Sec. Terrel H. Bell. 2 Feb. 1981. NCTE Archives, Record Series 15/71/9, Box 7.

"Standards in Your State." *Common Core State Standards Initiative*, http://www.corestandards.org/standards-in-your-state/. Accessed 16 Sept. 2019.

"Statement on Dual Credit/Concurrent Enrollment Composition: Policy and Best Practices." *Conference on College Composition and Communication*, 2012, https://cccc.ncte.org/cccc/resources/positions.

Stenberg, Shari J., and Darby Arant Whealy. "The Chaos Is the Poetry: From Outcomes to Inquiry in Service-Learning Pedagogy." *College Composition and Communication*, vol. 60, no. 4, 2009, pp. 683–706.

Stock, Patricia L., editor. *Composition's Roots in English Education*. Heinemann, 2012.

Stoller, Eric. "Strategic Enrollment Management Keeps the Lights On." *Inside Higher Ed* blogs, 7 Aug. 2014, https://www.insidehighered.com/blogs/student-affairs-and-technology/strategic-enrollment-management-keeps-lights.

Stotsky, Sandra. "Common Core's Invalid Validation Committee." The Changing Role of Education in America: Consequences of the Common Core Conference, U of Notre Dame, 2013, http://www.uaedreform.org/downloads/2013/11/common-cores-invalid-validation-committee.pdf.

Stratford, Michael. "DeVos Tightens Rules for Forgiving Student Loans." *Politico*, 30 Aug. 2019, https://politi.co/30KmjyO.

Strauss, Valerie. "Everything You Need to Know about Common Core—Ravitch," *Washington Post*, 18 Jan. 2014, https://www.washingtonpost.com/news/answer-sheet/wp/2014/01/18/everything-you-need-to-know-about-common-core-ravitch/.

Strickland, Donna. *The Managerial Unconscious in the History of Composition Studies*. Southern Illinois UP, 2011.

Suhor, Charles, and Diane Allen. "NCTE to You." *English Journal*, vol. 70, no. 5, 1981, pp. 90–94.

Suitts, Steve. *Overturning Brown: The Segregationist Legacy of the Modern School Choice Movement*. NewSouth Books, 2020.

Sullivan, Patrick, and Howard B. Tinberg, editors. *What Is "College-Level" Writing?* National Council of Teachers of English, 2006.

Sullivan, Zola. Letter from Zola Sullivan to Marjorie Farmer. 17 Feb. 1981. NCTE Archives, Record Series 15/71/9, Box 7.

Summary of Public Feedback on the Draft College- and Career-Readiness Standards for English-Language Arts and Mathematics. Common Core State Standards Initiative, http://www.corestandards.org/assets/CorePublicFeedback.pdf.

Summerfield, Judith, and Philip M. Anderson. "A Framework Adrift." *College English*, vol. 7, no. 6, 2012, pp. 544–47.

Swanson, Joni Lynne. *An Analysis of the Impact of High School Dual Enrollment Course Participation on Post-secondary Academic Success, Persistence and Degree Completion*. 2008. U of Iowa, PhD dissertation.

Taczak, Kara, and William Thelin. "(Re)Envisioning the Divide: The Impact of College Courses on High School Students." *Teaching English in the Two-Year College*, vol. 37, no. 1, 2009, pp. 7–23.

"TAG Background." Ohio Department of Higher Education, https://www.ohiohighered.org/transfer/tag/background.

Tagliaventi, Maria Rita. *Liminality in Organization Studies: Theory and Method*. Routledge, 2020.

Tampio, Nicholas. *Common Core: National Education Standards and the Threat to Democracy*. Johns Hopkins UP, 2018.

Thomas, Nina, et al. *Dual Credit and Exam-Based Courses in U.S. Public High Schools: 2010–11.* NCES 2013-001, US Department of Education, National Center for Education Statistics, Feb. 2013.

Thompson, Thomas C., editor. *Teaching Writing in High School and College: Conversations and Collaborations.* National Council of Teachers of English, 2002.

Thomson, Alec. "Dual Enrollment's Expansion: Cause for Concern." *National Education Association*, 2017, https://eric.ed.gov/?id=EJ1156162.

Tobolowsky, Barbara F., and Taryn Ozuna Allen. "On the Fast Track: Understanding the Opportunities and Challenges of Dual Credit." *ASHE Higher Education Report*, vol. 42, no. 3, 2016.

Turner, Victor W. "Betwixt and Between: The Liminal Period in Rites de Passage." *Reader in Comparative Religion: An Anthropological Approach*, 4th ed., edited by William Armand Lessa and Evon Z. Vogt, Harper & Row, 1979, pp. 234–43.

"2019 Policy Recommendations." *NCTE*, https://ncte.org/get-involved/volunteer/take-action/policy-recommendations/. Accessed 11 May 2020.

Tyack, David B., and Larry Cuban. *Tinkering toward Utopia: A Century of Public School Reform.* Harvard UP, 1995.

United States Code. 20 U.S. Code § 7801 – Definitions. Cornell Law School, *Legal Information Institute*, https://www.law.cornell.edu/uscode/text/20/7801.

University Completion Plan. U of Toledo, 2018, https://www.utoledo.edu/offices/provost/docs/FINAL.UT%20University%20Completion%20Plan%20Update%202018-2020.pdf.

Vinovskis, Maris. *From a Nation at Risk to No Child Left Behind: National Education Goals and the Creation of Federal Education Policy.* Teachers College Press, 2009.

Wardle, Elizabeth. "Intractable Writing Program Problems, *Kairos*, and Writing about Writing: A Profile of the University of Central Florida's First-Year Composition Program." *Composition Forum*, vol. 27, 2013, https://compositionforum.com/issue/27/ucf.php.

Webber, James. *An Alternate Pragmatism for Going Public.* Utah State UP, 2017.

Weir, Kirsten. "Inequality at School: What's behind the Racial Disparity in Our Education System." *Monitor on Psychology*, vol. 47, no. 10, 2016, pp. 42–47.

Wells, Susan. "Claiming the Archive for Rhetoric and Composition." *Rhetoric and Composition as Intellectual Work*, Southern Illinois UP, 2002, pp. 55–64.

"What Is Concurrent Enrollment?" *National Alliance of Concurrent Enrollment Partnerships*, http://www.nacep.org/about-nacep/what-is-concurrent-enrollment/.

"What Parents Should Know." *Common Core State Standards Initiative*, http://www.corestandards.org/what-parents-should-know/.

White, Eric Charles. *Kaironomia: On the Will-to-Invent*. Cornell UP, 1987.

Wible, Scott. *Shaping Language Policy in the U.S: The Role of Composition Studies*. Southern Illinois UP, 2013.

Williamson, Ben. "The Hidden Architecture of Higher Education: Building a Big Data Infrastructure for the 'Smarter University.'" *International Journal of Educational Technology in Higher Education*, vol. 15, no. 1, 2018, article 12, doi:10.1186/s41239-018-0094-1.

Wilson, Carter A. "Policy Regimes and Policy Change." *Journal of Public Policy*, vol. 20, no. 3, 2000, pp. 247–74.

Winalski, Amanda. "Bam." *What Is College-Level Writing?*, edited by Patrick Sullivan and Howard B. Tinberg, National Council of Teachers of English, 2006, pp. 302–08.

Wolcott, Harry F. *The Man in the Principal's Office: An Ethnography*. AltaMira Press, 2003.

Wood, Martin, et al. "Achieving Clinical Behaviour Change: A Case of Becoming Indeterminate." *Social Science & Medicine*, vol. 47, no. 11, 1998, pp. 1729–38.

Wu, Hui. "Historical Studies of Rhetorical Women Here and There: Methodological Challenges to Dominant Interpretive Frameworks." *Rhetoric Society Quarterly*, vol. 32, no. 1, 2002, pp. 81–97.

WWC Intervention Report. US Department of Education, 2017, https://ies.ed.gov/ncee/wwc/interventionreport/671.

Yin, Alice. "Education by the Numbers." *New York Times*, 8 Sept. 2017. *NYTimes.com*, https://www.nytimes.com/2017/09/08/magazine/education-by-the-numbers.html.

Young, Vershawn Ashanti, et al. *Other People's English: Code-Meshing, Code-Switching, and African American Literacy*. Teachers College Press, 2014.

Zeppos, Nicholas W., and Phillip A. Wallach. "Tracking Deregulation in the Trump Era." *Brookings Institute*, 2017, https://www

.brookings.edu/blog/fixgov/2017/12/05/tracking-deregulation-in-the-trump-era/.

Zinth, Jennifer, and Elisabeth Barnett. "Rethinking Dual Enrollment to Reach More Students." *Education Commission of the States*, 30 Apr. 2018, https://www.ecs.org/wp-content/uploads/Rethinking_Dual_Enrollment_to_Reach_More_Students.pdf.

INDEX

Tyler S. Branson is an assistant professor of English and the associate director of composition at the University of Toledo. He has published articles in *College Composition and Communication*, *Composition Studies*, and *WPA: Writing Program Administration*, and he has essays in the edited collections *Bad Ideas about Writing* and the *Cambridge Handbook of Service Learning and Community Engagement*.

WRITING
RESEARCH,
PEDAGOGY,
AND POLICY

The Writing Research, Pedagogy, and Policy series publishes cutting-edge empirical scholarship about writing, broadly conceived, with a particular focus on work that impacts pedagogy, practice, and policy at various levels and locations, such as elementary, secondary, postsecondary, national, and international. The series takes a particular interest in empirical research on writing centers, writing across the curriculum, multilingual writers, assessment, and writing center–library collaborations—all subjects related to the work of the Howe Center for Writing Excellence, which provides financial support. The focus of the series includes not only institutional research sites but also cross-institutional research sites.

This series draws on the definition of empirical research used by the Dartmouth Summer Seminar for Composition Research: "systematic or replicable inquiry in response to [one or more research questions] that generate interpretable data; inquiry that is grounded in previous research and designed to extend existing knowledge and, through scholarly publication or other public contributions, to be extended itself." Systematic research may include archival and ethnographic methods, among many others.

Please send all queries via email to
Elizabeth Wardle, Director
Howe Center for Writing Excellence
King Library 133
Miami University
Oxford, OH 45056
writingresearchseries@miamioh.edu